July 4, 2013

To Vince and Olive,

Were so grateful for the heritage
we share and the love that binds
us together.

Thank you for being with us on
this Independence Day. Our hearts
are with you always.

Love,
Cliff + Marilyn + Family
Christine Whyte
Craig Whyte

Published and Distributed by:

Granite Publishing and Distribution, L.L.C.
868 North 1430 West • Orem, UT 84057
(801) 229-9023 • Toll Free (800) 574-5779
FAX (801) 229-1924

First Printing; April 2002
10 9 8 7 6 5 4 3 2

ISBN: 1-930980-79-5

Library of Congress Control Number: 2002106399

Layout design by Steve Hansen (H2 Design, SLC, UT)
Cover by Edward Walter Design, Inc. (NY, NY)
Artwork and maps by Chrystine Whyte
Photography work by Dave Otvos
Photo collections: Freedom Bird Organization and Larry Petersen

WHAT PEOPLE ARE SAYING ABOUT
REASONS TO REMEMBER

As a U.S. Senator, while serving on the Armed Services Committee and chairing the Personnel Sub-Committee, my deep respect and appreciation grew for the men and women who proudly wear the uniform of the United States Armed Forces. Now, as Governor and Commander-in-Chief of the Idaho National Guard, I continue to see, firsthand, the commitment and sacrifice of our soldiers as they serve our country.

History records their bravery as they defend our Nation from the enemies of freedom. To those courageous individuals who gave their life, for those who now serve, and for the Veterans who continue to live as patriotic Americans, we are forever indebted.

Reasons to Remember is a moving tribute to the many Idahoans who fought and died for the ideals of freedom in Southeast Asia during the Vietnam War. We will never forget their love of country, their legacy of service and their ultimate sacrifice. May we be so committed.

—*DIRK KEMPTHORNE*
Governor of Idaho

Idaho's Vietnam Veterans receive a fitting tribute with the publication of *Reasons to Remember*. This book gives a fresh look at the stories of the individual Idahoans who fought for our nation, but failed to receive the respect and recognition of its people. With her book Marilyn Whyte helps to heal those old wounds while putting into the words the horror, bravery, fear, friendship and many other emotions our young soldiers faced half way around the world more than a generation ago. Whyte's book gives Idaho Veterans special recognition by being the nation's first comprehensive, statewide account of the Veterans' stories from Vietnam.

—*U.S. Senator Larry Craig*

In the times in which we live, we have learned through sad experience that heroes are born when ordinary people are put into extraordinary circumstances. As I read through the stories of the Idahoans who fought and died for their country in Vietnam, I am struck by this simple truth about heroes. Like Flags of Our Fathers, this book brings home the fact that these heroes were sons, brothers, fathers, and friends; that they played football, ran track, set up practical jokes, and, most of all, are missed every day, in every way by those they left behind. It weaves those sacrifices into the fabric of the conflict in Vietnam, and gives us one of the most complete pictures of how battles unfolded and how lives were saved and lost by these Idaho soldiers. Fittingly, it brings us into the present-day to share how we can honor the memory of their sacrifice today.

—U.S. Senator Mike Crapo

Marilyn Whyte gives readers 251 reasons to remember the Vietnam War. These individuals, in addition to the 45,000 Idahoans who served in the Vietnam War, are a stark reminder of freedom's high price. Many of these men were plucked from youth, just starting their lives when their country called. *Reasons to Remember* reveals the personal price paid by our military and the contributions of Idahoans to liberty's defense.

—U.S. Congressman Mike Simpson
Chairman of the House Veterans Subcommittee on Benefits

Reasons to Remember is a historic tribute to the 45,000 brave Idahoans who served in the Vietnam War and to the ultimate sacrifice 251 of them paid on battle-fields so far from home. For the families and friends who lost loved ones, I pray that this book helps heal their wounded hearts. For those too young to remember, I hope that this great work serves as a window into the generation who fought in the Vietnam War, so that they might finally comprehend the sacrifices so many Idahoans made in service to our nation.

—U.S. Congressman C.L. "Butch" Otter

Because of the divisive nature of the Vietnam War, many of its fallen heroes have yet to be properly recognized for their valor and courage. This book pays tribute to the Sons of Idaho: our brothers, fathers, neighbors, and friends who answered the call of their Commander in Chief and gave their lives in the cause of freedom. This is their story—beautifully interwoven with the dates and historical facts of the war. I stand in deep respect for their ultimate sacrifice.

—*J. Stanley Williams*
Idaho State Senator

The men and women who stepped forward to serve in Vietnam deserve the thanks and appreciation of their countrymen. Those who gave their lives should have our undying gratitude. As Marilyn Whyte has shown in this outstanding tribute, those who served and died from Idaho were among the best and brightest of their generation.

Members of the Freedom Bird group are to be commended for conceiving the idea for this tribute and Marilyn Whyte is to be greatly thanked for carrying it through to completion. In this book and in our everyday lives, we can never forget those who made the ultimate sacrifice for the benefit of us all.

—*Jim Jones*
Former Idaho Attorney General

In honor of the 45,000 Idaho enlisted men and women
who answered the call of duty…
and the families and loved ones
of those who never returned.

A Mother's 'Back Porch Memorial'

FOREWORD

"In God's good time it will appear. A treasure for generations to come."
(Mother of Chad Carson, Idaho Casualty)

In 1991, I became acquainted with a group of veterans in the Idaho Falls area known as "The Freedom Birds", whose tireless efforts conceived and constructed the Idaho Vietnam Veteran's Memorial in Freeman Park, near the banks of the Snake River. For several years they had worked tirelessly to gather and compile the records of the 250 plus Idaho men and boys who had lost their lives in the Vietnam War.

When first asked to assist in the overwhelming task of compiling the mounds of priceless information and stories, I was immediately impressed that this work needed to be accomplished. Little did I know it would lead me on a journey beyond anything I had ever experienced or imagined.

Initially, I assumed the project would require a few months work. But more than ten years have passed as my search for understanding took me to the homes of family members, county courthouses, historical societies, cemeteries and monuments, (including the Wall in Washington, D.C.) and through countless books and written accounts looking for answers.

In the interim, my three teenage sons grew to manhood. As I saw in their faces, the faces of so many (from my generation) whose lives were cut short in service to their country; the project took on an emotional intensity I could hardly bear. The task to tell the story fairly and with sensitivity, to the loss of so many good people, became astronomical. Many times I was tempted to give up. Thanks to the support and patience of the Freedom Birds Veteran's group, this priceless record will now be preserved for generations to come.

The past decade has also brought me in contact with many young high school and college-age students, of whom I always asked the same question. "What did you learn in school about the Vietnam War?" Their minds were bright and their backgrounds varied, but the answer was always disappointingly the same.

"Nothing," they replied with vagueness I too, could comprehend. What did we as a people and as a nation learn from the Vietnam War and whom have we thanked for carrying the burden we largely ignored and blocked from our collective conscience?

A mother's tribute sits in the corner of a small patio, against a backdrop of bushes and freshly mowed grass. A pair of shoes—but not just any shoes. High topped laced boots that carried her son through the jungle terrain of a far off mountain range. Boots lifted from the mud by a buddy who carried his friend from the nightmare of the battlefield—"personal effects" that accompanied his body home at the tender age of twenty.

Combat boots now overflowing with petunias, a seasonal touch of beauty added each year in remembrance of cherished memories of a baseball field and the sound of the backdoor at his return—the door he hasn't opened for 34 years.

Still she waits—and remembers.

And where was I?

Much has been said of 'survivor guilt'—those who returned from battle bearing the psychological burden of surviving when others died. Mine is an 'observer guilt', derived from watching and even ignoring, the tremendous sacrifice and pain of those who bore the burden and fought the fight; without ever stopping to express thanks or acknowledge their contribution to the freedom I so freely enjoyed.

Reasons to Remember is a book whose time has come, culminating years of extensive research and study. A collection created from countless hours of compiling, analyzing and searching to understand what really happened in that far off corner of the world; while I and others enjoyed lives of ease and were largely unaware.

This intricate study represents a "sifting for truth", compiled from the insight of gifted historians, military analysts and political experts. Combined with "true-life" human drama and sacrifice, it becomes a journey; taking us to the stark reality that 'freedom isn't free.'

Since the early inception of our nation, 226 years ago, some 1.3 million Americans have given their lives in defense of liberty and the struggle for freedom. In the 20th Century alone, 130,000 died in World War I (the War to end all wars), and another 354,000 died on the battlefields of World War II and Korea.

Each of the 2.5 million men and women who served in Vietnam saw war through different eyes, and their combined experience spanned more than two decades. When the war that 'couldn't be won' finally ended, some saw the deaths of 58,000 Americans as useless.

But regardless of personal or political views, the lives and sacrifice of those who served have great meaning. A meaning and sacrifice made crystal clear by the 1967 inscription on an "in-country" dedicatory plaque:

"I tried. I did all I could do. I just couldn't do anymore."

Specialist Four Billy Jones and Private First Class Herbert E. Frenzell were on an "eagle flight" on January 21, 1967, when their unit met a well-entrenched VC force. The unit, caught in open terrain and without cover, was in a desperate situation. PFC Frenzell, who was not at the time directly involved in the ambush and was in a safe location, chose to open fire on the enemy, thereby drawing fire away from the exposed positions. After everyone had withdrawn, PFC Frenzell started his attempt to move back to rejoin his squad. As he left his concealed position he was shot and killed. Specialist Four Jones crawled through the mud and enemy fire to recover Frenzell's body. After contact was broken, Sp4 Jones carried PFC Frenzell's body for over two hours through thick jungle growth and hazardous swamps to place PFC Frenzell on the waiting helicopter. However when he saw another man hit and fall, he lowered PFC Frenzel's body to the ground and rushed to assist the newly wounded soldier. It was at this time that he was fatally wounded. His final words were, "I tried. I did all I could do. I couldn't do anymore."

Official Military Report
(Redcatcher! Yearbook, Vietnam 1969)

The following pages have been compiled and written to honor the lives and sacrifice of young Idahoans "who did all they could do", and to remember the families and loved ones of those whose lives were "forever changed" by the tragedy of war.

VIETNAM: "A thousand different stories...a thousand different wars."

Pieces of a puzzle, so difficult to understand—even by those who lived through it. But one by one, the pieces appear and a clearer picture emerges— a picture designed to bring greater understanding and appreciation for a time and place called Vietnam.

—The Author

INTRODUCTION

Vietnam: "Too painful to remember –
too important to forget."

Situated high above the banks of the Snake River, and hidden from the pace of a hectic world, the crest of a lofty green hill lies in quiet majesty.

Here on this hallowed corner of mother earth, arises a stately pillar—a modern monolith bearing the image of an inverted V. Poised serenely against the open sky, the understated edifice stands in silent repose.

Once again, a new day awakens as mists rise from the river below and rays of sunlight reflect against the glow of the highly polished beam. In stately prominence it rises to the sky, then drops sharply to the ground like a fallen wing. Still proud and unbroken, it stands as uniformed posts of chain link fence wait in quiet sentinel.

The morning dew glistens against the reflection of silver and bronze, and in the fading shadows moisture escapes the lines of a forgotten map. Beyond the noise and routine of the day, the striking silhouette bears at its base a list of names—forever sealed in polished steel. Brothers, sons, fathers—unnoticed by the casual passerby, but never forgotten by those who loved them.

Decades have passed, yet it seems like only yesterday, as the cool morning breeze rustles the waves of the American flag and rays of sunlight reflect against the metalic frame that bears the image of another time.

To those who listen, voices whisper from the past. Strains of laughter, silenced by the battle's roar, and words of assurance—longing to be heard—echo in the chambers of a reverent heart.

Keeping silent vigil as seasons come and go, time waits on bended knee.

Beneath the shadow of the stately obelisk, the waters of the mighty river flow steadily onward. Thirty years have passed since the last youth's name was added to the ranks of the fallen dead.

While annals of time chronicle the perplexing narrative, history waits to be understood. But here, etched in bronze and silver, names and faces forever-sealed preserve a legacy of honor and duty.

Faces. Faces that only yesterday left the football fields of local high schools and universities, the farmlands and valleys of rural Idaho. Faces of hope and promise. Faces bearing the image of unfulfilled youth and the missed opportunity of a bright new future. Faces of fathers, lovers and friends longing to be remembered.

This book is their collective story: a story of sacrifice, honor and duty— "never-ending tales" bearing the timeless message that 'freedom isn't free.'

A book written to celebrate the lives and acknowledge the contribution of the unsung heroes of my generation, men and boys who became veterans of the longest conflict in the history of the United States. A tribute to Idaho's brightest and best who answered the call of duty and gave of their tomorrows that others might have today. Waiting to take their place in history— a place of honor and respect— these heroes were born of sacrifice and duty, as were their fathers and grandfathers who paid the ultimate price for freedom.

The time has come to look back—and to see the future.
For these are the reasons to remember.

—*M. Whyte*

★★★

Idaho Vietnam Veterans Memorial
Idaho Falls, Idaho
PHOTO: DAVE OTVOS

REASONS
TO
REMEMBER

*A Tribute
to the
Unsung Heroes
of the
Vietnam War*

CONTENTS

PART 1

HISTORIC TIMELINE

*U.S. Involvement
in
Vietnam*

HISTORIC TIMELINE

"There's history being made over there and I want to be a part of it."

(Idaho Casualty Kenneth Turner)

Vietnam: An era so complex and obscure, even those who lived through it find it hard to understand. Piece by piece the puzzle comes together and a picture of a troubled past appears.

Recent renewed interest in the World War II era has led to the insightful work of Tom Brokaw's tribute to the 'Greatest Generation'—aptly broadening America's appreciation for the men and women that survived the tests of the Great Depression and trials of the second world war. The initial focus of this historic overview begins at the post World War II era, and explores the international climate that led to the longest and most divisive conflict in America since the Civil War. The subsequent decades become a sobering commentary bearing the message 'Those Who Fail To Learn From History Are Destined To Repeat It.'

Compiled from military records, historical accounts, political commentaries and personal information submitted by family members and expert advisors; the following timeline is designed to help the reader follow national and international events leading up to and through the Vietnam War. Much effort has been expended to present a clear, objective and accurate account of military strategies and political issues—inviting the reader to draw his or her own conclusions.

Selected stories and experiences of Idaho servicemen have been incorporated into the story line to broaden understanding and increase appreciation for the service and sacrifice of thousands of young Americans in a land called Vietnam.

October 24, 1945

The United Nations was established soon after Germany surrendered in World War II. The aims of the new organization were to 'encourage international peace and security, promote cooperation in solving international, social, and economic problems, and to develop friendly relations among all nations.' The UN's effectiveness was seriously hampered soon after it was established by complications of the Cold War era.

As World War II ended, the Soviet Union and the United States emerged as the world's two great political powers. Soon the two nations were in conflict over ideology, and divergent plans for political and economic expansion. The powerful competitors were also engaged in a great arms race, developing and improving weapons to be used in case of war. These pressures dominated the political climate of the postwar years, and the Cold War era emerged.

October 24, 1945
The United Nations was established.

Cold War tensions first developed when the Soviet Union set up Communist governments in the East European countries it had occupied during World War II. Between 1945 and 1948 Albania, Bulgaria, Czechoslovakia, Hungary, Poland, Romania, and Yugoslavia all came under Soviet control.

In addition to confrontations (the Berlin blockade), and warfare (in Korea), the Cold War also bred the nuclear arms race and spurred space exploration.

SOUTHEAST ASIA & INTERNATIONAL CONCERNS

1946 The Indochina War

The Indochina conflict between the French and Vietnamese broke out in the spring of 1946. By late 1949 both the East and the West had a real stake in its outcome. Fear that the communists (led by the Soviet Union's Stalin) had their eyes on all of Southeast Asia, prompted President Truman to approve aid to France.

1947

Truman pledged U.S. support for "free people who are resisting attempted subjugation by armed minorities or by outside pressures." Every move was seen as critical. Lack of resolve or signs of weakness could easily lead to a crisis. The reality of the Cold War made the conflict in Indochina an international war.

1950-53 The Korean War

As North Korean forces launched an invasion across the 38th parallel into South Korea, Douglas McArthur was named Commander of the UN forces. The world hovered close to the brink of a third world war when Chinese Communist troops entered the Korean campaign. After 3 years of intense fighting, the Armistice was signed July 27, 1953. The war ended where it started, at the 38th parallel and resulted in 54,000 American deaths.

1952

Dwight D. Eisenhower was elected President with Richard Nixon as Vice President.

1954

President Eisenhower declared his foreign policy would be dedicated to regaining the initiative in the world fight against communism and to winning the confidence of U.S. allies.

1947
The U.S. responded with the TRUMAN DOCTRINE which offered aid to countries threatened by Communism (then Greece and Turkey).

1948
The Marshall Plan gave the countries in Western Europe large-scale U.S. aid to rebuild their war-shattered economies and to strengthen them against Communist pressures.

1949
The North Atlantic Treaty Organization (NATO), was established to bring the European nations together to insure their common defense.

THE CONCLUSION OF THE INDOCHINA WAR

The war between the French and Viet Minh took eight long years with France suffering a humiliating defeat in 1954. The treaty divided Vietnam at the 17th Parallel and the foundation was in place for America's war in Vietnam.

In 1950 the U.S. began sending aid directly to the South Vietnam government which was supported by the French. Congress approved a mutual defense assistance act that called for the deployment of U.S. military advisers to Asia. The National Security Council produced an important paper entitled, "Position of the United States with Respect to Asia" which Truman approved as official policy.

According to the "Domino Theory" accepted by America's foreign-policy makers in the early 1950's, if Vietnam went communist, it would not be long before the rest of Indochina would follow suit. The first American military advisors assigned to Vietnam in 1950, set up MAAG—the Military Assistance Advisory Group. The next four years, the U.S. would provide more than two-thirds of the money required for the French war effort, until the war ended in 1954 with the partition of Vietnam at the 17th Parallel.

In 1954 Ngo dinh Diem was appointed as prime minister. He would become the central figure in South Vietnamese politics for the next nine years. Foreign policy experts in Washington were optimistic about their ability to keep the communists out of South Vietnam, but recognized the Diem regime could not go it alone. North Korea and China had already been lost and if South Vietnam went communist, Laos, Cambodia and other Southeast Asian nations would undoubtedly follow.

The American crusade against communist expansion soon picked up momentum. In 1955 the United States expended $355 million in military and political aid into South Vietnam. The salaries of South Vietnamese government employees were paid by U.S. dollars and a rural police force was instigated. Foreign Service officers trained the Vietnamese in the ways of Western democratic government, while American engineers developed projects to improve the country's roads, airports, and harbors.

Throughout the late 1950's the communists exerted more and more pressure on the South Vietnamese government. Assassinations of village chiefs unsympathetic to the revolution occurred with alarming frequency. In 1959 more than 1,000 government officials were killed and by 1961 the toll was reported to be around 4,000.

By the time John Fitzgerald Kennedy assumed the presidency of the United States in January of 1961, South Vietnam had received more than $1 billion in aid since 1955. Vietnam was considered the cornerstone of the free world in Southeast Asia, and Kennedy had no intention of permitting a communist takeover.

The Kennedy years were filled with crisis and promise. At home Kennedy committed the government to civil rights, and abroad he actively opposed Communism, bringing the world to the brink of nuclear war in the Cuban Missile Crisis. His administration marked the beginning of the military involvement of the United States in Vietnam. The Kennedy years ended in tragedy when he was assassinated November 22, 1963 in Dallas, Texas.

After seizing power in Cuba in 1959, Fidel Castro (1927-) joined the Soviet bloc in 1961. Soon afterward, Cuban exiles trained by the U.S. Central Intelligence Agency (CIA) staged what is called the Bay Of Pigs invasion in April of 1961. The exiles hoped to spark an uprising against Castro, but the attack was quickly crushed, becoming a major embarrassment to the Kennedy administration.

THE BERLIN WALL

As Cold War tensions increased in 1961, the Communists moved in August to end the flow of refugees from Communist East Germany into West Germany. The result was the Berlin Wall, a 29-mile-long barrier separating East and West Berlin. In the West, the wall quickly became a symbol of Communist oppression.

CUBAN MISSILE CRISIS

In October of 1962, the United States discovered the Soviets were building missile sites in Cuba. President Kennedy's demand that the missile sites be dismantled and withdrawn brought the United States and the Soviet Union to the brink of nuclear war. On October 28, Radio Moscow announced the arms would be crated and return to Moscow and disaster was averted. However, the incident heightened public awareness of the dangerous possibility of a nuclear war and American citizens were advised to build or buy shelters against atomic fallout.

1963
Idaho's First Casualty

August 3, 1963
29-year-old **DONALD MCGREGOR** from Paul, Idaho became Idaho's First Casualty of the Vietnam War. A 1952 graduate of Paul High School, Donald was Student Body

1961
A Russian cosmonaut Yuri A. Gagarin became the first man to orbit the earth. In 1962 John Glenn became the first American to orbit the earth. But on July 20, 1969 the United States won a clear victory by landing the first men on the moon (Neil Armstrong and Edwin "Buzz" Aldrin, Jr.) Meanwhile, satellites and other space vehicles were perfected for peaceful and military purposes on both sides.

1961
Bay Of Pigs invasion of Cuba.

June 1961
Two U.S. Army officers were killed in an ambush by guerrillas north of Saigon.

February 8, 1962
The Defense Department announced the creation of a new U.S. Military Assistance Command (MAC) in South Vietnam.

February 10 U-2
pilot Francis Gary Powers was released in Berlin by the Soviets in exchange for Soviet Spy Rudolf Abel.

President his senior year and later graduated from the University of Utah. The father of three sons, Captain Mc Gregor was stationed at Quang Ngai at the time of his death.

August 28
A Freedom March on Washington D.C. brought an estimated 200,000 participants who listened to Dr. Martin Luther King's "I Have A Dream" speech, describing a U.S. free of divisiveness, hatred, and injustice.

August 30
The 'Hot Line' went into operation as an emergency communications link between Washington D.C. and Moscow to reduce the risk of accidental war.

November 1
South Vietnamese armed forces overthrow the government of Pres. Ngo Diem and assassinate Diem. Nov. 7th the U.S. recognizes the provisional government of Nguyen Ngoc Tho, Diem's vice president.

November 22, 1963
The death of President John F. Kennedy shocked the nation and the world. The 34th person elected president of the United States was the fourth to die from an assassins bullet while riding in a motorcade in Dallas, Texas. Vice President Lyndon Baines Johnson was sworn in as the 35th President of the United States and inherited the problems escalating in Southeast Asia.

December 6, 1963
27-year-old **GARY BITTON**, airforce pilot and father of three from Blackfoot, becomes Idaho's second fatality when his B-26 airplane is shot down in South Vietnam. The crew bailed out and it appeared Gary lost his battle to fight the river currents trying to swim to shore. His body was later recovered several miles from the crash site, south of Saigon at the mouth of the Mekong River.

A 1954 graduate of Blackfoot High School and 1958 graduate of BYU, Gary was "in country" less than one month before losing his life. In a letter home dated November 25, 1963 he wrote: "…the war games here are ridiculous and very frustrating. We have "Rules of Engagement," kind of like fighting with one hand behind your back. We are controlled by the VNAF (Vietnamese Airforce) and cannot move unless they have approved and marked our targets. If we saw 10,000 V.C. (Viet Cong) marching we couldn't strike until it was approved. Apparently, we have V.C. in our chain of command because all of our strike missions seem to leave an escape route for the V.C. We know where the V.C. headquarters are but have never struck it."

Describing his quarters in Bien Hoa as 'luxury living,' he shared descriptions of huts with asbestos roofs, wood sides and floors, ceiling fans and mosquito netting over their steel cots. The latrine hut had a pull type commode with hot water (only) in the sink and shower. The compound also included the central dining room, a hut with a theatre, an officer's club and PX. A perimeter ditch, Spanish concertina and barbwire that reminded Gary of a Chinese concentration camp secured the entire base. A Memorial Service for President John F. Kennedy interrupted his writing on this day.

Another letter reflected: "This is quite a place—if the world needed an enema they would insert it here. You cannot possibly imagine the filth. 80% of the population have VD. The people are very small (their) life span is 38 years. A girl working for us is 19 years old and has 5 children and she lost 2 others. The hunting season here is in full swing all year round—after people."

Three days before his death Gary wrote he had been transferred to Saigon. He surmised, "The only way we will ever win this war is by pulling out. We must train the Vietnamese to train their own and (then) we could win."

"Supplies are scarce. But that's because Sec. of Defense Mr. Mac Namara said we would win the war in one more year." The U.S. (reports) thousands are being returned, but fails to mention replacements have already arrived."

Bamboo pole used for carrying water.
PHOTO: LARRY PETERSEN

December 14, 1963

Major **JAMES ALLRED**, career soldier and father of five from Twin Falls, Idaho dies in an offshore Med-Evac helicopter mission.

A 1943 graduate of Twin Falls High School, James dedicated most of his adult life to military service. A veteran of WWII and Korea, he had flown fixed wing and rotor type airplanes in Vietnam since May of 1963. With the first half of his tour completed, James was in the Officers Club waiting to leave on R&R when a request for a medical rescue mission came over the radio. Dressed in civilian clothes, off-duty James immediately left to assist.

On the ground jeep lights guided the Huey to the extraction area, but also alerted the enemy to the precarious position. After successfully loading the casualties aboard, James and his crew were shot down over the sea before they could clear the area. The surviving co-pilot reported James' last effort was attempting to save a crewman who couldn't swim. The medic and wounded passengers and pilot all perished less than a mile from safety. The man who had given his life to service, including the gift of a vegetable seed program to help the Vietnam highland Montagnard tribes earlier that year, had given the ultimate gift of sacrifice to his country.

Montagnard Village.
PHOTO: LARRY PETERSEN

December
By the end of the year President Johnson had increased the number of American advisors to 16,300 and the U.S. had sent $500 million to South Vietnam.

January
General William Westmoreland (b.1914)
was appointed deputy commander of
Military Assistance in Vietnam (MACV),
and in June was promoted as com-
mander.

August 4
President Johnson reported to congres-
sional leaders that a second attack had
been made on the Maddox, although this
attack was never confirmed and was
later shown not to have taken place.

August 7
The Gulf Of Tonkin Resolution, a joint res-
olution approving U.S. action in
Southeast Asia was passed by Congress.

February 7
Following a VC raid against the American
base at Pleiku, in which nine soldiers
were killed and five aircraft were
destroyed, U.S. Airforce planes initiated
Operation Flaming Dart against North
Vietnamese military bases just above the
17th Parallel.

February 24
The U.S. begins Operation Rolling
Thunder, the sustained bombing of North
Vietnam.

Lyndon Baines Johnson was elected President.

Racial violence and protests in many U.S. cities marked the year. Deterioration of the situation in Southeast Asia resulted in greater U.S. military and economic assistance to South Vietnam.

August 2 Gulf Of Tonkin

While conducting electronic surveillance ten miles off North Vietnam, in the Gulf of Tonkin, the American destroyer Maddox was pursued by three North Vietnamese torpedo boats. As the patrol boats closed in, the Maddox opened fire and the patrol boats responded with torpedoes, which missed. The destroyer called for air support from the nearby carrier Ticonderoga, and three United States fighter planes attacked the boats. The Maddox sank one patrol boat, crippled the other two, and withdrew. Two days later the Maddox and a second destroyer, the Turner Joy, were ordered back to Tonkin to "reassert freedom in international waters."

August 5

Johnson ordered U.S. planes to bomb North Vietnam in retaliation for the "attacks" on the U.S. ships. The American bombing mission was called "limited in scale", but more than sixty sorties (a sortie is one flight of one plane) are flown, destroying oil depots and patrol boats. Two American planes were shot down resulting in the capture of downed pilot Everett Alvarez Jr., the first Prisoner of War (POW) of the Vietnam War. He remained in Hanoi prisons for eight years.

August 7 The Gulf Of Tonkin Resolution

The Tonkin Resolution granted authority to the president to use " all necessary measures" to repel an armed attack and to help any SEATO nation asking assistance in defense of its freedom. U.S. Senators Wayne Morse and Ernest Gruening challenged the resolution on grounds that Congress alone had power to declare war. The Tonkin Gulf Resolution had the effect of transferring that power to the president. But Congress had already supported one aid package after another to save Vietnam and overwhelmingly voted in favor of the resolution.

The American people also approved of the resolution and the president's swift reply to aggression. Communist China and the Soviet Union felt differently and pledged to support North Vietnam, seeing that country as a victim of U.S. imperialism. North Vietnam called the bombing of their territory criminal and denied they were sending large numbers of troops down the Ho Chi Minh Trail.

Not long after the Tonkin Gulf incident, Saigon was in a state of near anarchy as Catholics and Buddhists battled each other in the streets.

October 30

In a Viet Cong attack on the U.S. airbase at Bien Hoa, six B-57 bombers are destroyed and five Americans are killed. Bien Hoa was only twelve miles from Saigon, prompting Washington that something had to be done to improve security.

December

The number of American military advisors in Vietnam rises to 23,300.

1965

U.S. participation in the war in Vietnam was protested by many in demonstrations across the nation. Before year's end, U.S. losses in Vietnam since January 1961 exceeded 1300 dead and 6100 wounded. The use of helicopters for medical evacuations helped keep the fatality rate of those hospitalized below 2%.

March 8

The Supreme Court Decision on "conscientious objectors" unanimously ruled a person holding a sincere belief in a Supreme Being, even though differing from the beliefs held by accepted religions, may be exempted from military combat training and service. (A favorable ruling for young men with no college deferment who wished to avoid the draft.)

March 8-9

The first U.S. combat forces waded ashore on the beach at Da Nang. More than 3500 Marines (two battalions) land in South Vietnam to guard the airbase at Da Nang, joining 23,500 other Americans serving as advisors in South Vietnam. With no air power capability, the Viet Cong strategy was to attack American Bases. Westmoreland requested 40,000 additional ground combat troops. In early April 3,600 sorties were flown against North Vietnam.

Another 50,000 troops were slated for deployment by the end of the 1965. Cautious over dissension at home and on the international front, Johnson did not commit America to the Vietnam conflict in one dramatic move. Instead, he was hopeful the gradual measures taken would be enough to kill Hanoi's will to carry on a war against South Vietnam.

July 28
Pres. Johnson announced U.S. troop levels in South Vietnam would be increased from 75,000 to 125,000 and the Draft would be doubled from 17,000 to 35,000 a month.

August 16
Total U.S. Casualties since Jan. 1, 1961 were 561 killed, 3024 wounded, 44 missing in action (MIA), and 269 dead of noncombat causes.

August 26, 1965
An announcement from President Johnson that the "draft marriage deferment" would be struck down at midnight resulted in 132 couples rushing to be married just before midnight in Las Vegas, Nevada. (The marriage deferment was dropped short months later).

Three Years of Escalation Follow:

April 15
Students for a Democratic Society (SDS) sponsor a large antiwar rally in Washington.

June 17
The first mass bombing raid in the Vietnam War, Guam-based B-52's bombed a Viet Cong concentration, 30 miles north of Saigon. It was the first combat use of the heavy jet bombers since they were placed in operation in 1952.

July 12, 1965
Twenty-eight-year-old **FRANK REASONER** from Kellogg, Idaho risks his own life in a fire fight with Viet Cong insurgents and is posthumously awarded the Congressional Medal of Honor for 'conspicuous gallantry above and beyond the call of duty.'

SUBMITTED BY: FRANK REASONER FAMILY

"1st Lt. Reasoner was leading a reconnaissance patrol deep within enemy territory when his men came under extremely heavy fire from 50 to 100 Viet Cong. Accompanying the advance party and [acting as point which consisted of 5 men], Frank immediately organized his men to fend off the assault that came from numerous concealed positions. Boldly shouting encouragement and completely isolated from the main body, he organized a base of fire for an assault on the enemy positions.

The slashing fury of the Viet Cong machine gun and automatic weapons made it impossible for the main body to move forward to assist. Repeatedly exposing himself to the devastating attack, Frank skillfully provided covering fire, killing at least 2 Viet Cong and silenced an automatic weapons position in a valiant attempt to evacuate a wounded man. As casualties began to mount, his radio operator was wounded. When the radio operator was hit a second time trying to reach a covered position, Frank courageously ran to his aid through grazing machine gun fire and fell mortally wounded."

The honorable citation presented to his family continued: "His indomitable fighting spirit, valiant leadership and unflinching devotion to duty provided the inspiration that was to enable the patrol to complete its mission without further casualties. In the face of almost certain death he gallantly gave his life in the service of his country. His actions upheld the highest traditions of the Marine Corps and the U.S. Naval Service."

Army
Medal of Honor

"The Medal of Honor dates back to 1862, when it was authorized by Congress during the Civil War. Its long history is marked by many acts of bravery, conspicuous gallantry, and (most often) the sacrifice of one's own life for others in combat."

AIR FORCE & SPACE DIGEST MARCH 1967

October 17, 1965

Navy Pilot L. Cdr. **RODERICK MAYER** Listed as Missing in Action (MIA) and taken Prisoner of War (POW).

A 1957 graduate of Lewiston High School, Roderick Mayer attended the University of Idaho on a Navy ROTC scholarship. Following graduation in 1961, he was commissioned an Ensign in the Navy and sent to the Naval Academy in Annapolis, MD. There he and three others were chosen from 52 colleges and universities to attend the first class in Space Navigation. He also received the award for the most outstanding academic student in advanced Navy Flight Command, Jet Carrier Phase. Before receiving orders for Vietnam, Roderick had passed screening tests as a potential astronaut for NASA.

In Vietnam, this promising young Idaho native was stationed aboard the USS Independence. A pilot of the F4 Phantom Black Aces, he had flown more than 70 missions when he was shot down over the Thai Nguyen bridge near Hanoi on October 17, 1965. He and his co-pilot, Dave Wheat ejected and were taken prisoners. Dave Wheat spent 7 1/2 years in a North

Navy Pilot Roderick Mayer

Vietnamese prison camp and was released in 1973. There has been no word on the fate of Rod.

A Sunday, September 10, 2000 Internet Tribute posted thirty-five years later reads:

"Florida Waiting for you to come home."
"Lt. Mayer's aircraft was one of three our airgroup lost on October 17, 1965. I was working on the flight deck and can remember the feeling of despair when his aircraft did not return…He was a likeable man that took care of his men."

(Ed Elster)

★★★

October 30, 1965

Pocatello, Idaho loses its first man in Vietnam. 20-year-old **GRANT CLARK** dies near Da Nang from enemy fire.

A fun loving boy who was always found on the baseball All Stars Team and surrounded by friends, Grant graduated from Pocatello High School in 1963 and immediately joined the Marine Corps. With a strong sense of responsibility and achievement, he went to Vietnam in August of 1965 where his abilities were immediately noticed and he was promoted to a Corporal.

On April 12, 2000 the untold story appears from the past as Grant's Platoon Sergeant offers Internet tribute for the 'boy who took his place.'

"I picked up Grant between (my) tours. He stood out as a level-headed leader as we trained up at Pendleton. I was acting Plt. Sgt.….and we were sent back to Nam in a hurry after the attack on Da Nang, July 2. He continued to act as my most trusted L/Cpl. A ground surveillance radar unit, we were sent to remote OPs with a sweeping view of the terrain. Grant's perseverance netted us the only proven success of the system that I know of in the conflict. I recommended him for the Naval Commendation, but I don't think it ever came through. As I was also an interpreter, I was pulled out for an extended tour as Marine Liaison to the nearby Vietnamese District Headquarters, and Grant, now a Corporal took my place. That night my old position was hit by enemy mortar fire, and my friend Grant Clark was killed."

(John J. Burke)

★★★

The buildup of American troops during 1965 allowed the unstable South Vietnamese government time to gather strength. While the Viet Cong (or VC—the shortened form of the words *Viet Congsan,* meaning *Vietnamese Communists*) had been held at bay, the North Vietnamese Army (NVA) had been storing tons of

November 14-16
First major conventional clash in the war: U.S. forces take the offensive and defeat North Vietnamese units in the Ia Drang Valley.

supplies (ammunition, heavy guns and medical supplies), near the border of South Vietnam in Cambodia.

The Communists plan was to attack South Vietnam and attempt to cut the country in half. The staging for the first major engagement between American and North Vietnamese soldiers was in place. It began with an attack on the Special Forces camp at Plie Me situated east of the Ia Drang Valley, about thirty miles south of Pleiku. U.S. First Air Cavalry Division helicopters were called in and the enemy force was annihilated. American forces now took the initiative as a "search-and-destroy" mission in the Ia Drang Valley commenced.

November 17-1965

22-year-old **JIMMY NAKAYAMA** from Rigby, Idaho dies of severe napalm burns and is listed among the fallen at Ia Drang, "The Valley Of Death."

Thirty-five years after that fateful day in the central highlands of Vietnam, on May 27, 2000 Doug Connor, a former comrade and friend posts an Internet remembrance entitled:

"Friend Of The Cav."
"A tribute to Jimmy, one of the 234 young Americans who died in three days of fighting in LZ-Xray, and Albany, November 1965 in the Valley of Death, the Ia Drang. Lest we forget our fallen heroes, those who gave the last measure of devotion. May their souls be cradled in the Arms of the Lord forever."

November 17

Following several days of intense combat and hand-to-hand fighting, B-52's dropped enormous payloads on NVA positions. As the battle continued, American fighter bombers were called in to drop naplam (jellied gasoline) on the NVA, engulfing men and vegetation in fire. After the napalm sorties, The NVA's will to carry on the fight seemed to disappear. The punishing American firepower caused the remainder of the North Vietnamese regular troops to flee into the jungle or back to the base camps in Cambodia.

The success of the Ia Drang campaign gave encouragement to the military strategists in Washington and Saigon. If the U.S. could inflict enough battlefield defeats on the North, Hanoi's will to fight would eventually deteriorate. Superior technological know-how and American military expertise would ultimately result in such a high "body count" that Hanoi and the VC would be forced to withdraw. The cycle of escalation increased as the U.S. accepted an even greater role in the war in Vietnam.

November 27
Anti-Vietnam War demonstrations were held in Washington D.C. with 15,000 to 25,000 protestors.

December 25
President Johnson suspends bombing in an attempt to get North Vietnam to negotiate. By year's end, American troop strength is 184,000 and combat losses total 636 Americans killed. At home, draft quotas have doubled.

Unlike the front lines of other wars, fire bases in Vietnam had a 360° perimeter. A favorite tactic of the enemy forces, was to attack the perimeter at night.
PHOTOS: LARRY PETERSEN

November 20

U.S. Casualties in Vietnam after a week-long battle in the Ia Drang Valley were placed at 240 dead, 470 wounded, and six missing, exceeding the Korean War weekly average of 209 killed.

Hundreds of soldiers were arriving "in country" on a regular basis, as engineers built new airfields and harbors to support the ever-growing military installations of South Vietnam.

Conditions Soldiers Faced

The following condensed account of James A. Warren's writings in "Portrait of a Tragedy" aptly describes Vietnam as a much different war than American troops had been trained to fight.

"Like all foreign troops who fought in Indochina, the Americans faced great difficulties in adjusting to the climate and to the unorthodox methods of a determined enemy. The monsoons and excessive heat for much of the year made moving in the bush an agonizing experience. The terrain of South Vietnam varies considerably. Many infantry soldiers, as they humped the trails through jungles, across rice paddies, and over mountains, came down with malaria or jungle rot, a condition affecting the skin which makes movement of any kind excruciatingly painful. Snakes, red ants, scorpions, leeches, and mud were their constant companions.

The American soldier frequently carried sixty pounds of equipment, sometimes even more, while on patrol. With all that weight, including a hot steel helmet, heat prostration was a real danger. Some soldiers died from it.

In pursuit of an elusive enemy, American troops often found themselves in combat at the time and place of the enemy's choosing. In the Mekong Delta, U.S. troops could be pinned down for hours at a time in the hot sun in flooded rice paddies. In the jungle areas, dense undergrowth had to be chopped down by hand, yard by yard. Firefights in the jungle often took place at very close quarters, a few dozen

yards or less, and were extremely intense, with everyone firing on full automatic and lobbing grenades.

...By 1966, American ground forces had an awesome array of weaponry and equipment to hunt down and destroy the enemy's armed forces. The helicopter became the symbol of the war... Soldiers could be lifted into small isolated LZs (landing zones) in a hurry, allowing American units to close in on an unsuspecting enemy... Once troops had finished their mission, the helicopter could extract them quickly as well. Many a wounded soldier's life was saved by heroic "medevac" pilots, who risked their own lives by landing on "hot" LZs to evacuate the wounded... Helicopters ferried the wounded to Army surgical hospitals or to hospital ships offshore. In Vietnam, 19 percent of the wounded died, compared to 30 percent in World War II.

...Reconnaissance was another function of the UH-1Huey... The choppers performed an essential role in clear-and-hold and search-and-destroy missions. The strategies developed by General William Westmoreland were essential in a war without a single front. American and South Vietnamese troops were... to find, fix in place, fight, and destroy enemy forces... As the infantry troops patrolled on the ground, their activities had to be coordinated with artillery support... Airplanes, helicopters and communication devices used in the war required extensive maintenance. Coordination between base camps, the smaller fire-support bases, and airfields had to be accurate and precise... or American lives would be needlessly lost.

To meet the...needs of the war effort, the vast majority of Americans in Vietnam were assigned to supply and support functions, not actual combat operations... Twenty-seven major base camps were built in the country, many of them resembling small cities.

[The enemy initiated much of the actual fighting during 1966 and 1967. The VC and NVA knew the subtleties of the terrain] and could avoid contact unless they felt they could escape from American heliborne troops and artillery... Patrolling in Vietnam in search of the enemy was a nerve-racking affair. [In] a war without fronts, the soldier never knew when or where a firefight might occur. [Experts at camouflage techniques the enemy ambushed many American patrols.] Even more unnerving than the unexpected fire from the VC or NVA was the wide assortment of booby traps—pungi stakes dipped in poison and placed in carefully hidden pits and "bouncing Betty" mines, designed to blow up at crotch level [were a constant danger].

A favored NVA and VC tactic was the night frontal assault upon isolated American fire bases...

[When bad weather prevented superior American air power to save the day]... it was not unheard-of for NVA or VC units to overrun entire American companies."

(Portrait Of A Tragedy, pp.79-84)

Scenes of typical fire bases in Vietnam
PHOTOS: LARRY PETERSEN

January 31
President Johnson announced resumption of bombing raids on North Vietnam which had been suspended on Dec. 24 in hopes of furthering negotiations.

February 22
Operation White Wing, a month-long search and destroy mission by more than 20,000 U.S., South Vietnamese and South Korean (ROK) troops in Quang Ngai Providence in South Vietnam, ended after enemy resistance collapsed. Communist troop deaths were reported at 1130.

March 10
A Green Beret camp was overrun by about 2000 North Vietnamese troops after a 72 hour siege. About 200 U.S. and South Vietnamese troops were killed or captured at the Special Forces base in the A Shau Valley.

Steadily escalating participation in the Vietnamese War resulted in 5008 U.S. troop deaths and 30,093 wounded in 1966, bringing the total casualties since Jan.1, 1961, to 6664 killed and 37,738 wounded. By the end of the year, the U.S. had almost 400,000 troops in Southeast Asia. Among the antiwar demonstrations were the International Days of Protest (March 25-27), during which parades and rallies were held in seven U.S. and foreign cities.

March 10, 1966

BERNARD (BERNIE) FISHER from Kuna , Idaho (1927-) Airforce pilot and father of five, becomes the second Idaho native to receive the Congressional Medal of Honor for gallantry above and beyond the call of duty in the historic battle of South Vietnam's A Shau Valley.

The U.S. Special Forces camp at A Shau was located in the northwest corner of South Vietnam, near the border of Laos, about 60 miles west of Da Nang. Situated in a valley seven miles long at the juncture of three canyons, and surrounded by 1,500-foot hills, the camp consisted of a triangular fort next to a small steel landing strip.

The enemy's ground attack was launched during extremely bad weather, with rain and mist and low-hanging clouds obscuring the surrounding hills down to the 800-foot level. When enemy troops (estimated at 2,000 to 3,000 men) opened fire with machine guns, mortars and light artillery in the hills, the besieged camp of 450 personnel called for air support. Weather conditions made it extremely difficult to deliver, but jet and propeller-driven fighter-bombers were sent hoping some would be able to penetrate the heavy overcast.

Bernie reports, "All during my tour of duty in Vietnam, we had a lot to do with the Special Forces people. They were our babies—great bunch of guys—and we looked after them real carefully."

Bernie's squadron was based at Pleiku, about 140 miles south of A Shau, or about an hour's flying time in the A-1E Skyraider, the aircraft he was flying at the time. With a 14-foot prop, the heavy-built plane could fly low and carry a lot of ordinance. The A Shau camp had been under attack for several days with Navy and Marine F-4 Phantoms and F-Cruisers "on top" unable to get down into the valley with adverse weather conditions. The only support they could offer was bombing from radio coordinates. When an AC-47 Dragon Ship was shot down, along with a helicopter that went in to try to rescue the crew, the A-1E Skyraiders were called in.

Bernie led the first Skyraider flight, followed by wingman Bruce Wallace. Other flights followed, but when the command first arrived they couldn't find the valley. "All we could see were clouds with an occasional mountain peak sticking up," Bernie recalls. "So down we went, looking for the camp. Twice we ran into a dead end—either solid overcast or a mountain wall and had to make a fast one-eighty and pop back up on top."

On the third attempt the team found their target and made a number of strafing runs on the enemy trenches. "The ceiling," Bernie said, " was so low that when Bruce and the other pilots made their steep turns over the camp, you'd see one wing right in the treetops and the top wing would be up in the overcast. Sometimes you couldn't see anything except the trees right underneath you, and you had to be real careful without any forward vision. But we gave the people in the camp as much close support as we could, using up all our ordinance."

When Bernie heard the anxious call from camp for rescue helicopters, he led the huey's flight leader down through the 'soup' and into the dangerous box canyon. Realizing they were getting low on fuel Bernie and Bruce needed to head back to Pleiku. "But we'd been listening to the guys in camp talking on FM... and they were yelling for blood plasma and morphine. When you start calling for this kind of stuff, you're hurting, so I knew they had a lot of dead and wounded."

"If a man is down, you just don't leave him there . . ."

Major Bernard F. Fisher
United States Air Force
☆ ☆ ☆
The Medal of Honor
for action above and
beyond the call of
duty on March 10, 1966

THE AIRFORCE AND SPACE DIGEST MARCH 1967

A couple of C-123s were overhead, carrying the medical supplies the Special Forces needed, so with Bernie in the lead and Bruce following, the two guided the big 123s down the hole and through the 7 mile canyon to the camp. Under enemy fire they dropped their bundles, hitting most of their targets. After declaring an emergency because of low fuel, Bernie and Bruce landed in Da Nang before refueling and returning to their base at Pleiku. All through the night the Special Forces camp fought on. The next morning, before daylight, word came they had lost the camp. At least, contact had been lost during the night and new targets were assigned for the day.

While in flight that day Bernie recognized the coordinates as A Shau—the ground defenders had made contact again. Once again, dense overcast prevented the larger planes from descending. Joined by five other A-1s Bernie searched for a light spot in the clouds. Seeing a plowed field below he called over the radio, "Tally-Ho, let's go." The cloud cover had lifted to around 800 feet and under intense .50-caliber fire that looked like 'a fireworks display,' the six brave commanders proceeded to making strafing runs on enemy positions—resulting in some 300 to 500 enemy dead. Making radio contact with a soldier on the ground, Bernie reported he was the A-1 that had just buzzed him and they were there to help.

Relieved to see the planes he reported, "We've been overrun. They've got us except we've got some troops in this little northwest bunker—a mortar bunker—and we've only got one corner of it. There's about 180 of us left."

One plane was hit and another was down when Colonel "Jump" Myers called and said he had been hit too. Spotting his plane at about 200 feet 'off the deck' Bernie could see he was on fire and his cockpit full of smoke. Next to the camp was a landing strip made of steel planking that appeared to be about 2,500 long. A Skyraider needs 3,000 feet of runway to land, so Bernie checked with the Aerial Command overhead whose maps indicated 3,300 feet. Myers' plane was burning quickly as Bernie lined him up for the final approach and talked him through his landing checklist.

With all the confusion and smoke in the cockpit Myers was coming in too fast and Bernie yelled, "You're too hot. Jump! Pull your gear and belly it in. YANK YOUR GEAR!" Myers pulled his gear and settled onto the ground on top of his 300-gallon drop tank that no one noticed had not released on time. The tank blew as instantly as it hit the steel planking. Flames from the burning fuel raced him all the way down the runway. As the plane skidded down the strip and nosed over in the underbrush a huge fireball surrounded him. Thinking no one could survive such an explosion Bernie banked down to get a closer look. To his relief and surprise, Jump had climbed over his wing and was running through the flames before diving beneath an overhanging where the enemy couldn't hit him.

Calling for a rescue helicopter, the four planes that were left continued to strafe the area around Myers so the enemy couldn't get to him—their hits at times as close as 20 feet, although they couldn't actually see where he was hiding. He later said, "The sweetest pain I ever felt was those empty shell casings hitting me as you guys went over me on your strafing runs." Sooner or later they would run out of ordinance and with a helicopter some twenty minutes out, Bernie decided to go in alone. Supported by cover from the other A-1s, he set up for a normal landing thinking he could pick Jump up about two-thirds down the runway, turn around and take off downwind.

Heavy smoke blinded Bernie's view and mortar hits on the steel runway had made big mushroom-shaped craters with steel prongs standing up about a foot and a half around the hole. 55-gallon fuel drums at the end of the runway and debris from the camp buildings that had been blown out on the strip made a landing next to impossible.

"I couldn't stop the first time," Bernie recalls, "so I just threw the power to it and lifted back off." Circling back in a tear drop pattern and staying only 50 feet off the ground, he came back in the other direction. Maneuvering back and forth to avoid all the garbage on the strip, the plane barely stopped at the far end of the runway. Hitting the brakes hard, Bernie pulled a one-eighty and came back down the strip in the other direction. Taxiing pretty fast he spotted

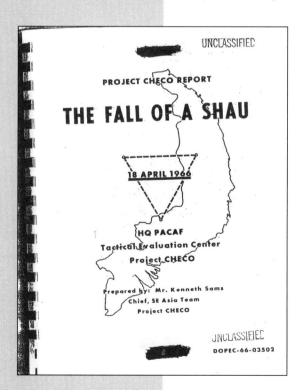

Jump crouched under the bank waving his arms to say, "Here I am!" Traveling another 150 feet before he could stop Bernie waited for a minute thinking, "Where in the blazes are you?" Then three bullets hit the airplane.

"One went through the cockpit right in front of me, in one side and out the other. It's funny. With all the trouble I had getting that bird on the ground, I'd forgotten about enemy fire. In fact, I wasn't even too concerned until they hit me...but that snaps you to attention all right."

When it dawned on Bernie that Jump might not be able to make it, he determined he would go after him. As he started to get out of the plane Jump was crawling up the backside of the right wing. "All I could see was these bloody red eyes—you know, the term everybody uses, and boy he had 'em. He was burnt and bruised and covered with mud, but he was there."

Exhausted from the ordeal Jump was too weak to climb inside so Bernie grabbed him by the seat of the pants and dragged him in headfirst onto the floor of the airplane. Only two-thirds of the runway was left, but with flaps up and riding the rudder hard, Bernie lifted off—barely missing the trees at the end of the runway. Making a couple of quick turns to throw off any enemy gunners that might be tracking them, the courageous Idaho Major didn't stop climbing until he reached 11,000 feet. As he leveled off and looked around, there was his trusted wingman—Paco Vasquez—right beside him. Radio trouble earlier had prevented them from communicating through the harrowing escape.

When Bernie and Jump arrived at their Pleiku base medics were waiting to assist with injuries and three star generals were on sight to congratulate them. Bernie's plane had been hit eleven times and to his great sorrow the camp at A Shau was lost. Only a small number of Special Forces personnel and South Vietnamese troops were able to escape in groups of two or three; the rest were killed or captured.

For his action in rescuing Colonel Myers, Major Fisher received the Medal of Honor, presented to him by President Lyndon Johnson at a White House Ceremony on January 19, 1967. The first living Air Force recipient of the Medal of Honor since World War II, Bernie remains a humble and unassuming man. When asked 30 years later why he did it, he replied with a quiver in his voice and tears glistening in his eyes, *"If there's a man down...you just don't leave him there."*

Bernard Fisher—fellow Idahoan, and true American hero.

(Compiled from interview with Mr. Fisher and featured articles in "Popular Aviation" May/June 1967, and "The Air Force and Space Digest", March 1967.)

April 11, 1966 Easter Attack

For the survivors of Charlie Co. perched near the village of Xa Cam, 40 miles east of Saigon, the horror of war was concentrated in one day—April 11, 1966. The com-

April 23

April 23
North Vietnamese aircraft for the first time attacked U.S. aircraft flying over North Vietnam.

May 1
The first intentional shelling of Cambodian targets occurred when U.S. artillery fired on forces attacking U.S. troops operating along the Caibac River.

May 15
More than 10,000 persons picketed the White House in antiwar demonstrations.

May 30
In the heaviest air raids on North Vietnam to date, more than 300 U.S. planes bombed targets. On May 31st an important North Vietnamese arsenal was virtually destroyed by U.S. bombers.

June 3-13
A major battle was fought in the Kontum Province in the Central Highlands of South Vietnam. No figures on U.S. casualties were announced.

June 29
Hanoi and Haiphong were bombed for the first time in the Vietnam War. Oil storage and loading installations, highways, railroads, bridges, and ships were attacked. Approximately two-thirds of North Vietnam's oil supply was destroyed within a week. Meanwhile the intensity and size of ground operations grew as American troops tried to counteract the ever-increasing flow of NVA troops into the south.

pany, consisting of four platoons of infantry, was poised to engage in Operation Abilene, a strategic plan to send small units of American soldiers to search out and destroy the Viet Cong. Usually the company was 291 men strong, but 157 men were in the rear or out of action, as the remaining 134 soldiers prepared to snake through the dense jungle in search of D-800, (a powerful Viet Cong battalion—triple the size of the pared-down Charlie Company.) Soon enemy intelligence determined they had located an isolated American unit and a horrific battle ensued. The Viet Cong attacked at dawn and the American sightings of khaki uniforms were ominous. First-line officers of the NVA were directing the farmer-soldiers in black pajamas. The American troops were surrounded.

Heavy casualties continued throughout the day and in the afternoon Air Force Huskie helicopters arrived to evacuate the wounded and dead. Troopers first cut a hole in the treetops so the choppers could lower a bullet-shaped jungle penetrator down to the jungle floor. As the pilot skillfully maneuvered his helicopter to hover above the hole in the trees, a steel cable would lower a man to the smoking battleground 200 feet below. Once he was on the ground, the hoist cable was reeled up and attached to a litter basket and then re-lowered to the airman below. Under intense enemy fire the familiar scene of the Med Evac helicopters occurred on a regular basis throughout the jungles and mountainsides of Vietnam.

The intense fighting of the Easter attack continued through the night before Bravo Company could hack through the jungle terrain and come to the rescue. As day lightened, 28 survivors heard Air Force Huskies and Army Chinooks overhead. With no place to land para-rescue men rode cables down from their choppers to the jungle floor below. Rope ladders tumbled out from the rear doors of the Chinooks and engineers descended the swinging ladders. Chain saws and other gear were dropped and soon trees were falling and helicopters landing. With 106 of 134 men killed or wounded, Charlie Company had suffered a casualty rate of 80 percent. "Unwritten in any of the after-action reports, were the wounds this battle and others like it would inflict on the men who fought them and on their families."

(Condensed from "The Washington Post Magazine", May 1989 by George C. Wilson, author of "Mud Soldiers".)

July Operation Hastings

The Marine effort in Vietnam was primarily restricted to the northernmost military tactical zone in South Vietnam, known as I Corps. Operation Hastings, the largest enemy Marine Operation in Vietnam, was triggered by enemy troop movement. During the first week of July, helicopters dropped a recon (reconnaissance) squad in behind enemy-controlled territory. The squad found signs of large-scale NVA activity, as an entire division (up to 20,000) of North Vietnamese soldiers were moving across the Ben Hai River into South Vietnam. General Westmoreland believed General Giap planned to attack the highly populated coast of Quang Tri Province. He ordered six marine infantry battalions, some 8,000 men, along with ARVN (Army of the Republic of South Vietnam) troops to find the North Vietnamese and drive them back across the DMZ (the demilitarized zone) separating North and South Vietnam at the 17th parallel.

July 15, as the first Marines were being airlifted into the Ngan River Valley, about five miles south of the border between North and South Vietnam, two large CH-46 choppers collided and crashed, killing a number of marines. A third helicopter crashed trying to put men on the ground. The remaining choppers descended under heavy attack and the battle began. The marines found themselves in thick jungle and tall grass, and as darkness fell the NVA mounted a frontal assault on a battalion of marines it had managed to surround. But the tough infantrymen held their ground throughout the night. The following night brought more of the same as air strikes and artillery had to be called in dangerously close to marine positions in order to fend off the NVA soldiers, more than a hundred of whom were killed that night alone.

As the battle continued, clever lures would draw American troops out of their foxholes into carefully prepared ambushes, then NVA soldiers would retreat into the darkness of the jungle waiting for another chance to draw the Americans onto dangerous ground. Two weeks later on August 3rd, sporadic fighting continued as the assault was officially ended. Although the NVA had been successfully pushed back up north beyond the DMZ, Operation Hastings became a frustrating success for the marines who suffered heavy losses. The rules of engagement set by Washington prohibited the troops from crossing the DMZ in pursuit of the enemy. 126 Americans had been killed and 448 wounded.

⁓

Body Count

Throughout America's involvement in Vietnam there was constant pressure from Washington to "quantify" the war, and provide actual evidence of the losses inflicted on the enemy. One result was the policy of "body count," based on the presumably simple process of counting the number of enemy dead after each firefight or battle. The daily statistics would then be relayed up the chain of command, enabling the Department of Defense (DOD) to issue figures that would show progress in the war.

But the grisly process of body count was more difficult in practice. Quite often enemy remains were physically impossible to identify, even if the Americans succeeded in occupying the disputed ground. Many times it was equally impossible to distinguish between combatant and non-combatant dead, leading to distorted figures and unreliable reports.

July 30
The demilitarized zone (DMZ) separating North and South Vietnam was bombed by U.S. planes for the first time.

August 6
Antiwar demonstrations were held across the country on the anniversary of the atomic bombing of Hiroshima in 1945.

Sept.18-24
U.S. weekly casualties hit a record 970: 142 killed, 825 wounded, 3 missing. During the same period South Vietnamese losses were 98 killed, 280 wounded, 71 missing.

Sept 23
Aerial defoliation of areas immediately south of the demilitarized Zone (DMZ) between North and South Vietnam had begun. The U.S. military command announced the chemical defoliant, Agent Orange would be used to deprive infiltrating North Vietnamese of protective cover.

Oct. 13
The heaviest air strike on North Vietnam to date was made by 173 U.S. bombers. The next day 175 bombers renewed the raid. On Oct. 15 it was announced that 403 U.S. planes and three helicopters had been lost over North Vietnam since Feb. 7, 1965.

October 25
A conference between President Johnson and heads of Six Allied Nations involved in Vietnam issued a peace plan— Australia, the Philippines, Thailand, New Zealand South Korea, and South Vietnam.

Oct. 26
A fire at sea on the U.S.Carrier Oriskany in the Gulf of Tonkin, killed 43 men and injured 16.

November 4, 1966

A Sandpoint Idaho soldier, 31-year-old **WILLIAM HUNT** is Missing In Action (MIA) after voluntarily leaving his aircraft to assist troops on the ground.

Serving as a replacement Special Forces Platoon leader ten miles from Dau Tieng, William ignored his own wounds while assisting an injured comrade. The Sergeant then sent the rest of his patrol ahead to prevent the Viet Cong from overtaking their dwindling ranks. A Nung (native tribesman) soldier stayed behind with William and later reported he had died, but no body was ever recovered. William left a wife and two sons.

After studying the anti-war furor, William's grown son believed the U.S. was right in entering the Vietnam War. But the conflict dragged on too long because politicians didn't let the military carry out the war operation to end it sooner. "Protestors," he writes, "were taking it out on the wrong people. They were protesting against the government but the backlash came down on the individual soldier."

December 17, 1966

Thirteen days of hell begin for 19-year-old **JOHN LARSON'S** family in Blackfoot, Idaho. The telegram reporting he was missing in action arrived as they were decorating the Christmas tree. With no word from the military or Red Cross of his hospitalization, they learn December 30th their only son had succumbed to his wounds and would not be returning home.

In an enemy assault near Vong Song above the Central Highlands, John's company came under heavy fire from well-entrenched enemy positions hidden by hedgerows less than 40 meters ahead. Several key men, including the company commander, a platoon leader and one of the platoon medical aide men were wounded in heavy point-blank fire. John rushed forward through the withering fire and began treating the more seriously wounded men in his platoon.

Despite pleas from his platoon leader to wait until the firing subsided, Larson made several trips to help treat and evacuate the wounded. After he had treated the more seriously wounded in his platoon, he moved to another platoon where the medical aide man was down and began treating injuries in that unit as well. As casualties continued to mount, John moved back and forth between the two units, repeatedly exposing himself to hostile fire. When a close friend was hit he raced forward still another time and shielded his buddy with his own body while working feverishly to revive him. John was critically wounded at that point and subsequently died from the wounds he sustained while attempting to save his friend's life.

The former Snake River High School student wrote home September 27, 1966:

Dear Folks:
"Hope this letter finds all is well. I am writing this by moonlight overlooking a rice paddy. All is well, we moved into this area today to help another company that was hit here this afternoon.

We have been walking in the mountains since the 13th and they are straight up and down, and covered with brush. Can't even see the sky most of the time. So this flatland is nice. We are in the Bong Suon area...in the Central Highlands (and) could see the China Sea yesterday, must be 10-12 miles from it. Sorry about having to write like this but no time. Had no deaths in the company, had to patch up a few—will be in the field until the 15th of Dec.

This place is beautiful...I should be a missionary here instead of a soldier, these people need help and I'd like to help them. Write even if I can't write you. I am eating C rations out of a can 3 times a day, shave every once in awhile, haven't washed or bathed since the 12th, but I'm used to the smell now, have my hair cut in a mohawk.

I think I became a man a couple of weeks ago when a 50-caliber machine gun cut down on us. And the first man in the platoon got hit with a booby trap. A 50 round is as long as this paper. I really do like it over here except for the leeches, the place is full of land and water leeches. My body is home for many different animals or crabs or what have you. But that don't bother me as I say live and let live. Well be good, write and don't worry I am keeping my head down. See you in 11 months." Love, John

John's father writes, *"Every day I see the Purple Heart and Silver Star on the wall with your picture. My only consolation is that you didn't shirk your duty. Then I think of what might have been..."*

★★★

American Troop Strength at the end of the year is nearly 400,000. Casualties for 1966: 5,008 killed and 30,093 wounded. Totals since 1961 are 6,664 killed, 37,738 wounded.

1967

By mid-November of this year, more than 17,000 Americans had died in Vietnam since 1961—2,000 more in the first ten months of 1967—than in the

Scenes from the North Central Highlands Song Dong Ni River (bottom)
PHOTOS: LARRY PETERSEN

January 8, 1967

30,000 combined American and South Vietnamese troops begin Operation Cedar Falls, an offensive against enemy positions in the "Iron Triangle." (Among Battalion commanders in this operation is General Alexander Haig, who later becomes secretary of state under Ronald Reagan.)

January 28-1967

North Vietnamese announce U.S. bombing must stop before there can be peace talks.

period of 1961-1966 combined. U.S. and UN efforts to achieve peace were entirely unsuccessful, with UN Secretary General U. Thant asserting that the impasse was caused by the U.S. bombing of North Vietnam.

January 8, 1967

Twenty miles northwest of Saigon, the capital of South Vietnam, was an important Viet Cong stronghold known to the military as the "Iron Triangle." The Viet Cong had remained concentrated in the area since the early 1950's when the French lost their war. Until now, American and South Vietnamese troops who periodically occupied the area had lacked enough strength in numbers to uproot the VC activity there.

Under Operation Cedar Falls, General Westmoreland determined the entire area would have to be leveled because the Viet Cong were so securely established in the countryside. For several days B-52 sorties hammered the sixty-square mile plot of land. Next followed the airborne infantry. American ground troops uncovered an amazing system of underground complexes, complete with offices, hospitals, supply rooms, arsenal and sleeping quarters. The Viet Cong military headquarters for much of South Vietnam was concealed in the gigantic network.

"Tunnel rats", some of the bravest American soldiers in Vietnam, were required to search the underground complexes to eliminate any remaining VC. Very few were found however, as advance reports of the American operation allowed most of the enemy time to escape into the jungle.

Nearly 16,000 rural villages in South Vietnam were vulnerable to the grasp of the Viet Cong, and the elimination of the VC fortified village of Ben Suc was a primary objective of Cedar Falls. Under the direction of Lt. Colonel Alexander Haig, U.S. soldiers secured the village and evacuated the entire population. Nearly 6,000 people, along with their belongings and livestock——were relocated to a resettlement area. The Vietnamese people held extremely strong and emotional ties to their ancestral lands and resented the army that forcibly removed them from the triangle—even when the soldiers tried to tell them it was for their own good. Military strategists considered Cedar Falls neither a success nor a failure. A trouble spot had been cleared of the enemy, but it required the destroying of an entire village to accomplish it. At home, American television coverage of the leveling of Ben Suc alarmed viewers and policymakers alike.

An estimated 25 percent of the rural Vietnamese population became refugees of war. Poor villagers and farmers fled to the cities of Saigon, Hue, and Da Nang as American bombs and artillery destroyed the countryside. Settling on the outskirts of town, the displaced refugees survived in shacks made from American garbage and refuse. Corrupt importers frequently stole supplies and funds intended for the homeless, while disease and prostitution flourished in the abject poverty.

As the war continued the South Vietnamese forces (AVRN) became more and more content to let the Americans do much of the fighting. Security leaks threatened

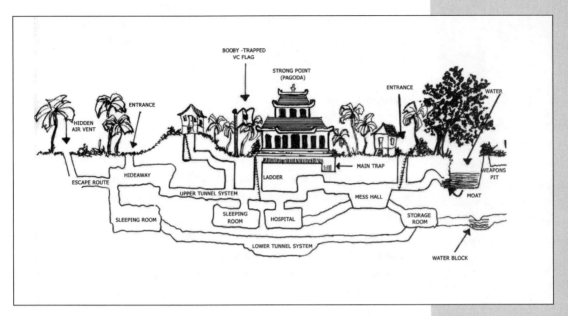

military strategy and many times American soldiers wondered who the real enemy was. Slowly but surely, South Vietnam became more and more dependent upon America to keep it afloat. Countless military engagements between the Americans and Communists continued for the remainder of 1967. By the gruesome standard of body count, the U.S. was the victor of every major battle. The North appeared undaunted by the high death toll it was paying to defy the American military.

February 16, 1967

22-year-old Medic **RONALD MOTTISHAW** from Pocatello, Idaho dies near Cu Chi when the ambulance in which he was transporting the wounded hit a landmine. The 1963 graduate of Pocatello High School was assigned to the 12th Evacuation Hospital. Upon his arrival in Vietnam he wrote:

> Oct.14, 1966 —"Today I got my first look at Vietnam. It is rugged. The mountains seem to rise right at the coast. They are proud and green with long golden beaches along the base. The ocean is jade green and calm. To look at all these things you would never guess the struggle that is going on with those mountains."

> Oct. 16, 1966 —"Flash news! C Company just had contact with a two platoon size unit of Viet Cong. The Aide man came over wanting morphine and other medical supplies. I feel that we have a job to do over here… I am really positive that we should be here and what we will accomplish in the end."

Can Ranh Bay
PHOTO: LARRY PETERSEN

April 4

Military officials announce the 500th U.S. plane had been shot down over North Vietnam since the bombing began in 1964.

April 15

In antiwar demonstrations 100,000 to 400,000 people marched in New York City from Central Park to the UN headquarters. A similar protest in San Francisco drew about 50,000.

April 20

The North Vietnam port of Haiphon was bombed by U.S. planes which destroyed two power plants and struck at North Vietnamese Mig Airfields for the first time.

May 19

The first U.S. air strikes on central Hanoi, North Vietnam's capital begin.

June 1

U.S. Casualties in Vietnam for the week of May 21-27, were reported as 313 killed and 2616 wounded, the greatest weekly casualty toll of the war.

July 2-7

U.S. Marines at Con Thien, just south of the DMZ, suffered heavy casualties in fierce fighting against North Vietnamese units.

Nov. 14, 1966 — "Last night Company C was ambushed but none of the good guys were hurt. We got one of "them" though that is nothing to brag about, killing another human. It's really too bad there has to be wars."

Jan. 10, 1967 — "We went on a 5-day search and destroy mission right after the Christmas truce. We had captured 6 Viet Cong and had no casualties ourselves, that is, until I ran over a mine. The force of the blast blew one track and the rear door off. I didn't get so much as a scratch but everything I had with me burned. Somebody upstairs must have been looking out for me." (Ronald died the following month when the ambulance he was driving hit another concealed mine.)

⋆⋆⋆

June 18-1967

WILLIAM LEMMONS, H-23 helicopter pilot radios to Chu Lai Base that he is 10 miles south. After the communication he is never heard from again. Following a fruitless search, army officials speculate the 25-year-old may have hit an unusual wind sheer that caused him to crash in the river. Listed as Missing In Action, William is officially declared dead on 6-12-78.

One of Idaho's brightest and best, William Lemmons graduated from Pocatello High School in 1960 and Idaho State University (College) in 1965. While serving as Student Body President and President of the ISU Associated Men Students, he helped to get legislation passed that changed the college to University status.

A graduate of ROTC, Bill went to Vietnam in January 1967. There he was in the same company and flew many combat missions with Major Darrel Savage who had served in 2 tours in Vietnam, the first as a Military Training Advisor in the Mekong Delta. During the six months they were together the men developed a strong bond but never discussed where they were from. The day prior to Darrell's return to the states, Billy asked him where home was. When Aberdeen, Idaho came up in the conversation, Bill's eyes lit up as he said he used to live in Aberdeen as a kid. Suddenly the connection became clear. The 31-year-old Major immediately recognized the fleet-footed lad who used to throw rocks in the potato cellar so many harvests ago. About the time Darrell was entering the service in 1953, the Lemmons family had moved from Aberdeen to Pocatello, Idaho. It had been several years since he had last seen Billy and the memories flooded in. On the morrow he would depart from Vietnam, and unknowingly say good-bye forever to the special friendship reunited by war.

No sign was ever found of Major Lemmons' helicopter. He was listed as MIA for 11 years before being officially declared dead by the U.S. government in 1978. He left a wife and two children.

⋆⋆⋆

July 18, 1967

29-year-old **DAVID CHATTERTON** from Twin Falls, Idaho loses his life on a rescue mission to save a downed pilot.

A 1956 graduate of Twin Falls High School, David was a talented musician who enjoyed Pep Band and Marching Band. He entered the Navy the August after graduation and there he met and married a young woman who was also a WAVE. In the Marines his musical talents were utilized as he played drums in the Drum and Bugle Corp. While stationed on the Carrier USS Hornet in the Gulf of Tonkin, David's brother Larry was also serving on the USS Providence.

Chatterton, an anti-submarine warfare technician, was off the coast of Vietnam on his second tour of duty when volunteers were asked to go inland to pick up a downed pilot. Five men went in by helicopter, including David who served as the forward gunner. During the daring rescue the Viet Cong opened fire. The helicopter made it back to the ship but David had been shot in the chest and was mortally wounded. He was the father of three children.

July 27, 1967

Recipient of two Purple Heart Medals, **BOBBY PETERSON** of Bonneville County dies four days before his 20th birthday.

When Viet Cong mortars and rockets unexpectedly attacked Bobby's base camp at Phuoc Vin, 30 miles north of Saigon during the night, the nineteen-year-old's last letter had already reached his family's home in Idaho Falls, Idaho.

June 10, 1967 Bobby wrote that his battalion was going into a hot landing zone the next day and it was certain that many men would die. He was in a cold sweat and said there would be very little sleep that night. In the lonely hours before the conflict, he wanted to write and tell his family that he loved them very much—fearing he might not live through this battle. He expressed the hope that he would be able to send another letter after it was over, letting them know he was all right. The courageous 19-year-old lived another month before the attack at Phuoc Vin, but his family never received another letter.

July 29

An aircraft carrier fire aboard the U.S.S. Forrestal in the Gulf of Tonkin, kills 129 and injures 64.

The USS Forrestal, the Navy's first super Carrier with 5000 men aboard was on assignment in the Gulf of Tonkin the summer of 1967. Saturday, July 29th was another routine mission. Airplanes were loaded and lined up along the sides of the

August
Defense Secretary Robert McNamara testi-
fied before Congress, that the bombing of
of North Vietnam was ineffective.

August 21
The Defense Department announced two
U.S. Navy jets had been shot down over
the People's Republic of China after stray-
ing off course from a bombing mission
over North Vietnam.

September
Major Communist offensives begin.
General Westmoreland fortifies Khe Sanh.

Sept.1-Oct 4
A siege of the U.S. Marine base at Con
Thien, just south of the DMZ in South
Vietnam, raged for more than a month
before U.S. firepower forced North
Vietnamese gunners to withdraw from
their artillery positions in the DMZ.

October 21-22
An Anti-War March in Washington D.C.
drew some 50,000 protestors. At least 647
were arrested, most after a clash between
police and troops at the Pentagon.

October 26
Cancellation of draft deferments of college
students who violated draft laws or inter-
fered with recruiting was ordered by
director of Selective Service.

carrier runway, and several pilots were seated in their cockpits ready to start their engines. Generators were used to start the planes and a possible faulty circuit could have set off the fire that caused the deadly chain reaction.

A rocket misfired hitting several planes as (now) Senator John McCain had just started his Skyhawk. With flames all around him, there was only one way out. Climbing over the nose and jumping over the fire he escaped just as the two 1,000 lb. bombs on his plane exploded, causing more planes to catch fire. With rockets, missiles and bombs going off it was difficult to control the catastrophe. Thinner casings on older bombs being utilized from WW II exploded quickly. Water hoses were riddled with shrapnel and many of the firemen were killed. The rest of the crew quickly took over their jobs—their inexperience sometimes causing more problems, as water on certain substances caused the fire to spread even more rapidly. The men worked for 4 1/2 days before the fire was finally under control. Before its quenching, it had engulfed the entire deck below the carrier airstrip. Overcome by fire and smoke, 70 men died in their berths as they slept. Many below deck were killed when hatches had been closed to control the flames. One minute and 28 seconds after the faulty circuit ignited—the chain reaction of death and destruction began, ravaging the USS Forrestal—and taking the lives of 128 sailors and leaving 64 others with burns and other serious injuries.

Among the initial missing was **CHARLES GREGORY**, a young sailor from Montpelier, Idaho.

A popular and well-liked student at Montpelier High School, Charles had been the captain of the football and wrestling teams. While in school he ran track, was voted Junior Prom prince and also served as Student Body Vice President. Following graduation in 1965, he joined the Navy and two years later departed for the high seas on the USS Forrestal on June 5, 1967. Charles' body was recovered a few days after the carrier fire and transported home to Montpelier for burial. He was 19.

★★★

October 16, 1967

CLAYTON MARTIN of Burley, Idaho dies from wounds received September 4 while carrying his squad leader to safety at Nui Ba Den Mountain in Tay Ninh Province.

Clayton graduated from Burley High School in 1963 and Idaho State University technical school in 1965. After joining the army in October 1966, he went to Vietnam in March of 1967.

October 24, 1967 a Twin Falls "Times News" Editorial reports his loss:

" A YOUTH IS DEAD"

"Another one is dead. He didn't want to die. Army Spec.4 Clayton Martin, Burley, died in action against the enemy near the Cambodian border in South

Vietnam. He was 23. This is not the only area death in that war. It is another to be added to the staggering toll in that terrible conflict. By mentioning the death of Spec.4 Martin we are not neglecting the deaths of those other brave men who have given their lives in the defense of their country's ideals. But the death of Spec.4 Martin makes it all the more apparent that there is a war going on. We deplore this waste of human life, this waste of our country's most valuable resource. But we recognize the need. Many have died before to protect America. Many will die in years to come.

Spec.4 Martin leaves behind a young son and daughter. They will be taken care of by a grateful America and a grateful community. But to his relatives, the loss cannot be measured, either in words or deeds. Army Spec.4 Martin is gone. He fought the Viet Cong since last March, then he fought for his life beginning Sept.4 when he was wounded. He lost that battle last week in a Japan Army hospital. Now he will be returned and buried. We do not look forward to the next death."

★★★

October 30-Nov.4
The North Vietnamese assault on Loc Ninh, on the Cambodian border about 90 miles north of Saigon, was broken after six days by U.S. air strikes and artillery. The attack on the town and the U.S. Special Forces camp was "unusually determined," possibly because Communists wanted a victory to offset the October 31st Inauguration of Nguyen Van Thieu as President of South Vietnam.

Resettlement village
PHOTO: LARRY PETERSEN

November 15, 1967
Platoon Leader **WILLIAM PETERSEN**, a 1954 graduate of Boise High School was mortally wounded in a search and destroy mission near HaTay. After knocking out an enemy position with a grenade, he exposed himself to heavy enemy fire while helping move his wounded men from an open area.

After two years of college at the University of Idaho and Boise State College, William joined the army in 1958. He re-enlisted after a two year tour of duty in Germany and was sent to Fort Benning, Georgia for 6 years. While there he broke two World Marksmanship shooting records. Although his service to his country never allowed him to attend, he was invited twice to compete at the World Olympics in sharp shooting. Thirty-one-year-old Petersen was the father of three daughters.

During the eight-month period William served in Vietnam, letters to his wife aptly reflect his disciplined thinking and dedicated service to the country he loved.

April 1967— "This has been about the most uncomfortable night I've spent here yet. We have been up in the An Lau Valley for some time and have done a lot of moving around. One of the companies ran into trouble yesterday and we went in to help. Of course we didn't start until late afternoon and we air-assaulted into another rice paddy. Then (we) climbed up behind the company of enemy they were supposed to have holed up. We got all wet with perspiration and on top of that (they) couldn't supply us like they normally do in the evening. Most of us were out of food and water this morning, but they can drop food and water through the canopy of trees which is about 50 feet up.

We haven't had much fun in this area. It is so infected with leeches that it was unbelievable. Just going through the brush I picked up six on one arm and numerous ones on my clothing. Nearly everyday up here we have been seeing the enemy and giving chase, but most of the time he gives us the slip. We are in the middle of a hard core area now. There are also a lot of reluctant farmers around here. We have given them the ultimatum to leave their farms and offered them new accommodations and even better farms, but these people are just like us. We wouldn't want to be forced off of our land, especially when a burial ground of our ancestors is part of the farm."

Government issued military money for U.S. troops
LARRY PETERSEN

A couple of days later —"We have been busy. Day before yesterday we were air assaulted into another area to help another company and we have had our hands full. My platoon has really been up on top.

We were lucky day before yesterday and were able to kill one of the NVA regulars who was carrying a Chinese Ak-47 which is a very effective automatic weapon. We were moving into an area just behind another company emplacements when out pops Charlie. He must have not seen us as he didn't even have a round in the chamber of his weapon. One of the guys back there shot him and knocked him down but he got up on the other side of a tree and was just about to shoot one of our guys in the back when another guy here shot him in the head. We got some documents, weapons, lots of ammo, and a Chinese grenade off of him. He also had about 30 cents on him. He was young, but quite large for Vietnamese. They say they are a lot bigger from up north. (The) area where we killed that one was about 50 yards up from a very hotly disputed area. In the same area Co. B had lost 3 dead and 17 wounded. The one we got was sneaking around some of Co. B's positions and could have done a lot of harm if he had made it.

That night we camped right there on the hill with Charlie and in the morning went down the hill and found two more dead ones and one had

American equipment, camera, wallet and ID card. It was good that we could at least recover the effects of the American. Also nice to see the one probably responsible for the American dead. We moved from that hill top yesterday after an almost sleepless night. Charlie was moving around in the brush a lot. We are staying (in) the area long enough to destroy about a ton of rice and about 100 bunkers. We are right in the middle of a large bivouac area. Charlie built everything out of vines and surrounding vegetation and earth, etc. Actually they are quite ingenious. We also found a large cache of cloth and packs, etc. We burned most of it. This morning we are waiting for demo people to come to blow up the bunkers."

July 15, 1967 — "Got up early and went on a patrol NW of our position in Na Lao. We captured (a) NVA Sgt. with a weapon and about 250 pounds of rice and some clothes and cooking utensils. I went in (the) hole and brought him out at knifepoint. On the way back to camp my temp came back and am sure it reached 104-105, but made it back under my own steam."

November 1967 — (Shortly before William's death) "We made a three day assault through some very nasty country. We also met some nasty resistance and ended up with some casualties. Two men from my platoon were killed just ten meters from me, and another one (was) wounded a little later. The two who were killed walked to within 10 feet of the NVA soldiers who shot them. I was off to the left of them and couldn't see the guy and I'm sure neither of our men (saw) him at all. I ran over to help them but saw it was too late for one and happened to look into the hole that the VC was in and right down the barrel of his weapon. Luckily I shot the weapon out of his hand and then put a grenade in the hole with him. This all happened so fast that I didn't have time to think. Our medic and I pulled the two out of the line of fire with rounds snapping around us all the time. It was just like the movies—but this was tragic—it was real. All total we lost in the company...2 dead and 8 wounded. We just got alerted to another assault we have to make through the same area." (William died later the same month while again trying to rescue the wounded.)

Enemy cache of food and ammo.
PHOTO: LARRY PETERSEN

(Note: Family connections indicate Dennis Golden from McCall, Idaho was on the same Hill Sgt. William Petersen was killed on 11-15-67. The battle appears to have been on Hill 875.)

November 30, 1967

20-year-old Marine and graduate of Vallivue High School, **JIMMY WARD** is killed by small arms fire in the vicinity of Quang Lin Providence, South Vietnam. A former bull rider and high school rodeo star, the Nampa native wanted to become an auctioneer. He had been in country only 2 months.

" ...10 months and 20 days left..." young Jimmy Ward writes home to his mother from the battlefield of Vietnam. "I'm doing fine...being a good boy and keeping my head down. Did you hear about Chaun Yu? I was there 15 days. It was the worst thing I have ever seen in my life. Well Mom, I have to get ready for an ambush now. I'll write soon. May God keep you and bless you always."
Love Ya, Your only son, Jim
P.S. Write Soon

Dear Dad, "How are you? Boy it is bad up here. We get shelled all the time. It takes a day to walk two miles because(it's so) rough. They said we can have one beer and it was hot but it was good... Tomorrow we have to take a hill as soon as the sun comes up. They had 3 M-60's on top of it (and) the Lt. said we lost about 20 men before it was over. But I don't worry... Well I have to get my gun ready to go. It will be a big day tomorrow. So tell Mom I'm all right and don't worry, I'm a big boy now. So write as soon as you can. I love you all very much." Love Always, Jim

★★★

"...I'll soon be old enough to vote, I'm getting to be an old man."

LeRoy Damiano

When Thanksgiving Day 1967 arrived, **LE ROY DAMIANO** from Kootenai County was out on patrol as he usually was, sometimes up to 60 days at a time. But on this day helicopters deliver real food to the LZ—"turkey with all the trimmings." General Westmoreland visits the soldiers closer to base and delivers a troop message. Le Roy sends home the printed folder he received in the field.

COMMANDER'S MESSAGE

On this traditional Thanksgiving Day, as we find ourselves half way around the world from home, we should pause for a few moments to count our many blessings as Americans. We should never forget that in Vietnam, our actions are defending free men everywhere. We pray that peace will come to all the world and that all of us can return to our loved ones in the not too distant future.

W. C. WESTMORELAND
General, United States Army
Commanding

"When I have spare time, I dream of the big plane that will take me home."

(The Freedom Bird)

The men sometimes held church in the jungle, but as the Harrison, Idaho native wrote, " I guess you can have church anywhere you want." He mentioned the filth and the Vietnamese people having to dig through the garbage to find leftover food to eat. In one raid his platoon captured 16 rifles, 1,000 rounds of ammunition and 3 tons of rice. All of the rifles were broken but what the VC used. The cache was found beneath a false floor in one village shack. The 1965 graduate of Kootenai High School said one of the things he missed most was a plate of fried spuds. On his first Christmas away from home, he was grateful for so many cards. Le Roy died February 12, 1968 at Ap Bein. He was 21 years old.

★★★

"…twenty days and twenty nights"

A letter from Green Beret Medic **DENNIS GOLDEN** dated November 1967:

"Dear Family,
Just got in last night but was too tired to answer your letters. Right now I've got mono plus I came through a living hell so I don't feel too good.

The hell I speak of was the battle of Dak To and Hill 875. We fought steady for twenty days and nights. I saw things that I'll have nightmares over for a long time…

Things like Americans with legs and arms blown off. What used to be American machine gunners burned to a crisp… I worked on one poor (guy). His name was John,

but he died. So I just held his head in my lap until he went. For about four days I was so covered with blood it was like I had taken a shower in the stuff.

The VC would throw grenades at us but after the first day you got used to it. They would knock (you) into the air, slam (you) back on the ground, and then you would feel yourself all over to see if any frags hit (you) then back to work.

And all the time the artillery and air strikes were going in. Sometimes with all the booming, firing and screaming from the wounded you almost would go crazy. And then the VC would scream, especially when napalm hit them. It's an awful sound when you hear humans burning to death.

This was the only time that I figured I was going to die. It wasn't a good feeling."

A native of Boise and raised in McCall, Idaho, **DENNIS GOLDEN** graduated from Donnelly High School in 1962. An avid outdoorsman who enjoyed skiing, fishing, scuba and sky diving, he joined the army after two years of college and became a medic with the Green Berets. In 1966 he went to Vietnam as an advisor to the Montagnards (a highland native tribe) and then joined ranks with a Green Beret A Team consisting of 12 men. After a one-year tour of duty, he extended for another year and was stationed at Pleiku.

24-year-old Dennis had received 2 Army Commendation Medals for Heroism in March and April of 1967. The following September he was awarded the Silver Star and Purple Heart for a serious wound to his thigh. Dennis' brother Mike was also serving a second tour of duty in Vietnam, when Dennis was mortally wounded by an accidental hand grenade explosion, while he was engaged in a friendly discussion with members of his detachment. The two brothers had made an agreement that if anything happened to one of them, the survivor would bring the other home. Shortly after Dennis' death on June 9, 1968 Mike escorted his brother's body home.

November 1967 HILL 875 *
Media Report from Associated Press Correspondent Peter Arnett: 14 miles west of Dak To in the Central Highlands.

"While U.S. planes and artillery pounded dug-in North Vietnamese gunners, helicopter crews removed today the last of 140 American paratroopers wounded since Sunday in bitter fighting on the slopes of Hill 875. One of the most brutal fights of the war was underway as men of the 173rd Airborne Brigade attempted to take the remaining enemy bunkers on the hill in the Central Highlands southwest of Dak To.

Short of food and water, the paratroopers battled stiff enemy fire as they continued their push to the summit. They used flame-throwers against the enemy's intricate bunker system. U.S. jets pounded the entire area, attempting to keep to a schedule of one strike every 15 minutes. U.S. artillery gunners filled in the gaps.

U.S. casualties have mounted to at least 239 dead and 822 wounded during the 19 days of fighting around the Dak To Valley. Although the North Vietnamese repeatedly drove off medical helicopters, five wounded men were lifted out Monday night. U.S. crewmen sped in and out of a clearing cut in the jungle growth and removed all the rest today in a two-hour period. This was the second most costly battle of the Vietnam War for American Forces. It rivaled in intensity the 1965 fighting in the Ia Drang Valley—also just before Thanksgiving in the Central Highlands—in which 147 Americans were killed and 570 wounded."

(* Hill 875: Name designated by the number of meters above sea level.)

By the end of 1967 public confidence in the Johnson administration was beginning to wane, and a number of senior advisors and civilians in the Defense Department were questioning whether the United States could ever win the war in Vietnam. Each night on the news, the gruesome body-count figures of American, South Vietnamese and Communist soldiers grew. President Johnson granted Westmoreland more troops with a new ceiling of 525,000 men. The increase could hold off defeat, but was not enough to win the war.

At years end: U.S. troop strength stands at nearly a half a million—474,300.

1968

January 2 Signs of Trouble in Quang Tri Province

Marine guards stationed at Khe Sanh, a strategic base 18 miles south of the DMZ, kill 5 NVA officers all wearing U.S. Marine uniforms—signaling something big is brewing on the horizon.

General Westmoreland saw the base as a key blocking point to stop the communists from invading the northern provinces and ordered the Marines to dig in, both on the base itself and in the surrounding hills. They built mortar proof bunkers, put out German razor wire, and dug trenches for protection against the powerful Soviet and Chinese artillery the NVA had within range of the base. The enemy controlled Route 9, the main road leading to Khe Sanh, so the marine's supplies had to be brought in by air.

January 21 The Battle of Khe Sanh begins with the siege lasting until April

When communist guns began to shell the combat base, a rocket landing inside the main ammunition dump explodes 1,500 tons—90% of the marine's ammo—starting a fire that would rage for 24 hours. Supplying the base by air became more than difficult with continual enemy shelling on the runway. The NVA's next move was to overrun a nearby Special Forces camp at Lang Vei and for the first time in the war they had used tanks. The fate of 6,000 marines—now surrounded by as many as

Aerial view of the winding
Ho Chi Minh Trail

20,000 crack North Vietnamese forces, becomes even more ominous with the threat of tanks being used against their isolated positions.

The siege is seen by many Americans including Westmoreland, President Johnson and the media, as a repeat of the 1954 communist attack on the French stronghold at Dienbenphu. A military catastrophe such as the French suffered is averted by massive B-52 bombings. But at home, Americans watch the siege unfold like a nightly TV drama. In an unprecedented move, President Johnson has a model of Khe Sanh built in the basement of the White House and asks each of the Joint Chiefs of Staff to sign a document claiming the base *could* and *would* be held.

In Operation Niagara, 2,000 aircraft saturated the area surrounding the base with heavy bombing. On an average day American planes flew 300 sorties, dropping massive payloads every ninety minutes. Still the NVA continued to shell the base day and night. The weary marines were on constant alert knowing the enemy was digging tunnels closer and closer to their perimeter. Nightly patrols sent out to monitor NVA positions began to encounter few and fewer firefights, and as the weeks continued signs of enemy activity diminished. Intelligence reports in late March confirmed the eerie truth. The communists had abandoned their tunnels and trails, leaving behind only their dead. More than two months had expired before the First Cavalry Airmobile Division was finally able to relieve the Marines, who had been living in half-blown-up, rat-infested bunkers. The siege of Khe Sanh resulted in 205 Americans killed, and some ten to fifteen thousand enemy dead.

Ironically, the base was abandoned one year later when a planned strike against the Ho Chi Minh trail was cancelled.

Two Idaho men were among the casualties of Khe Sanh.

When M. Sgt. **HOWARD WALDRON** from Couer D'Alene, Idaho learned Platoon leaders were desperately needed at Khe Sanh, he volunteered to leave his post in Okinawa, Japan to offer assistance. Howard had joined the Marines at the age of 17 and had served in the South Pacific in World War II and also in Korea.

A recipient of the Purple Heart in the battle of Iwo Jima, he was later wounded at the Chosin Reservoir in Korea. After 22 1/2 years in the Marine Corp, he decided to retire, but returned to active duty at the request of the Marine Training Program to help train an advance contingent in Okinawa.

On March 6, 1968 Howard left for the Khe Sanh Airbase in Vietnam to serve as a replacement Platoon leader. When he arrived, the base was under siege. While the Air Force was trying to bring in reinforcements and keep the strip open, his plane (a C-123 transport) was shot down, killing all 47 aboard. Howard left a wife and child.

After years of dedicated service to his country, the 41-year-old veteran was interred with the remains of the other 46 men on board, in a common grave in St. Louis, MO.

20-year-old Cpl. **HERMAN LOHMAN**, a Marine from Twin Falls, Idaho was killed while walking "point" for his squad when he tripped a landmine at Khe Sanh. A 1966 graduate of Twin Falls High School, he had been a member of the wrestling team and a member of the Twin Falls Squadron of the Civil Air Patrol, where he served as a Cadet Officer. Herman joined the Marines shortly after graduation at the age of eighteen.

In December of 1999, 31 years after Herman's death, Joseph Olszewski posted the following Internet Tribute:

"I was Platoon Commander of the Third Platoon, Golf, 2/6 from September, 1967 until February, 1968. Corporal Lohman was one of my Squad Leaders. He was tough, experienced and loved being in combat. He was on his second tour, as during the Vietnam years a Marine could receive a bonus by extending his first thirteen month tour. Corporal Lohman did this and was in Vietnam over eighteen consecutive months before he became a casualty. He never complained. Corporal Lohman and many of his Golf Company comrades were KIA on April 6, 1968 on Hill 700 just outside the main Khe Sanh combat base. I think of them every day and pray for them on Sunday..."

Herman Augusta Lohman Jr. CPL

Retired Colonel Jack Layton of Rexburg, Idaho is the pilot of the SR-71 "Blackbird" Reconnaissance plane that discovers the initial sighting of the Pueblo.

Conceived and built nearly 40 years ago, the SR-71 holds the record for having flown faster than any other turbo jet at the speed of Mach 3+ (in excess of 2,100 miles an hour). Reaching altitudes of 80,000 feet and more, its titanium alloy skin reached temperatures of 750 degrees Fahrenheit.

PHOTO: LARRY PETERSEN

Colonel Jack Layton stands before a YF12. Photos of the SR-71 "Blackbird" were prohibited for intelligence reasons.

Only 32 SR-71s were ever built, all in the 1960's. Put into service by the Air Force, the plane gathered vital military intelligence on virtually every military and political crisis in the world for more than two decades of the Cold War. The jet's high-resolution radar imaging system could survey 100,000 square miles in an hour, flying twice as fast as a .357 magnum bullet.

The Air Force retired the highly classified aircraft in the 1990's and there are now fewer SR-71 pilots in the world than there are space shuttle astronauts.

January 31 THE TET OFFENSIVE

During a brief truce set to celebrate the Vietnamese Lunar New Year, (similar to New Year's Eve or Christmas) the Viet Cong launch a major offensive throughout South Vietnam, and the American Embassy in Saigon is attacked. U.S. forces were surprised by the scope and size of the operation, whose key targets included Saigon, the Marine Base at Khe Sanh and the provincial capital Hue.

In a twenty-four hour period on January 31st the well-fortified American base at Cam Ranh Bay had been rocketed and General McArthur's headquarters at Long Binh (15 miles north of Saigon) attacked. During the same time frame, 13 Provincial Capitals in the southern Mekong Delta region were attacked simultaneously. Taking advantage of President Thieu's decision to allow South Vietnam soldiers in charge of guarding important installations to go home over the Tet Holiday, the Communists raids were devastatingly effective. General Westmoreland's attention and strategies had been drawn north to the siege of Khe Sanh, and American troops throughout South Vietnam were shocked at the ferocity and extent of the more than one hundred carefully coordinated attacks.

In the United States, the bloody Tet Offensive is seen as a major defeat and symbol of the Viet Cong's ability to strike at will anywhere in the country. The optimistic views General Westmoreland and other military leaders had been sending to Congress were permanently damaged in the public eye. Meanwhile, U.S. troops continued to fight valiantly to regain lost ground and secure strategic strongholds, inflicting on the North Vietnamese and Viet Cong a shattering military defeat of 50,000 dead. A high price the Communists seemed more than willing to pay for the psychological and propaganda victory they had gained.

The Battle of Hue

Within three weeks, Communist forces had been pushed out of every major stronghold in the three southern military regions. But up in I Corps, the NVA had captured Hue, one of Vietnam's oldest, and most prized cities.

Before Vietnam's partition in 1954, Hue had been the capital. Until the Tet Offensive in 1968 the city had been spared the carnage and destruction that had plagued so much of the country. Hue was the home of a large university and located at the center of the city was the Imperial Citadel, a huge stone fortress built at the beginning of the nineteenth century. Here, U.S. and South Vietnamese forces would do battle for three long weeks against communist troops.

The surprise attack began in the early morning of January 31. American Marines stationed at a nearby base, and the South Vietnamese responsible for the defense of the city were caught off guard as two NVA battalions charged the gates of the city. Additional enemy units launched an assault to the south. Within hours the Communists had control of most of the city, including hospitals, schools, and residential areas. The NVA command post was strategically set up inside the Citadel itself. Rockets and mortar fire met the Marines called in to relieve the South Vietnamese troops, as they attempted to cross the Perfume River.

Hand to hand combat in the streets and alleys continued for several weeks, and U.S. and South Vietnamese casualties were extremely high. Unable to get adequate reinforcements, the tenacious Marines persevered in unusually cold and stormy weather with little or no sleep. Fierce house to house fighting cost them dearly in blood as enemy soldiers retaliated from well-entrenched positions. On the morning of February 24, South Vietnamese units were finally able to penetrate the walls of the Imperial Palace itself. Expecting heavy resistance, they surprisingly found none. The NVA had vanished in the night, fleeing into sanctuaries westward in Laos and leaving only their dead.

The battle for Hue was the longest, most vicious and costliest battle of the Tet Offensive. The communists executed 500 to 5,000 innocent civilians and many more were killed in small arms fire in the streets or by the naval gunfire the Americans used to dislodge the NVA and Viet Cong. More than 200 Marines and other U.S. troops lost their lives in the fighting, and 1,200 were wounded. The communist forces lost as many as 8,000 men.

March 11, 1968

TERRENCE (TERRY) THOMAS from Hammett, Idaho is mortally wounded on patrol north of Saigon. The 20-year-old graduated from Glenns Ferry High School in 1964 where he played football and served as Senior Class President. He attended Idaho State University for a year before being drafted into the army. Terry had been in Vietnam 5 months and was looking forward to his R&R the end of March.

On Christmas Day of 1967 he wrote from Song Be near the Cambodian border:

" …They flew in a Chinook helicopter full of beer and coke for the troops… and a Red Cross lady (Donut Dollie) came out and walked the lines with us. We had three hot meals and most of the day off and even a Santa Claus, except you could see the 45 under his costume which pretty much ruined the effect."

★★★

February 20
Defense Secretary Robert McNamara resigns after concluding the war cannot be won. He is replaced by Clark Clifford.

February 25
After 26 days of fighting since the Tet Offensive began Hue is recaptured by American and South Vietnamese forces. Mass graves reveal enormous atrocities committed by retreating Vietcong and North Vietnamese troops against civilians suspected of supporting the Saigon government.

"Stand Down" Troop entertainment for the 101st Airborne.

March 16
Robert Kennedy announced he will campaign for the Democratic presidential nomination.

Early Spring
General Westmoreland requested additional 200,000 troops be sent to Vietnam as the full extent of the Tet Offensive became known.

March 31
President Johnson announces in a television address a bombing halt to all of North Vietnam except for the area just north of the DMZ in hopes such an act would bring the North to the bargaining table. The President, noticeably exhausted from the strain of an unpopular war, stuns the nation by announcing he will not run again.

April 4
Martin Luther King Jr. is assassinated in Memphis Tennessee by a sniper's bullet. The event was followed by a week of rioting in urban black ghettos. The nation's capital was seriously disrupted. King's funeral in Atlanta, Georgia on April 9th was attended by 75,000 people.

April 5
The Seige of Khe Sanh—at the site of the U.S. Marine Base was officially lifted.

U.S. polls showed approval for the President's handling the war had fallen from 40 to 25 percent. Increasing numbers of young men had served and died in Vietnam over the past three years. Americans were demanding proof that progress was being made, and questioning the "defensible cause" so many were dying for. A task force, assembled by President Johnson to examine future U.S. policy in Vietnam, delivered an ominous recommendation from many highly respected foreign-policy experts. The United States could not win the war at any time soon, and should begin decreasing the American military presence in Vietnam.

"I think it's worth it…what about you?"

March 18, 1968

Cataldo Marine, Pfc **MARSHALL SCHAFFNER'S** heroic efforts as a forward artillery observer saves many lives near the village of Vinh Quang Throng. While providing cover fire for a fellow wounded Marine, Marshal was hit by enemy fire and fell mortally wounded. While a member of the 9th Marine Amphibious Brigade, the 20-year-old writes home to the students at Kootenai High School, November 1967:

> "I hope we can end this war before any of you have to fill your military obligations, because war is hell. But remember our fathers before us fought so we could be free, and I hope you realize if you want freedom we will always have to fight to keep it. I think it's worth it. What about you?"
> P.S. "Good Luck with basketball."

Marshall turned 21 two weeks before his final battle.

April

A combined force of 50,000 American and ARVN troops in the southern Mekong Delta deploy a large-scale enemy assault. Severe forest fires assist in the offensive and the communists are driven out of the U Minh Forest.

April 8

Operation Complete Victory involving 100,000 allied troops in Vietnam began. Its aim was to drive enemy forces from the provinces around Saigon. In addition to leaving 14,000 civilians dead, the Tet Offensive had put many South Vietnamese government services out of action for months after the attacks.

April 23

At New York Columbia University, members of SDS (Students for a Democratic Society) seized five buildings in protest of Columbia's involvement in war related research.

April 28, 1968

Kootenai County boy, **STEVEN MCARTHUR** loses his life near Hue. Born and raised in the Coeur d 'Alene area, Steven played football in high school and was on the Jay Cee's boxing team. While stationed at Fort Gordon, Georgia he boxed competitively and served in Vietnam in the 101st Airborne division. Steven had just turned 19.

May 1968

In Operation Delaware, a strategic base camp for more than 5,000 North Vietnamese soldiers in the northern A Shau Valley is overcome by combined U.S. military forces. As the battle commenced in I Corps, thousands of bombs from B-52 "sortie" raids were not enough to silence the NVA guns. Ten helicopters were lost on the first day alone, but communist forces opted to evade the onslaught of U.S. ground forces and unexpectedly abandoned the base. Huge supplies of ammunition and weapons were left behind.

May 5

Another major enemy offensive was launched in South Vietnam against all allied strongholds. Saigon came under attack from mortar and sniper fire. The assault, though not as serious as the Tet Offensive, came in two waves and the fighting was bloody and intense. As U.S. and ARVN forces used napalm and other highly explosive materials to expel the communists, civilian casualties were exceptionally high. Thousands of Saigon residents were left homeless and resentful.

May 10

The Peace Talks open in Paris, France.

May 10, 1968

Terreton Marine **VERLE SKIDMORE** dies in an attack at Kham Duc near the Cambodian border. One hundred and twenty five men are wounded during the evacuation of the Special Forces camp and twenty-one-year-old Verle is one of twenty American casualties. A 1965 graduate of West Jefferson High School, he joined the Marines in 1966 and was married the following year. The couple had a son before his departure to Vietnam and a baby daughter was born the fall after his death. Verle was in country 3 months.

May 27, 1968

Marine Rifle Platoon Commander, **RALPH GORTON**'s unit was pinned down by intense enemy fire during an assault on the village of Phu Con. As Ralph maneuvered across the firing line to deploy his men and "point squad," his familiar words of encouragement and assurance were suddenly silenced by an enemy bullet.

Ralph's words home to his family aptly describe the seasoned experience of a man who had led his men through 5 major combat operations in Vietnam.

May 7, 1968 — "We were sweeping a village. When we got within 75 meters all hell broke loose. They were waiting for us and had us pinned down in a wide, open rice paddy. All we could do was call in air strikes, napalm and 250 lb. bombs and artillery. There were many heroic deeds during this battle but before we finally extracted ourselves we suffered 65 casualties in the company. That was by far the longest day of my life and many more like that I will be an old man. This was a terrible ordeal but a necessary one to keep a river open to U.S. boats supplying all military units in this area."

"The weather here is much like Boise on a humid day. Temperature between 90 and 100 degrees with a lot of humidity. The thunder clouds build up over the mountains during the day but disappear at night. The evenings cool off about 7:00 and it's just right all night.

This is rice harvest time so all the local inhabitants are busy cutting, hauling and reaping. It's interesting how they do it. First they cut it in the paddies and tie it in bales. Others take the bales back to the villages where it is spread out on hard courtyards. Then they walk water buffalo over it until all the grain is knocked off the stalks. They then pitchfork the stalks into stacks and sweep the grain up for husking. Very primitive, but it gets the job done for them."

15 May 1968 — "Evenings are the best part of the day. It cools off and a slight breeze blows. There are usually a few clouds in the sky, so the sunset is a bright orange and red reflection off the clouds. It is also the interlude between the flies and mosquitoes. Any respite from those two insects is a gift in itself… Evening also allows one a few moments to thank God for another day and for His guiding hand without which our tasks would be so much greater."

Three weeks later Ralph's unit was pinned down again. It was the 26-year-old's final battle in Vietnam.

✮✮✮

June 23, 1968

The war in Vietnam became the longest war in U.S. history.

Strategists and military officials who ran the war were more divided than ever over the best course of action in Vietnam. Disagreements between bureaucracies continued as military men pressed to enlarge the war. Meanwhile, a group of civilian planners were insisting no amount of military force would ever solve the conflict of South Vietnam.

June 5
Following his victory in the California primary, Robert F. Kennedy was shot by Sirhan B. Sirhan. He died the following day.

June 10
General William Westmoreland turned over command of U.S. forces in Vietnam to General Creighton W. Abrams.

In July 1968 South Vietnamese President Thieu met with President Johnson in Honolulu and obtained a promise that no coalition government would be agreed to in Paris. The Saigon government was also assured it would participate in the drawing up of any final settlement. Fear of abandonment was quickly growing in South Vietnam. America was in the process of changing course in Vietnam and those changes suggested the U.S. was no longer seeking an unconditional victory.

Meanwhile, Hanoi hoped that America's will to continue would diminish with each new American casualty. One of the prevailing myths of the war in Vietnam was that the North Vietnamese and Viet Cong had inferior power and ability to resist a superpower like the United States. In reality, the enemy enjoyed several advantages the allied forces struggled to overcome. On the battlefield, experienced communist soldiers had fought in the mountains and jungles for decades. They understood the complexities of the terrain and capitalized on U.S. limitations with climate and weather conditions. Fierce defenders of their native land, they enjoyed the safety of neighboring Cambodia and Laos where they could retreat without fear of harassment. More importantly, the communists benefited from a strict set of limitations on where and how the allied forces could fight. "The Rules of Engagement" prohibited Americans and South Vietnamese soldiers from chasing after them as they fled into sanctuaries across the border. The single greatest advantage the communists had was their unbending will. Millions of lives would be sacrificed if necessary to achieve their objective. It simply did not matter how long it took, or how many men were killed. Every means would be taken to expel the Americans, destroy the GVN, and gain control over South Vietnam.

August 8
The Republican National Convention nominated Richard M. Nixon.

August 29
The Democratic National Convention opened in Chicago in the midst of anti-war protests and violence. The police respond to the unrest as the Democrats nominate Hubert Humphrey.

September 8
Idaho's 116th Army Corps of Engineers reach Vietnam.
In response to the escalating fighting of the Tet Offensive and the USS Pueblo capture, President Johnson authorized the mobilization of 24,500 Reservists and National Guardsmen across the nation.

The farewell ceremony at Ravsten Stadium was not dampened by rain

116th

(Continued from Page B-1)

Chevelle," Burtenshaw said. "I had had it for only a month after ordering it from the factory. I was kind of shocked."

Most of the battalion's soldiers were members of the Church of Jesus Christ of Latter-day Saints. Some were students. Many were farm boys. Others worked as loggers, mechanics and truck drivers.

The 116th was every bit the hometown National Guard unit. Many of the men had known each other most of their lives. Others were related, including about 90 brothers and several fathers and sons.

After years of American involvement in Southeast Asia, eastern Idaho was not untouched by the war. At least two eastern Idaho men had been killed in Vietnam by the time the 116th was activated.

The anti-war movement was also on the rise in the United States. And the Tet Offensive, a bloody campaign by North Vietnamese troops and Viet Cong guerrillas against South Vietnamese cities, was only

> "It was really hard, very difficult to leave family and friends. But that's what we were there for.'
>
> **Tom Chriswell**

attitude, because everybody felt we weren't going overseas."

One man who knew the 116th was headed for Vietnam was Ghormley.

"I was informed when we were called up and I was even given a date, but it was top-secret and I was the only one in the battalion that was privy to the information," he said.

Some of the Guardsmen were full-time employees of the Guard, but, for most, going on active duty meant leaving civilian jobs, and their families.

mother. "I di should be sent really upset. A were upset, too.'

"But the order active duty stat talion would e and that the uni to Fort Lewis, W

The battalion on May 13. The review was held at Idaho Falls. filled the bleach able drizzle.

The bulk of leaving for Fort

Most traveled and airplane. Th went by convoy jeeps, trucks, b front-end loade equipment mad the Army post.

Mrs. Burtens

(EDITOR'S NOTE: This is the second of a five-part series on the Idaho National Guard's 116th Combat Engineer Battalion and the time it spent in Vietnam.)

The 116th

Combat Engineers

PREPARE THE WAY

Idaho's guardsmen passed muster in '68

By DAVID FIELDS
Post-Register staff writer

Training at Fort Lewis, Wash., for Idaho's 116th Combat Engineer Battalion in 1968 was a busy 2½ months of instruction, practice and field exercises.

U.S. Army officials expected a lot out of the National Guard unit and planned to send them to war-torn South Vietnam as combat-ready as possible.

"It just seemed like it went by so fast," said Forrest Hanson, Idaho Falls Headquarters Company commander. "We were busy all the time. It was just kind of like one event leading into another. We did so many things. Weapons training. Grenade training. First aid training.

The battalion was the largest U.S. Army reserve component to serve in the war. Four of the 116th's companies came from eastern Idaho. Another was based at Grangeville and Orofino.

Notice of the call-up came in April 1968, when Secretary of Defense Clark Clifford ordered an additional 24,500 troops for the U.S. war effort in South Vietnam.

Most of the battalion began arriving at Fort Lewis on May 16. The men traveled by bus, air and convoy.

The training the 116th received there differed little from the work it had done over the past 2½ years, said Battalion Commander Don Ghormley of Ashton. The men still practiced mine-sweeping, building

At Fort Lewis

IDAHO NATIONAL guardsmen, above, line up for chow at Fort Lewis, Wash., where they trained before going to Vietnam. Below, Rexburg Mayor Whitey Brock visited Fort Lewis and spoke with Platoon Sgt. Fred Clemons of Company B. (Post-Register file photos)

gotten themselves into, I guess," Ghormley said.

But the 116th was well-trained by the time it reached Fort Lewis. In spite of the stigma attached to what regular army troops call "weekend warriors" and "sunshine soldiers," the National Guard unit began earning a sterling reputation at Fort Lewis as a well-trained, well-disciplined battalion.

As proof of its ability, the 116th in late July passed the Army Training Test, a comprehensive examination covering all aspects of the 116th's operations.

It was a test that one California

and they serve and do what's expected of them. It kind of antagonized some of our people, to be called to active duty and do what that unit did."

The squadron never went to South Vietnam as a unit. However, some of the unit's soldiers eventually were ordered to South Vietnam as replacements for other units.

As for the 116th, official notification of its destination was withheld from everyone except Ghormley, who knew at the time of the call-up that the battalion was headed for Vietnam.

Some officers and senior non-com...d officers were told shortly...he deployment where the...headed. But rumors were...information the other men... on.

...ation among the troops took...accurate turn when they were...othing and gear for a jungle...ment.

...s very evident we weren't...ent to North America,...we were being issued jungle...jungle boots," Parke said. ...nit in early August began...y for the deployment. Bull-...ackhoes, trucks, jeeps and...hicles and equipment were...o port facilities on Puget...Wash., for transport to South...by container vessel.

...he loading was done, most...en were released for a two-...ve. The exceptions were a...t of soldiers that accompa-...116th's equipment on its...oing voyage to Vietnam, and

an advance party that left for South Vietnam in late August.

Jerry Jensen, first sergeant with Rigby's A company and a veteran of World War II and two other call-ups with the Idaho National Guard.

"It was pretty intense," he said. "We had this place we have now at the Palisades and it was just a summer home then ... We tried to enjoy that. And it rained about every day we were up here. It was kind of a bummer."

The main body of the battalion began leaving for Vietnam the week of Sept. 8. They left by airplane from McCord Air Force Base, Wash., at

the rate of about one company per day.

John Farrow, a squad leader with D Company, said he wasn't notified about his destination until his plane was enroute to Vietnam. The word came from Company Commander Donald Burris, who called Farrow and the other men to attention and broke the news.

"It was a pretty somber ride," Farrow said. "Everybody was pretty quiet and doing a lot of thinking in those sorts of times. It wasn't any great shock. We knew where we were going."

(Next: Arrival in Vietnam and first encounters with combat.)

Roadbuilders

MAJOR TASK of the 116th Engineering was maintaining and constructing | mortar shells.
supply roads. Most of the contact with the enemy came through mines or

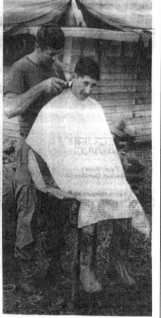

'Gas-saving' gadgets eyed by agencies

By WILLIAM GLANGALL
AP Business Writer

NEW YORK (AP) — Claims by mail-order promoters that their "miracle" gadgets can cut gas consumption dramatically are being investigated by two federal agencies.

Tests have shown some of the gadgets actually reduce gas mileage. State and federal officials, consumer organizations and car industry spokesmen say that at best, the devices are only marginally useful.

But "you and I know what's on everybody's mind these days — it's energy," said Inspector

we saw them around was in 1954 and 1955," said Norman Kayne of the California Air Resources Board Laboratory, which tests many of the devices.

"We've tested more than 800 of them, and none of them works to the extent that it would be worth installing," said James Sibbonon, a spokesman for the Environmental Protection Agency.

"We investigate them all, and so far we have found none that $2.95.

Government officials say Ball-Matic's operation resembles several other "air-bleed valve" devices, including the "Super Gas Saver," the "Ram-

extra miles per gallon" and "up to 70 ... 90 ... even 100 extra miles from every single tank-

Ball-Matic purports to increase mileage by allowing additional air to enter the fuel mixture. It is assembled by Ball-Matic Corp. of Orange, Calif., and sold wholesale for $2.95 to Cliffdale Associates Inc. of Westport, Conn., which resells the item by mail for $2.95.

The little guy chose a straight razor for a equalizer and believed the bypass won't damage on his opponent.

ordered Cooper and four companies involved to stop claiming the gadget can save gas.

In 1974, the Postal Service tested Ball-Matic on a Jeep and found it produced "slightly greater fuel consumption."

In tests at the California state lab in 1975, mileage fell in one, increased in two and was unchanged in one. Overall, mileage rose an average of 3.6 percent in the state tests.

In 1976, the EPA concluded the device "had no significant effect on fuel economy." Last year, Consumer Reports magazine found Ball-Matic produced "no significant change in gasoline

advertisements."

Tests performed for Cliffdale last spring indicated Ball-Matic cut fuel use by 9.2 to 6.91 percent when a 1985 Oldsmobile engine was run in a lab at steady speeds. But Cliffdale's ads say the device is most useful when a car is accelerating, rather than cruising.

Cliffdale ads also cite a series of road tests showing a gas saving of up to 40 percent, but reports supplied by Cliffdale says "it would be unfair" to imply that all cars would get the same results.

Cliffdale vice president Phillip Barnett said he disagrees with the results of the state and

On April 11, 1968 Idaho residents learned the list included the 116th Combat Engineer Battalion of the Idaho National Guard. The battalion consisted of more than 800 men who for the most part lived within a fifty-mile radius of Idaho Falls. One hundred of the men of the 116th were also from the northern Idaho communities of Orofino and Grangeville. Although U.S. Army regulations required that no more than one man per family go to war, there were more than eighty teams of brothers and two father-son combinations who declined exemptions and accepted the call together.

The average reservist in the 116th was in his mid-twenties and married with children. Many were college graduates with careers, while most were farmers, mechanics, loggers and construction workers used to strenuous outdoor work. A number of the men had enlisted as recently as 1967 to minimize their chances of active duty. Although no one was happy that the Guard was required to provide a battalion in Vietnam, each family and new enlistee understood the SRF (Selective Reserve Force) classification and special training of the 116th meant increased likelihood of activation. The majority of the men viewed the call with stoic acceptance, reasoning it was a job that had to be done and what the Guard's preparedness program was all about. Sharing similar backgrounds and values, the units quickly developed a close camaraderie and reputation of excellence.

With only a few short weeks before the scheduled departure, the small communities of southeastern Idaho banded together to say goodbye to their fathers, sons and brothers. Parades and patriotic programs were organized and the city of Idaho Falls hosted a major event for the men as school children were dismissed from classes to witness the troops' formal farewell. Orofino and Grangeville in northern Idaho also hosted their own send-off before the more than 800 men of the 116th Battalion traveled to Fort Louis, WA in mid-May for nine weeks of intensive training for duty in Vietnam.

While at Fort Lewis the men of the 116th distinguished themselves by finishing the course with high marks and good spirits while their counterparts, a unit from California protested their activation by staging sit-down strikes in the mess hall and refusing to eat.

As a result of the California men's lack of unit stability, commanders at Fort Lewis dispersed their ranks throughout the army. In recognition of the Idaho men's pride and comradeship, the 116th was rewarded by going overseas as a group—becoming the only National Guard battalion in the entire United States to actually serve in Vietnam.

As deployment in early September neared, dignitaries from Idaho were invited to visit Fort Lewis. In ceremonies at the base Governor Don Samuelson conveyed statewide appreciation and offered his personal "salute of respect and affection." Idaho mayors and city councilmen received praiseworthy reports from commanders on the units' preparedness and keen sense of duty. Orofino Mayor Bert Curtis observed, "Our boys are the salt of the earth. They're strong, tough and determined. We'll match our Idaho boys against any outfit in the world and we won't lose."

At home everyone's focus was on the men. While families coped the best they could some expressed opposition to their boys going to war. In response, Senator Frank Church met in Idaho Falls at a town meeting to hear concerns as letters flooded the office of the governor bearing the same questions: Why would the National Guard which existed for domestic protection be sent to a foreign war? And why were Idahoans activated when other states were not?

No one was surprised at the honest reactions of concerned families with the growing disenchantment of the war across the country. Upon receiving clarification that the president had legally called up the guardsmen, not only from Idaho but other states as well, everyone settled to the task at hand of providing support and encouragement to their loved ones abroad.

Soon after arriving in country, the 116th was assigned to the Thirty-fifth Engineer Group which was attached to the Eighteenth Engineer Brigade in South Vietnam, II Corps Tactical Zone. Companies Alpha (A), Charlie (C), Delta (D), and Headquarters (HHD) moved into the dense jungle of the central highlands in Lam Dong Province. Bravo (B) Company's location was on the coast of the South China Sea near Phan Thiet. Most of the men stayed in these regions throughout their tour of duty with the exception of Alpha and Charlie Companies who relocated to B'Sar in January 1969.

Idaho would lose 6 men from the 116th over the next 12 months and 67 would be wounded. Casualties include:

GARY SMITH of Pingree, Idaho became the first war casualty.
MICHAEL BROWN of St. Anthony lost his life when his base camp came under fire.
LONNIE HENDRICKSON of Orofino was fatally wounded by a mine detonation.
MICHAEL EARP of Grangeville was killed by small arms fire
while in a military vehicle.
KENNETH YOUNG of St. Anthony died from an accidental claymore mine detonation.
CONN CLARK of Rigby, lost his life when his truck hit a mine. Also a member of the 116th, his brother Hal escorted his body home.
RALPH CORDON of Idaho Falls was a former member of the 116th who went into duty with the 188th Engineer Battalion. He died from a landmine explosion 6 weeks before his tour of duty ended.

(Source: The above section compiled from interviews, Freedom Bird Files, articles from "The Post Register", "The Idaho Statesman" and "The History of the Idaho National Guard")

October 10, 1968

GARY SMITH from Pingree, Idaho becomes the first casualty of the 116th when an advance attachment of men are setting up a base camp near Bao Loc, west of Phan Rang about 50 miles from the Cambodian border. When enemy forces opened fire the engineers from D Co. could see the VC's firing positions, but had no heavy weapons in place to fight back. 24-year-old **GARY SMITH's** death had a tremendous impact emotionally upon the men he served with. Many of the Southeastern Idaho men had been close friends since childhood.

On September 24, 2000, the following Internet Tribute, was written by Mont (Eugene) Anderson, a former comrade from Virginia:

> "Gary I will always remember you as a hard working farm boy with a heart of gold. You were pleasant to visit with and I enjoyed the few times we shared our plans for the future. I regret your time being cut so short, you would have been a great asset to our society. I just learned about your fate and sensed the loss of not seeing you until I reach the other side. I always sensed they really loved you. Thanks for the good memories of long ago that seem just like yesterday."

November 12, 1968

A helicopter crash near Saigon claims the life of **DALE LARSEN** of Burley, Idaho. A 1966 graduate of Burley High School, Dale had been attending Ricks College when he was drafted into the army in 1968. Graduating 3rd in his class in Aviation Training, he was promoted to crew chief and then to Sergeant in less than one year. During his five months in the DMZ and Saigon areas the twenty-one-year-old had encountered some 50 combat missions in hostile territory.

Twenty years later his mother received a letter from a buddy who was on the ground when the two helicopters collided midair and crashed into mine fields surrounding the base. Prior to that time the family had no details concerning Dale's death and had never received any personal effects.

1969

Beginning of the Nixon Era

The administrations of Kennedy and Johnson had formulated the crucial decisions that committed U.S. troops in South Vietnam. When the Nixon administration took charge in January of 1969, the Vietnamese communists found an adversary whose

October 31
President Johnson orders an end to the bombing of the North in an attempt to break the stalemate at Paris and presumably help the chances of the Democratic ticket of Humphrey-Muskie.

November 6
In one of the closest Presidential elections ever, Richard Nixon defeats Hubert Humphrey. Third-party candidate George Wallace draws more than 9 million votes.

At Years End:
American troop strength in Vietnam is at 540,000. An entirely new phase of war in Vietnam is about to begin.

January 16
At the Paris Peace Talks, U.S. and North Vietnamese delegates finally agreed on the shape of the table to be used when the South Vietnamese and National Liberation Front (Viet Cong) joined the negotiations. Four party talks began January 18.

January 20
Richard M. Nixon is inaugurated president of the United States, with Spiro T. Agnew as Vice President. Anti-war demonstrations marred the Inaugural Ceremonies.

will was as decisive and unyielding as their own. With ample experience in foreign policy Nixon was a shrewd strategist, selecting former Harvard Professor Henry Kissinger as the main architect of his plan. Realizing an all out military victory was impossible, Nixon sought for "peace with honor" in Vietnam. Both men believed if the United States simply pulled out of the conflict, it's credibility as a nation would disintegrate, and free people everywhere would be in danger.

During the next four years, Nixon would preside over the most complicated and divisive of wars. For the American military, those years marked a time of disengagement, as U.S. soldiers fought on with the knowledge that an all-out victory was no longer the objective. Troop withdrawals would be slow but sure, in between periodic explosions of military might. Many times Nixon's strategy to intimidate and weaken Hanoi's will—deliberately widened the war. The fighting continued with the number of U.S. casualties steadily growing in the forefront of 'secret peace negotiations' to 'end the war with honor.' Ultimately, scandal and political cover-ups turned the pivotal tide of events. In the end, Congress would cut funding to Southeast Asia and American troops would leave South Vietnamese soil forever. In the process, Nixon would become the first and only American president to resign from office.

February 3, 1969

GLEN ATKINSON from Caldwell, Idaho loses his life in "HoBo" Woods, south of Saigon on a routine mission as a M-60 machine gun team leader.

Prior to leaving for Vietnam, Glen had been assigned to Fort Lewis. Unknown to him, his brother Jim (who was wounded in Vietnam) had been sent to the hospital on the same base. The two hadn't seen each other for 3 years and by 'chance' were able to spend time together before Glen shipped out to Vietnam. Another chance meeting took place when a friend from Middleton High School ran into Glen at the PX at Cu Chi. Their reunion was the last 23-year-old Glen would enjoy.

✯✯✯

February 19, 1969

Filer, Idaho Marine **RONALD "RONNIE" SHAFF** is mortally wounded during Operation Dewey Canyon. Pfc Shaff's platoon was conducting a search and destroy mission when the Marines came under heavy mortar, rocket-propelled grenades, and automatic weapons fire. Observing that his gunner's ammo was becoming low, and completely disregarding his own safety, Ronnie unhesitatingly left his covered position to procure an adequate supply. Ignoring hostile rounds nearby and intent only on his mission, he was maneuvering across the hazardous terrain when he was mortally wounded.

The posthumously awarded Bronze Star Citation for heroic achievement goes on to say, "His heroic and decisive actions inspired all who observed him and were instrumental in his platoon's routing of the enemy forces.

Private 1ˢᵗ Class Shaff's courage, bold initiative and unwavering devotion to duty were in keeping with the highest traditions of the Marine Corp and of the United States Naval Service."

In 1989 Ronnie's mother said she tries to forget about the war and look ahead. But, last week she saw a young Marine in his uniform walking down the street. *"Every time I see one, I am again reminded of Ronnie."*

March 9, 1969

When Blackfoot High School graduate **Douglas Rowe** becomes 1 of 52 casualties in a Company of 61 men, Senator Frank Church makes an emotional appeal to Congress over the terrible loss of life. Douglas was 22.

March 19, 1969

"68 Days To Go…" 21-year-old **Dean Moon** from Sterling, Idaho pens in his last letter home. Six days later on March 19, 1969 a sniper's bullet at Phan Thiet ended his tour of Vietnam. A member of the 101st Airborne Division Screaming Eagles, Dean graduated from Aberdeen High School in 1967. The soldier was a quiet unassuming boy, but never forgotten by those who loved him.

March 1989: A Letter To The Editor

But we…..shall be remembered;
We few, we happy few, we band of brothers,
For he today that sheds his blood with me
Shall be my brother….

Shakespeare

I remember my friend and my brother, Dean Moon. I remember him well. He was a member of my platoon in Company D 3/506th Infantry, 101st Airborne Division in Vietnam. I think of him often and will miss him always. I've cried and touched his name on the panel 29W, Line 81, etched in the polished black granite of that long black wall in Washington, D.C.

I never knew any of Dean's relatives or friends back in Idaho, but I want them and all the people who read this to know that he is remembered.

March 18, 1969
President Nixon orders the secret bombing of Cambodia.

Dean, and the over 58,000 of his brothers and sisters who made the supreme sacrifice of dying for their country in Southeast Asia, must always be remembered.

Larry Collins
Valencia, PA

Directly bordering Vietnam, Cambodia was known to be the staging ground for many Viet Cong and NVA operations. More importantly, the vast number of trails and roads constructed within its borders formed an essential part of the lifeline of Communism—the end of the Ho Chi Minh Trail. Hanoi had already been informed through French intermediaries that Nixon was ready to talk peace in Vietnam. The bombing of Cambodia was designed to convince Hanoi the United States would take harsh military action to bring the North around to negotiations.

April 1, 1969

Bingham County loses another son. Twenty-one-year-old **JON PETERSON** from Shelley, Idaho is killed while leading his men during an enemy engagement. In country only 3 months the young Sergeant writes of his first night in the field.

"…there was an explosion and when I looked up tracer bullets were going over my head and the mortars started landing." Jon was able to get to his foxhole but the man next to him was hit. He acknowledged, "I knew God was watching over me."

Everywhere they moved for the next 7 nights they were mortared. The first month of Jon's duty 10 men were killed in his company and 21 wounded. "It's hard to be walking along and come upon dead humans deteriorating away, but you seem to get used to it," he wrote.

When the Chaplain could come out, church services were held in the field. There was no particular religion, just a Christian service for all. "One time," Jon mentioned, "we met in the burned out hull of a C130 cargo plane." After 18 to 20 days in the bush, Jon and his men were looking forward to a 5-day rest at the LZ and a much longed for shower.

"I can't tell you where I'm at…"

When **REESE ANDERSON** packed his bags and gave final instructions to his family at their Arbon Valley ranch on Thanksgiving Day 1968—there was no way of

April 3

U.S. combat deaths in Vietnam since Jan.1, 1961 reached 33,641 topping the number killed in the Korean War.

knowing that in five short, but ever so long months, they would need to exercise the power of attorney their mature young son had signed and dated before his departure to Vietnam. Unable to handle a public farewell, Reese had asked his parents and three siblings not to come to the airport the following day.

After an emotional goodbye in the old cabin that he loved so much, the young Marine Officer spent the night at an apartment in town. Early the next morning before flying out of the Pocatello airport, he left his keys hidden safely in the car that his parents picked up later that day.

Reese reached Vietnam on November 30th assigned to the Dong Ha Combat Base in Quong Tri Providence. Excerpts from the 26-year-old's messages home tell the familiar tale.

December 12, 1968 — "...As of today I am here at Dang Ha, and I am Infantry Officer...We are going into virgin territory. It is known as the HOT SPOT of Vietnam. I undoubtedly will be seeing a lot of action in the very near future, a means of getting my feet wet."

December 22, 1968 — "...Here we are sitting atop a patch of high ground, got here yesterday, after three days patrolling and it seems we will be here till after Christmas. There are about 190 of us here. It looks like a tent city in the trees. Today my platoon has had nothing to do, so consequently myself, and (others) have built ourselves the D Co. Hilton. Tables, chairs and a fence clear around our Hilton, and each trail going and coming...looks like a cattle chute, with fences on both sides. It has been raining the past three hours and we are still good and dry."

December 26, 1968 — "Here it is the day after Christmas and we are on the move... We had a hell of a Christmas Eve. One dead and eleven injured from some of our own Mortar Rounds that fell into our Camp area."

January 20, 1969 — "...you asked how we got the mail out when we are in the bush. We usually have 2 or 3 people leave the bush each week, for some reason or another. They travel by chopper, so we send it out with them. We receive mail much less often, about every two weeks in the bush."

March 25, 1969 — "As for exactly where I'm at, I am close to the Laotian border in I Corps and that description will have to do for now. If I were to tell you where I am at and all the things that happen, and all of what we do—you would worry your head off. Also, if you don't get a letter from me for awhile, don't worry. It will be because I am busy."

April 2, 1969 — "General Davis, 1st Corps Commander asked the officers to submit a plan on how they would destroy Route 926. This had been used as the main supply route from Laos into Vietnam. Of all the plans offered, he bought my plan for mining the road, so this was my baby…I was working hand in hand with Lt. Colonels and Majors all doing my job. It was a blast, in more ways than one… Our mining of Route 926 is the first such mining of this type…in I Corps and by the 3rd Engineers in Vietnam. At the present time we are close to the Laotian Border and will be moving closer, if that is possible, as we are only 2000 meters from it now."

April 7, 1969 — "Here it is April and I have accomplished nothing this week. About three in the morning on Apr.3, I got the awfulest pain in my abdomen area. By 4:30 the doctor had me doped up to relieve the pain and at 0900, I was med-evaced …to Quang Tri and then my present location, the Hospital Ship Sanctuary. Due to the heat, lack of sufficient drinking water, improper diet, our daily stress and strains, I had developed kidney stones of all things. I have passed 2 stones…and I am to be released tomorrow, and it is about time. All the Officers are treated very well, but even with the Navy Nurses around all the time, I'll be glad to get off this ship and back to work with my men. They are a great group of guys."

April 13, 1969

Friday afternoon Reese and some of his men had returned to the Quang Tri Barracks from building a fire base near the Laotian border. While standing in his quarters, a stray bullet ricocheted off a nearby 2 by 4, struck Reese behind the ear and passed through the base of the brain—killing him instantly.

It was Monday, April 21st when a final message from Vietnam is delivered to the ranch Reese loved. The fateful telegram bearing the dreaded words, "We regret to inform you…"

"You may not be able to read this. I am writing in a hurry.
I see death coming up the hill."

(Extract from a GI's Letter Home.
Dong Apbia (Hamburger Hill) May, 1969)

May 1969

American ground troops fought one the most bloody and ferocious engagements of the entire war. The objective of the battle near the Laotian border, just west of the A Shau Valley, was to capture the Apbia Mountain (Hill 539) from NVA troops firmly entrenched there.

April 15

A U.S. reconnaissance plane was shot down by North Korea Mig jets over the Sea of Japan, 31 crewmen were lost.

April 24

In the heaviest bombing raid to date in the Vietnam War, U.S. B-52's dropped nearly 3000 tons of bombs on enemy positions near the Cambodian border northwest of Saigon

For ten days (May 11-20) American and South Vietnamese soldiers, supported by artillery and jet bombers struggled to expel communist forces from the jungle-covered slopes.

But the experienced and well-trained enemy had constructed bunkers so impenetrable that artillery and air power were ineffective. The only course remaining was costly frontal assaults from American ground troops. Casualties were extremely high and after several costly attempts the hill was finally captured.

Major Michael Davis O'Donnell's Tribute following the Battle of Apbia, expresses well the loss and sacrifice made by the men of the 101st Airborne Division at Hill 539. Major O'Donnell was listed as Missing In Action March 24, 1970.

If you are able,
save for them a place
inside of you
and save one backward glance
when you are leaving
for the places they can
no longer go.
Be not ashamed to say
you loved them
though you may not have always.
Take what they have left
and what they have taught you
with their dying
and keep it with your own.
And in that time
when men decide and feel safe
to call the war insane,
take one moment to embrace
those gentle heroes
you left behind.

Hamburger Hill
1969 May
101st Airborne Division (Hill 539)

May 20

U.S. and South Vietnamese troops captured Hamburger Hill after ten days of bloody battle. Senator Edward M. Kennedy of Massachusetts criticized such assaults as senseless.

June 8

Nixon announces the withdrawal of 25,000 American troops, the first step in the "Vietnamization" plan to turn the war over to South Vietnam.

September 3

Ho Chi Minh, Leader of the North since the 1950's dies at the age of 79.

September 25

Congressional opposition to the war grows as ten Bills designed to remove all American troops from Vietnam are submitted.

October 15

The first "Vietnam Moratorium Day" was observed by millions with prayer vigils, candle light processions, mass meetings, and black armbands. President Nixon ignored the demonstration. Coretta Scott King (widow of Martin Luther King) led a march of 250,000 protestors at Washington, D.C.

The hill was abandoned May 27 and later reoccupied by North Vietnamese troops. When "Life Magazine" published the pictures of 241 men who had been killed during one week in Vietnam, soon after the battle of Apbia, it set off a new storm of questioning and protest.

August 10, 1969

MICHAEL MOONEY, a Marine from Middleton, Idaho dies at Quang Tri. Vietnam was a long way from home for the young lad who had enlisted at 17. Proud to be a Marine, Michael was required to wait until his 18th birthday to serve overseas. Homesickness set in quickly for the teenager who wrote, " I sure do miss everyone and can't wait to come home. Man, I'm not ever gonna join anything again."

Adding to Michael's loneliness was the fact that he never received any of his family's letters from home.

"Last night I had to stand lines again," he penned, " It's pretty scary cause you can't see anything…all you do is listen and think."

On Michael's 45th day in country he was standing line again. In the darkness of the pre-dawn hours a fierce enemy assault attacked the camp. Moments later, the boy-soldier was mortally wounded by fragments from exploding mortar fire. Michael was 18.

October 28

Charges that an illegal war in Laos was being conducted without Congressional knowledge or consent, were leveled against the Administration and the Pentagon by Senator J. William Fulbright, Chairman of the Senate Foreign Relations Committee.

November 3

President Nixon said the secret U.S. peace proposals had been rejected. He asked the nation to support his plans to "Vietnamize" the war, that is, encourage Vietnam to pursue the war on its own and withdraw U.S. troops.

The Administration knew if the heavy casualties continued for long, the American public would refuse to support U.S. policy in Vietnam. If Nixon's 'peace with honor' was ever to be obtained, the South Vietnamese army must assume a larger role in fighting the enemy and providing national security. The President's strategy for ending the war committed American aid and equipment to support the local militias and re-doubled efforts by U.S. advisors to strengthen the South Vietnamese army.

The Phoenix Program, a controversial operation devised to uncover and destroy the Viet Cong, 'eliminated' some 6,000 Viet Cong officials. The Communist leadership called the combined efforts of the CIA and American Military Intelligence an 'assassination bureau.' Hanoi insisted the United States must withdraw its troops before a settlement could become a reality. Nixon refused.

November 11
Veteran's Day observances were marked by Pro-America demonstrations in support of U.S. policy in Vietnam. Nixon called it "the great silent majority."

November 14
The second "Vietnam Moratorium Day" began with a long single file "March Against Death" in Washington, D.C. The next day 250,000 people marched against the war. A similar protest in San Francisco drew 100,000 demonstrators.

November 16
News reports charged a U.S. infantry unit with the Massacre at My Lai 4, a village in the Songmy district in South Vietnam, on March 16, 1968. More than 450 villagers, including women and babies, were said to have been slain.

December 1
The first draft lottery of the Vietnam Era is instituted in an effort to reduce criticism of the draft as being unfair. It signaled an end to student deferments.

Propoganda "Free Passes" dropped from the air insuring safe passage to communist soldiers wishing to defect.
LARRY PETERSEN

February 20
National Security Advisor Henry Kissinger begins secret Paris negotiations with North Vietnam's Le Duc Tho.

April 20
Nixon promised to withdraw another 150,000 men from Vietnam by years end. The systematic withdrawals are decreasing American casualties.

April 29
A military invasion of Cambodia, called an "Incursion" by the White House, was launched by some 50,000 U.S. and South Vietnamese troops.

December 15
U.S. Troop strength in Vietnam would be cut to 434,000 by April 12, President Nixon announced, representing a total reduction of about 110,000 since he took office.

In 1969 alone, almost 10,000 U.S. soldiers had been killed in action.

1970

With the shrinking of the American presence on the ground, the Nixon strategists determined it would take a major military move to prevent North Vietnam from taking advantage of the situation. Knowing a ground thrust into Cambodia would trigger a public outcry, the decision was made to proceed. The President determined he would announce his plan to "go into the heart of the trouble" and clean out entrenched North Vietnam positions and supply bases in a nationally televised speech on April 30th. Some of the Cambodian positions the strategists correctly pointed out were as close to Saigon as Baltimore is to Washington, D.C.

April 30
President Nixon announces U.S. troops have attacked Communist sanctuaries in Cambodia, following the overthrow of Prince Sihanouk by U.S. aided Lon Nol. The incident sparked a nationwide shutdown of colleges and universities, violent demonstrations, and deaths on two college campuses.

May 4
As part of the widening campus protest against the war, a demonstration is held at Kent State University in Ohio. When National Guardsmen fired into the crowd of some 600 antiwar demonstrators, some of whom had been throwing rocks at the Guardsmen and taunting them, four students are killed. Ten days later two more students are killed, at predominantly black Jackson State College in Mississippi when state police open fire on demonstrators.

May 4, 1970 Another Mother's Son
CWO **Tommy Kearsley** from Buhl, Idaho dies in a helicopter crash at Phu Bai.

A 1965 graduate of Buhl High School, Tommy had shown an interest in the military from a very young age. On Mother's Day 1968 Tommy's mother watched her oldest son fulfill his dream to join the Marines. After basic training Tommy attended Officers Candidate school and graduated with high honors as a helicopter pilot.

The following Mother's Day 1969 Tommy hugged his mother goodbye again and left for Vietnam, commissioned to be a pilot and aircraft commander at Phu Bai. A difficult assignment during his year of service there, was the all too frequent need to drop body bags at specified locations and pick up the remains of battlefield casualties.

One week before the end of his 12-month tour of duty, Tommy was called on a final night mission, this time to drop flares for the troops below. In the midst of the battle, an unexpected collision in the fiery sky claimed the life of the young pilot who had so much to live for. Several hours later another mother's son dropped a bag for him.

On Mother's Day 1970 the heartbreaking telegram arrived. Tommy's body came home May 20th... the day of his expected return.

The 22-year-old's journal records:

Another uneventful day has come to a close; however, as I sit here on my cot with sweat oozing from every pore of my body I wonder what's going to happen. Why are things like they are? Why do people make other people suffer so much? Why is there so much killing? These are all questions that bother me very much, but the ones that bother me the most are, "Where do I stand? What is going to happen to me? What can I do to help if anything? Help is needed...Everywhere, help is needed!"

"Even though we were as close to death as I ever hope to be, it was worth it, because I saved a man's life."

On many occasions Tommy recorded in his journal how proud he was to serve his country and how grateful he was to be able to save as many lives as he did. In his personal belongings was a large plaque that had been given to him by the Marines for his excellent procedure in rescuing so many of them and lifting them safely off from "Box Hill" in the A-Shau Valley.

"What a thrill it was when I got everyone on board and departed to safety with them."

He further commented, "I really enjoy flying for the Marines. They are very appreciative. It gives me a good feeling to help them out when they are in trouble. *That's what I'm here for.*"

★★★

May 9
Another antiwar rally on Washington D.C. draws some 100,000 protestors to the nation's capital while similar demonstrations were held in many parts of the country.

June 15
The claim of 'Conscientious Objector' status on moral grounds alone, was found constitutional by the Supreme Court in the case of Welsh v. United States. Previously, such status was granted only on the basis long-standing religious belief and training.

October 7
President Nixon proposes a "standstill cease fire," and reissues a proposal for a mutual withdrawal the next day.

November 23
A covert raid into North Vietnam, in an attempt to rescue American POWs comes up empty-handed. Heavy bombing of the North continues. At years end, U.S. Troop strength falls to 280,000.

December 21
The Supreme Court rules the reduction of the voting age in national elections to 18 years is constitutional.

(Tommy Kearsley received the Silver Star)

June 24, 1970 Cambodia claims the life of Idaho man.

ALBARO GARCIA, an Army "point man" from Nampa, Idaho dies in a Cambodian ambush. In a letter three days earlier, the 21-year-old wrote that his company was struggling to keep from getting lost in the thick undergrowth and brush of the Cambodian hillside. It had been six weeks since his last shower and three weeks from his last change of uniform. " I sleep in the mud every night," he writes, "It rains three to four times a day, so we sleep in the cold and wet."

When he and six other members of his squad were wounded while on patrol, Albara courageously ignored his own wounds and held the enemy at bay until reinforcements could arrive. He died from his wounds later that day. Company C was scheduled to go back to Vietnam on June 26th two days after his death.

Born in Juarez, Mexico Albaro earned his high school diploma while serving in the Job Corps in New Jersey. Following one year at Boise State University, he joined the army and went to Vietnam in January of 1970. Giving his full measure to the country he loved, two Bronze Stars and a Purple Heart tell his story of duty well.

Cambodia
PHOTO: LARRY PETERSEN

 ★★★

When American intelligence sources reported the North Vietnamese were sending large quantities of military supplies into Laos and Cambodia, Nixon responded with a large-scale ground operation into Laos. Major bombing targets included the Ho Chi Minh Trail and also the docks and shipyards of Hanoi and Haiphong. A campaign to capture Tchepone, a major supply center in Laos was conducted almost exclusively by ARVN forces, but not before two of their battalions were completely overrun. When news of the operation in Laos reached the U.S., the Congress protested loudly. How could the administration be seeking peace by expanding the battlefield in Indochina? Senator J.William Fulbright proposed a repeal of the Tonkin Gulf Resolution, which originally expanded presidential power.

Late December U.S. troop strength in Vietnam had dropped to 340,000. By year's end the total death toll of U.S. personnel had passed 44,000.

February 8
The South Vietnamese with American support begin attacks on Viet Cong supply lines in Laos.

1971

The U.S. continued to disengage from combat in Vietnam. By December 1971 U.S. troop strength in South Vietnam had dropped to 184,000.

"…it's worse than anything I ever imagined…"

February 15, 1971

STEVEN ENGLAND, a 19-year-old Company Medic from Pocatello, Idaho dies in a chopper crash while picking up a wounded medic on a reconnaissance team. A 1969 honors graduate from Pocatello High School, Steven enlisted in the army in October of that same year. An honors graduate of Fort Sam Houston medical training and airborne school at Fort Benning, he volunteered for service in Vietnam in August 1970. Proud to become a medic with a Ranger Recon Team, capable and dedicated Steven was soon promoted as Company medic.

September 5, 1971 Stephen writes home from Vietnam:

"Sorry I've taken so long to write, but it's just been three or four days ago that I got a permanent address. I came in country at Cam Ranh Bay and was assigned there…with the 101st. Yeah, I'm a "Screaming Eagle"! I had a week or 9 days or so (of) jungle training at Camp Evans, about 10 miles north of Phu Bai. It's a damn funny thing to be in a trainee status and have real mortar rounds thrown at you during the night and live bullets during the day. Every night we were there they caught gooks crawling through the wire with home-made bombs.

Anyway, here I am under a poncho in the pouring rain (monsoons just started), in the mountains about five miles from the DMZ. How did I get here? Good question—I walked from a firebase two days ago. I never thought I could get this dirty, wet and cold. I'm a medic with (a) Recon Company and we live in the woods just like rats… "looney rats". I'm not sure when I'll get a chance to mail this letter or a chance to write again. This is the first time we've stopped other than just to eat or sleep in almost three days.

I won't even try to describe this country and the war to you, Dad. It's worse than anything I ever imagined or could hope to imagine. Living like this for a year, I'll come back to the world an animal. If I don't write much or often, believe me it's not because I don't care. It's just that there's so little time and so little good that can be said about what I'm doing. Please, though, write soon and often. You can't imagine how much I want to hear from home—even the smallest little things. Take care of yourself and write soon." All my love, Steve

An Internet Message posted July 31, 2000 pays Tribute to Sgt. Steven Glenn England and the men who died with him:

"Airborne Ranger Steven England (along with Lt. James Smith of Company L) was killed in a helicopter crash…trying to rescue a wounded soldier. The entire helicopter crew also perished.
Both England and Smith volunteered for this mission and knew how difficult the extraction was going to be. Because of the thick jungle terrain, the helicopter could not land but instead could only lower a McGuirre Rig (a steel cable

Extracting Troops by helicopter
PHOTO: LARRY PETERSEN

Swiss seat contraption). To make matters worse, the rescue mission was at night and in the middle of a monsoon storm. The pilot's visibility was almost zero during the entire mission. It would have taken a near miracle to pull it off. The helicopter crashed on the way back from the jungle and all were killed including the man they were trying to rescue. The loss of England, who was medic for the Rangers, and Smith, who had already been wounded once before on a similar mission, hit our company particularly hard.

The loss of Warrant Officer Concannon was also felt deeply for he had rescued many Rangers during some of the most harrowing situations. Gabriel Trujillo was the wounded soldier who died that night but I do not remember the names of Concannon's crew. All told, seven soldiers died that night... The relatives and friends of these men can at least take comfort in the fact that they died while trying to save another. Concannon, Smith, Trujillo, and Steve England were all friends of mine and they are forever in my thoughts and prayers."

Charles Reilly

 ★★★

Opposition to America's continued involvement in Vietnam, Laos and Cambodia made itself felt again in Washington, D.C. in early March when a bomb planted by a radical Weather Underground organization exploded in the Capitol Building. The device, planted in a restroom in the Senate wing, caused some $300,000 in damage but no injuries.

March 29

Lt. William Calley, Jr. was convicted of the premeditated murder of 22 people during the My Lai Massacre in 1968. The dropping of charges against 11 superior officers, fueled public outcry that Calley was being used as a scapegoat. On March 31 he was sentenced to life in prison. On August 20 Calley's sentence was reduced to 20 years imprisonment. He was later paroled.

June 13 The Pentagon Papers

The New York Times begins publication of the "Pentagon Papers" the top-secret history of American involvement in Vietnam. The original study entitled "The History of U.S. Decision Making Process in Vietnam" had been ordered by President Johnson.

Pentagon employee Daniel Ellsberg (who helped compile the report) handed it over to *Times* reporter Neil Sheehan. Outraged, Nixon tried to stop publication of the documents, which revealed much of the deceit within the government. On June 30th the Supreme Court ruled the *Times* and *Washington Post* could resume publication. Nixon was infuriated at its release claiming it compromised the intelligence-gathering process in Vietnam and decreased U.S. ability to bargain with the North Vietnamese. Revealing the doubts and reservations of many decision and policy makers in Washington, the *Pentagon Papers* left the American public believing the government had concealed the full story of the war.

On Nixon's orders, a unit known as the "plumbers" was set up to discover who leaked classified information to reporters. The "plumbers" soon expanded their activities to a break-in at the Democratic National Committee offices at the Watergate Office Building in Washington, D.C.

By mid summer of 1971 polls showed 58% of the American population felt the war was immoral. Only 31% approved of the administration's handling of the war.

Public view on the home front had a profound influence on American troops in the field. Without popular support from home, morale dropped significantly and the goal for many became simple survival to somehow get through 12 to 13 months of duty. Without the clear objective of a victory, the average soldier just wanted to get home alive. Incidents of fragging (the deliberate killing of officers) increased significantly to avoid situations that could be life threatening. Drugs were easy to obtain and soldiers were at times known to turn to marijuana, heroin and opium to escape the horrors of the war. At home, Americans erroneously believed that incidents like the My Lai Massacre were common occurrences, and as a result expressed little appreciation for the battlefield sacrifices being made.

Meanwhile, the fighting continued.

September 27, 1971

1st Lt. **Ronald "Lucky" Rueppel**, Cobra pilot from Latah County, Idaho dies in Vietnam. Ronald, a former Student Body Vice President, and 1966 Valedictorian of Deary High School enlisted in the army in 1968. After graduation from Ft. Benning Officer's Candidate school and Cobra flight training, he arrived in Vietnam on September 12.

15 days later after 24 combat missions Ronald's Cobra hit a tree in severe weather causing him to crash in the MeKong River.

In a letter to his parents from Ft. Lewis, Ronald wrote he had requested to go to Vietnam and felt it was "the right thing to do, not only for himself, but for America." The 23-year-old Lieutenant left a son and daughter. Carrying on a tradition of excellence and duty, his young son Ronnie later graduated from West Point.

November 12

President Nixon announces the withdrawal of 45,000 troops.

"The Cycle of Sacrifice Comes Full Circle"

June 30
The Twenty-sixth Amendment to the U.S. Constitution lowering the voting age for all elections to 18 went into effect when Ohio became the 38th state to ratify it.

March 8
The Supreme Court ruled draft exemption for conscientious objectors must be based on opposition to all war, not just to the Vietnam War.

May 3
In what was called the Mayday antiwar protest, thousands of demonstrators were arrested and confined when they tried to stop government activities by blocking traffic in the city. Most charges were dropped.

Paul, Idaho—Home of Idaho's First Casualty in Southeast Asia, again bears the sorrow of another lost son—and Idaho's Final Death in the Vietnam War.

December 14, 1971

GREG HOLLINGER from Paul, Idaho becomes the state's final casualty of the Vietnam War. A graduate of the University of Idaho and ROTC, he was commissioned in the army in 1965 and served in in Vietnam 1967-68 with the 101st Airborne Division. Upon his return he earned a Masters Degree at the University of Idaho and began his second tour of duty in Vietnam on Oct. 2, 1971.

Working as a logistics officer with the South Vietnamese army, Greg was presumably lost in a downed aircraft over the China Sea, five minutes from Da Nang. The plane was returning from the DMZ (demilitarized zone). The 29-year-old Idahoan had given six years of dedicated service to the country he loved.

★★★

December 26-30

Massive air bombardment of military installations in North Vietnam resumed. The heaviest attack since the November 1968 bombing halt was conducted by U.S. Navy and Air Force planes.

1972

Eastertide Offensive

As the stalemate continued, Hanoi was planning to go on the offensive again. The massive three-pronged attack from bases in Laos, Cambodia and North Vietnam would involve more than 120,000 troops. Failing to anticipate the scope of the invasions, the U.S. would face the biggest Communist offensive since Tet.

Early in Eastertide Offensive the North Vietnamese overran many ARVN strongholds in Quang Tri Province, including the city of Quang Tri. Farther south, they poured into the central highlands from bases in Laos. Without the previous concentration of U.S. ground troops, Hanoi undoubtedly believed that South Vietnam could be easily occupied. As the fighting continued several South Vietnamese generals had to be relieved of their command on the battlefield for incompetence or cowardice.

In late March, the North Vietnamese launched another massive offensive across the Demilitarized Zone and from Cambodia to the south. At the end of five weeks, Hanoi's troops had penetrated deep into South Vietnam. After serious initial losses, the South Vietnamese forces finally began to turn back the enemy as Nixon ordered massive B-52 strikes on advancing NVA troops. The offensive was ultimately a military defeat for the North, but American military men on the scene

January 13
President Nixon announces the withdrawal of another 70,000 troops.

January 25
The administration reveals that Henry Kissinger has been in secret negotiations with the North Vietnamese. The U.S. peace proposal calls for a cease-fire and release of all U.S. POWs. If accepted the U.S. will withdraw from Vietnam.

February 21-28
President Nixon enhances his chances for re-election and positions the U.S. internationally by taking a historic Presidential visit to China.

were unnerved by the ARVN performance. Some units had performed well, but the offensive could have not been halted without overwhelming American air power. This posed a great dilemma for the Nixon administration. Four-fifths of American troops had been withdrawn and Congress would be reluctant to provide funds to bail out the South Vietnamese.

May 22-30

The first U.S. presidential visit to Moscow was made by President Nixon.

Without the support of their communist allies, North Vietnam couldn't have survived the war for so many years. Knowing that China and the Soviet Union supplied the North's troops with weapons, food and ammunition, Nixon and Kissinger attempted to apply political as well as military pressure on the enemy. By the early 1970's, the Chinese and Soviets were in contention among themselves. Their border troops had clashed on a number of occasions and China refused to let Soviet aircraft carrying supplies for the Vietnamese war fly over its territory. By promising increased trade and better relationships with the Soviet Union and China, Nixon and Kissinger hoped to indirectly apply pressure to North Vietnam. One of the purposes of Nixon's highly publicized trips to China and the Soviet Union in 1972 was to leverage the U.S. position in the stalled peace negotiations with North Vietnam.

June 17

Five men, all members of the Committee to Re-elect the President are arrested at the Democratic National Committee offices at the Watergate Office Building, in Washington, D.C. When two former intelligence operatives, G. Gordon Liddy and E. Howard Hunt, are arrested for their involvement in the break-in, the White House cover-up begins to unravel.

After three exhausting weeks just prior to the 1972 Presidential Election, Henry Kissinger and Le Duc Tho reach a breakthrough in the Paris negotiations:

The U.S. openly agreed that it would no longer insist upon the complete withdrawal of North Vietnamese forces from South Vietnam. At the time of the cease-fire, whoever controlled the territory would continue to occupy it until a more complete political settlement could be obtained. In return, the North Vietnamese consented to the release of American POWs and no longer insisted on the ousting of the Thieu regime.

South Vietnam President Thieu resisted and was outraged when Kissinger presented the plan to him. The agreement would leave his government in political limbo and NVA troops would still occupy his land. President Nixon considered it crucial that Thieu agree to the proposal, otherwise, it would appear the United States was simply cutting its losses and getting out.

After ordering $1 billion in military hardware to be sent to Vietnam, Nixon warns South Vietnamese President Thieu that further aid will be cut off if there is more complaining about the U.S. government's failure to defend his interests. New plans for another round of bombing are also instigated.

April 15
Bombing in the North is resumed.

May 1
The city of Quang Tri is captured by the North Vietnamese forces.

May 8
President Nixon announces the mining of Haiphong Harbor and stepped up bombing raids against the North.

October 8
Kissinger announces peace is "within reach" two weeks before the election.

November 7, 1972
Richard Nixon is re-elected in a landslide victory.

December 18
The Paris peace negotiations reached an impasse.

December 18, 1972
In the next eleven days, 1700 sorties flown over Hanoi inflict heavy damage on power plants, factories and transportation networks. Americans react to the "Christmas bombing" with dismay and horror as U.S. pilots suffer heavy losses in the raids.

December 30
The bombing is halted and North Vietnam agrees to return to the negotiations.

1973

Kissinger resumes talks with the North. A cease-fire agreement is signed and formally announced on January 27th. Except for a few minor changes, the terms are similar to those Thieu had resisted earlier. A personal letter of assurance from President Nixon promising U.S. support if the North Vietnam broke the cease-fire brought the South's consent. Key provisions in the agreement included:

- A cease-fire throughout North and South Vietnam
- Withdrawal of U.S. forces and dismantling of U.S. installations within 60 days
- Release of North Vietnamese, Viet Cong and U.S. prisoners of war within 60 days
- Re-unification of the North and South through peaceful means
- The South Vietnamese government was to remain until new elections were held
- North Vietnamese forces in the South would remain, but could not be replaced or re-enforced

Defense Secretary Melvin Laird announces the end of the draft as the army shifts to an all-volunteer force. 2.2 million American men have been drafted during the Vietnam War.

February American POW's held in Hanoi are released.
At the end of World War II, military numbers reported 78,751 soldiers as Missing in Action (MIA), or Prisoners of War (POW). The Korean War resulted in 8,177 men unaccounted for. In 1973, the American military reported 2,338 men as MIA / POW in the Vietnam conflict.

Many of the captured servicemen were taken to a fortress-like complex called Hoa Lo Prison in North Vietnam, nicknamed by Americans as the "Hanoi Hilton." Common to the survivors' experience were some remarkable elements:

- Because the U.S. never declared war against the North Vietnamese, the "shoot-downs" were not regarded as prisoners of war, but as criminals.
- The vast majority of Americans in Hoa Lo Prison followed the Code of Conduct which precludes giving more than one's name, rank, serial number and date of birth. Only after being tortured did they "break" and allow themselves to say more.
- Orders for resistance were given by senior ranking officers via the "tap code" between cells. Anyone caught was beaten, but the POWs never relented.
- Because it was more difficult for the Vietnamese to kill a "known" prisoner, the POWs tried to "get the names out" by any means. One captive memorized the

names of 400 men to the tune of "Old MacDonald Had A Farm" and then, by pretending to be crazy, obtained an early release. The names got out.

- To prevent the Vietnamese from playing one captive against another, the POWs avoided taking early releases unless the entire group was set free and even refused to meet family members.

(Source: Parade Magazine, April 1987)

Among those released from the "Hanoi Hilton" in 1973 was Idaho's Captain **LARRY CHESLEY** from Burley, Idaho. Shot down over North Vietnam on April 16, 1966, Larry was one of 112 POWs released on February 12, 1973. Among his comrades were Lt. Everett Alvarez, the first American to be captured, Lt. Gerald Coffee and Major Sam Johnson who was shot down with Larry. With their loved ones and many more, the Chesleys had borne the burden of families held hostage for more than seven years.

"I don't remember him…but I still love him…"

were the honest words of Larry's eleven-year-old daughter when asked if she remembered her father the day of his return. Exactly seven years and three months had passed, since he had kissed his four-year-old daughter and two-year-old son goodbye. After four long years of no word and believing Larry was dead, Jolene had remarried leaving a painful void at his grateful return.

"Thousands Line Streets. Cheers, Tears Welcome Captain Chelsey Home" read the headlines of the "South Idaho Press" in Burley, Idaho. On March 10, 1973 the citizens of Burley, Idaho and surrounding regions put on a magnificent welcome. Some thirty thousand lined the streets for the local boy who was fortunate enough to come home. Larry writes, "Of all the official welcomes I received, …(this) was the most moving for me, being staged in the community where I had spent my childhood and whose scenes and people had been among the foremost of my recollections in prison. It was a profoundly humbling experience." The final chapter of Larry's book entitled, "Seven Years In Hanoi" reflects upon his time and sacrifice as a prisoner of war.

"I no doubt lost a lot by my seven years' captivity," Larry shares, " but I like to think it wasn't all loss. I believe I learned a thing or two there and reaffirmed others. One thing I learned was the futility of worrying over something one can't control… I came to realize in prison the value of learning.

…I believe I learned something about gratitude, especially appreciation for the "little" things in life. I'm thinking of little things like soap and toothpaste that we naturally take for granted in America.

National **POW MIA** Recognition Day, **September 21, 1990**

There were times when we didn't have such things in prison. It's hard to imagine how filthy and uncomfortable you can get if you don't have any toilet paper for days or weeks and can't bathe. And hot water to wash in? Seven years without hot water can do a lot to stir appreciation for what little things you *can* get.

Gratitude is something pretty hard not to have in prison. Virtually all the POWs were grateful for the little things we did have.... And we were deeply thankful for each other, thankful that we had a strong feeling of friendship and brotherhood.

As to my military service, I have no regrets about spending those years serving my country. I believe that any young man living in America should be willing to serve this country in the military if called upon to do so...this land is blessed of the Lord above all other lands even in a material sense...

More important is the American concept of freedom, a concept reaffirmed in prison by the POW's memories of home, the comments shared with his comrades, the contrasting philosophy and behavior of his captors, and that indefinable inner urge which is the heritage of every free man. We knew in prison of the "peace" marches in the States, the burning of the American flag, the riotous voices of dissent complete with the display of the enemy's flag, the visits to North Vietnam of U.S. citizens sympathetic to the enemy... It was discouraging in our circumstances and filled us with disgust, but it did not deflect our hearts from the ideal of freedom.

We managed to reconcile ourselves to all this with the thought that as servicemen it was our duty to fight for America's freedoms, among which is the right to dissent... There had naturally been divisions of opinion over the Vietnam War, and perhaps the returning prisoners have represented a common bond... although there were those who thought that the returning POWs would come back embittered by their long imprisonment, almost to a man we have come back with our heads high praising our country and our leaders.

While the other POWs and I hold the spotlight for this brief moment, before the lights dim and others move to center stage, let me briefly recall the great affirmation I experienced in my prison years. It is that, however tough the going gets, God never deserts us if we put our trust in him... It is under God's blessing the United States of America is the greatest country on the earth.

God and country—that is the great combination. Navy Cmdr. Jeremiah Denton said it at the end of the short speech... he gave as he stepped off the first plane from Hanoi. The military newspaper *Stars and Stripes* picked it up and headlined it "Three Words Say It All." With all my heart I reiterate those three words, with a prayer that the American people will increasingly comprehend the true implications of those words and live for their fulfillment."

GOD BLESS AMERICA

★★★

Fewer than 600 Prisoners Of War were released alive from Vietnam and since 1973, only 330 identified remains have come home.

"KILLED IN ACTION"

During President Jimmy Carter's administration, in an effort to bring some closure to the war, the Commander In Chief declared all remaining Vietnam POW MIA listings as Killed In Action (KIA). The League of Families, a national organization of family members still searching for answers, refused to accept President Carter's proclamation. Since that time, the Reagan and Bush administrations continued the effort to establish a final accounting through the Department Of Defense.

One of thirteen Idaho men listed as MIA/POW, the remains of Colonel **MARK STEPHENSEN** were returned to his family in 1988. An Internet posting from Mark's wife, Vickie brings solemn closure to decades of emptiness and loss.

MARK LANE STEPHENSEN COL
Mark was 36 years old. He was shot down on 29 April, 1967. His status was changed on 21 August, 1975. Marks remains were returned in April of 1988 and identification made 3 June, 1988.

Saturday, June 03, 2000

Air Force pilot Mark Stephensen began his 2nd tour of duty in Vietnam in 1966 where he flew 94 combat missions and 6 combat support missions before his was reported missing on April 29, 1967. He and his WSO Gary Siegler never returned from a night mission over the Paul Damieler Bridge. Captain Siegler was captured following the crash and held as a Prisoner Of War until his release in 1973. Nothing was ever heard regarding Col. Stephensen until his remains were finally returned in 1988.

Colonel Stephensen's son Mark, who was twelve years old when he last saw his father, has served on the Board of Directors for the National League of POW/MIA Families. Proud of his father's service, and recalling the sacrifice of 'tens of thousands of little white crosses' from the Vietnam era, Mark shares, "Dad went to fight—threatened they would take away his way of life, a piece at a time." *"He went,"* he adds with emotion, *"so I wouldn't have to."*

★★★

July 16
A Senate investigation into the secret air war against Cambodia begins.

August 14
The bombing of Cambodia is officially halted.

October 10
Vice President Spiro Agnew resigns after pleading "no contest" to charges of tax evasion. House minority leader, Gerald Ford is nominated by Nixon to replace Agnew.

Ocotober 16
The Nobel Peace Prize was awarded jointly to Sec. of State Henry Kissinger and to Lee Duc Tho of North Vietnam for their efforts in ending the Vietnam War. Tho declined the award.

August 9
Gerald R. Ford was sworn in as the 38th President of the United States.

September 8
Former President Nixon was pardoned by President Ford for any crimes he may have committed or may have participated in, while in office.

November 8
Charges against eight Ohio National Guardsmen stemming from the 1970 Kent State tragedy were dropped in federal court.

Another Idaho MIA/POW was one of 70 cases the U.S. government found most compelling in a 1987 Cover Story of *Life Magazine* entitled "Missing."

Lt. Comdr. Roderick L Mayer
Navy
Lewiston, Idaho

Shot down over the Thai Nguyen bridge in North Vietnam on October 17, 1965. Mayer and his crewman ejected. Sighted from the air, one appeared to have reached the ground safely; the other was seen for two hours sprawled on the ground with his parachute still attached. By the time a rescue helicopter arrived, neither could be found. Mayer's crewman was released from captivity in 1973. "I still send letters and packages," says Mayer's mother. "Some come back, some don't."

March 29, 1973

The last American ground combat troops leave Vietnam, but 9,000 or so "civilian" American advisors remain in the country. Most officially employed by the government of South Vietnam. Many of the men being recently retired U.S. servicemen.

November 7

Over the President's veto, Congress passed the War Powers Act, restricting the President's power to commit troops to foreign countries without prior Congressional approval.

1974

The Nixon Administration continues to be crippled by the scandals of the Watergate affair. President Nixon is charged with three 'Articles of Impeachment' by the House Judiciary Committee for: blocking the investigation of the Watergate affair, abuse of presidential powers, and for hindering the impeachment process by not complying with the committee's subpoena for tapes of White House conversations.

January 1974

South Vietnam's President Thieu announces that war has begun again as Communists proceed to build up troops and supplies in the South. Thieu depended on Nixon's secret promise to come to his aid should Hanoi threaten to overrun his country. But Nixon's ability to respond diminished daily, as did his ability to bargain with Congress and assert his will in matters of foreign policy.

August 8

President Nixon announced in a televised address that he would resign. Nixon told the audience of 100 million he had made some wrong decisions, but that he was resigning because he no longer had enough support in Congress.

September 16

A limited Amnesty Proclamation was issued by President Ford, offering clemency to thousands of Vietnam-era draft resisters and military deserters if they swore allegiance to the U.S. and performed up to two years of public service work.

1975

The Beginning Of The End

The final offensive of the Second Indochina War began in January 1975 with the capture of Phuoc Long Province, to the north of Saigon. One by one the southern provinces fell to North Vietnamese attacks. When the communists pushed into the central highlands, ARVN soldiers deserted their posts in a frantic effort to find their families and seek safety on the coast. Route 7B, an old abandoned highway running from the central highlands to the eastern coastal regions became a scene of carnage and death as more than 50,000 soldiers and 400,000 refugees tried to escape NVA artillery. Thousands died as the human caravan was shelled day and night.

March

Associated Press Release: Saigon

> "North Vietnamese and Viet Cong forces swept through Da Nang today (Sunday) to complete their month-long blitz of the northern third of South Vietnam. Phan Qang Dan, South Vietnamese deputy Prime Minister for refugee affairs, confirmed the loss of Da Nang, South Vietnam's second largest city. He called for immediate contact with the Viet Cong to provide humanitarian relief for the 1 1/2 million refugees said to be trapped in the

port city 380 miles north of Saigon. Only 50,000 of the estimated 1 1/2 million refugees have been evacuated by air and sea.

Da Nang, once a stronghold of the U.S. Marines, had collapsed into disorder and rioting as the end neared. Refugees and government soldiers battled each other Saturday to board aircraft or barges leaving the city as the Communist-led troops closed in. Frantic soldiers shot and kicked civilians trying to seize an evacuation plane and terrified refugees fell off crowded barges and sampans in the harbor."

Under contract with with the Federal Government, planes from Oakland based World Airways Airline, had been flying Vietnamese evacuation flights until operations were suspended by the riots in Da Nang and government hold ups. World Airways President Ed Daly had been in country personally overseeing the operation to airlift refugees in what was known as "Mercy Flights." By removing the seats of a Boeing 747, Daly planned to evacuate 1,400 people at a time. South Vietnam government officials refused his offer. Meanwhile, 461 sick orphan children were stranded on a Saigon runway while Daly and others worked frantically to obtain visas and required paperwork.

April 3, 1975
The Oakland Tribune reports:

"The pilots that flew 57 orphans from Saigon to Oakland yesterday are no strangers to harrowing flights." Ordered to "hold position" and knowing Viet Cong troops were in the facility, the pilot and co-pilot ignored instructions and prepared for take off. "As soon as we started the engines, they turned the lights out and wouldn't give us clearance...We turned and took off. After we were airborne we informed the ground that we had our radios back." A senior vice-president of World Airways was also on the flight. "It took eight hours to get the children that were on that plane," he said. "Originally we thought we had made arrangements with another organization that was going to bring between 400 and 500 children." Government officials felt the seatless cargo plane was unsafe for the large group of children. "We felt the aircraft was safe, and we knew the kids needed to be taken out... There was only one thing to do, and that was go."

April 17
Pnompenh, the capital of Cambodia (renamed Kampuchea), falls to Khmer Rouge.

April 23 President Ford calls the war "finished"

"Unfinished" for decades to come would be the effects of Vietnam on the veterans and their families. Nearly 58,000 men and women had died and more than 303,000 were wounded.

Unlike the soldiers of previous wars, the Vietnam serviceman came home alone. There were no parades or public thanks for his sacrifice, and more importantly there was no victory to celebrate. Relieved and anxious to put it all behind them, the American public viewed the war as anything but a popular topic of conversation. Conversations that needed to be spoken, remained in silence as tens of thousands suffered the psychological symptoms of post-traumatic stress. Many veterans experienced a sense of "survivor guilt" for living through the ordeal when so many of their comrades had died and thousands more lived with the effects of Agent Orange and other physical maladies.

Meanwhile, the vast majority of American servicemen would be able to put the war behind them and go on with productive lives. But it would be years before America was ready to face the painful truths of Vietnam—truths that had changed us forever as a nation.

Saigon was now near the verge of complete collapse and President Thieu was finally persuaded to resign. In the meantime, a final exit was being planned for the remaining Americans and their allies. The first communist rockets landed in Saigon on April 27 forcing the U.S. embassy to coordinate an emergency evacuation by plane and boat.

April 29

The last Americans are evacuated from Saigon. On the same day the last two American soldiers are killed in Vietnam.

On April 29th, at 11:00 a.m., President Gerald Ford ordered Operation Frequent Wind, the aerial evacuation of Saigon. 5,000 Americans were evacuated from Tan Son Nhut Airport by 9:00 p.m. The Marines continued the evacuation from the Embassy compound itself through the night and by 5:00 a.m. the following morning the helicopters had managed to remove another 2,100 people. Many South Vietnamese governmental officials who worked closely with the Americans escaped also. However, thousands of civilians who had assisted in America's crusade were left behind. Their fate left to the communists.

April 30 Communist forces take Saigon.

Fearful of what life would be like under communist rule, untold numbers of refugees fled their homeland, never to be heard from again. An estimated 400,000 South Vietnamese, many with no close relationships to the Americans or Thieu government, were shipped off to "re-education" camps. A small portion of the one million Vietnamese who tried to escape—made it to the shores of Thailand and other neighboring countries in rickety boats. Thousands had to be rescued from the water, with as many as 100,000 more perishing beneath the waves of the South China Sea.

1976

January 21
President Jimmy Carter unconditionally pardons most of the 10,000 men who evaded the draft.

1982

November 11
The Vietnam Veterans Memorial is unveiled in Washington, D.C. commemorating the 58,000 American lives lost in Vietnam between 1959 and 1975.

1990

August 4
The Idaho Vietnam Veterans Memorial is dedicated in Idaho Falls, Idaho.

(Military and battle descriptions of the above section formulated from the combined works of "Vietnam The Decisive Battles", "The Vietnam War Day By Day", "Portrait Of A Tragedy", and "Vietnam A History" Also see Note section.)

PART 2

PROFILES

*Idaho and the
Vietnam War*

*Images of war
and glimpses into
the hearts and minds
of
those who served.*

VIETNAM
THROUGH A SOLDIER'S EYES

LETTERS HOME:

During the long years of the Vietnam War, families across the state of Idaho anxiously waited for word from their sons and daughters. As rural carriers made their way down country roads and mailmen delivered door to door, words of relief coupled with messages of sorrow, arrived on a regular basis from Southeast Asia.

Treasured letters—some eloquently detailed and philosophic, with others being quickly scribbled notes by a homesick boy—were read and re-read, as the distance between heart and home grew momentarily near.

Postage was merely marked "free" and "return addresses" ranged from unit, division, and assignment to the simple inscription of "One Lonely Soldier." Notes on the back of the envelopes revealed the relief of "One month over" and the hope of "63 days to go." For many young soldiers, subjects of war—lightly discussed or intentionally omitted—were attempts to spare loved ones of worry and concern.

Scratches of paper, an occasional picture, and written feelings of gratitude and uncertainty in the middle of the night, reveal glimpses into the hearts and minds of those who served. Sacred communications really, and many times 'unknown' and 'final farewells.'

Go gently as you enter into the reality of those that served and died. May the truth of their combined experience bring greater understanding and appreciation for the sacrifices made, and the tremendous loss of loved ones left behind.

—*M. Whyte*

"....completed one month, only eleven to go...seems like a lifetime."
(DeVern Probart, 28 February, 1969)

May 18, 1969

Dear Family,
"Well, I'll write this today, but I don't know when I'll get it mailed. We left Xam Loc and went back to the jungle for a few days. It was a very bad operation and we really got wet. I also had words with my counterpart. Only a few contacts...

Then we left and came down to the ocean area. I haven't seen the ocean yet though. We are in the village of Gat So. The VC took over the village and our job has been to run them out and secure it. It's a rather large village. We are not doing what we expected to do, so I don't know what is going to happen. We don't have the secure compound and hootch we expected to have and the rain keeps us wet every night.

It's really a flat area down here except for…small in size, tall mountains. These the VC control. There are a lot of rice fields and other types (of) field areas. During the rain season it's a very wet area.

The jungle is very heavy, most things are starting to get real green and very beautiful, if you can call a country like this beautiful. I guess it's beautiful in its own way. Me, I'm homesick for the Tetons, the Bechler River, or the Gallaton Valley, for a clear stream, a horse, a fishing stream, and especially a nice clean smelling pine tree."

July 13, 1969
DeVern Probart's last letter home. He died four days later in a helicopter crash.

Dear Family,
"Here's just a short note to let you know that everything seems to be going OK. I got the cookies and tapes today. I've really enjoyed the tapes, and the cookies are real good. They got here in real good shape.

We are (expecting) to move. This is our permanent base area but apparently they think its (too) easy living. Anyway, they found an area where there is about 4 (Bus) of VC. They are moving a task force into the area. We are to be the controlling headquarters. Got to take our artillery and move into a new firebase for a few days. Live in a tent and in the mud again. Its what we call 'eagle flighting.' Set up for 4 to 6 days until the (enemy) moves out of our (artillery) range. Then we move to another to support them for another 4 to 6 days and continue…"

Kenneth Young of the 116th Army Corp of Engineers:

"Kind of wish I was home. It seems funny I would go places without packing a rifle and thinking someone is trying to kill me."

Journal entry of **Tommy Kearsley** from Buhl, Idaho:

"Today, upon opening my cupboard, I found a pile of paper shavings and a hole in the box of rat poison that Mom had sent me. War is really hell when it gets so bad the rats have to break in just to get some poison. Later, the rat decided to explore my bed. Needless to say, when the rat crawled up my leg and over my back, I bound out of my bunk and got very little sleep the rest of the night."

20-year-old Pocatello Marine, **MICHAEL CROUSON** writes home from shortly after his arrival inVietnam:

"…we're fighting the hot weather, mosquitoes, leeches and snakes more than the V.C."

In November 1966, Michael and two other soldiers were sitting in front of their machine gun foxhole when 2 or 3 "Charlies" sniped at them, shooting about 10 rounds and then leaving. Mike said they hit the foxhole in a hurry and he wished he "could have cut off his buttons so he could have gotten closer to the ground."

A 1962 graduate of Pocatello High School, Mike attended college at Idaho State University. Following in the footsteps of two older brothers he joined the Marine Corps in March 1966. Upon arriving in Vietnam in October 1966 he was assigned as a machine gun team leader. Two months later, Michael died on December 10th near Quang Tri, from fragmentation wounds while on patrol.

Six days before **DOUGLAS HOWES** of Canyon Country is killed, he writes home on "Snoopy" stationery to his family:

10 March 1970 — "I got all of today off and so earlier this afternoon I went to church…"

"There are only two of us left in the hooch now. The rest…are down in the new company. I'm supposed to move sometime this afternoon but I doubt it because I haven't heard anything about it yet.

It makes me feel so good to think how good we've got it back there in the world after seeing what these people have to go through to live over here. I was on trash detail yesterday and we had to haul a bunch of stuff to the dump. The

Vietnamese down there actually live on what we throw away. If you've got any wood or a rug or something like that on the truck, they'll unload the whole truck just to get it. They take it to the village and sell it."

Ross Bee, formerly of Georgetown, Idaho attended high school at Montpelier before his family moved to the Ogden area. Drafted in 1966, he left for Vietnam in Sept.1966 and arrived in Vietnam by ship on Oct.4th. Ross was hospitalized in Vietnam for a short while with a foot fungus he acquired from wading in the rice paddies and mud. In letters home he wrote how appalled and sorry he felt for the Vietnamese people's living conditions:

"The chicken coops back home are better than what some of them live in."

Just before Christmas, Ross' unit had pulled perimeter guard around a Special Forces Camp and he welcomed the break from his usual duty. The day before he was killed, while leading his patrol, Ross had been promoted to SpE5. He was 20 years old.

While attempting to drag a wounded comrade to safety, **Leonard Broenneke** was mortally wounded on a reconnaissance mission in Long Khanh Province. A 1968 graduate of Moscow High School, he died one week before his twenty-first birthday.

In a letter home he writes:

"Dear Sister: It has been quite a while since I wrote you a letter. I am really sorry because I have had a lot of free time, but I have been writing everybody else. There's really not much going on over here. We are on another mountain; it is really pretty nice. The main reason why it is nice is because there are not any gooks on it. Also, there is a stream and we can take baths about every day. The other day while we were taking a bath, a wild pig came walking out of the brush. We shot him and roasted him over an open fire, boy, was it ever good…"

"The bugs over here are really bad. It is really getting hot over here. Today we were out walking in this field, it was really hot then we cut down into the trees by a stream and the change in the temperature was so much that the steam starting rolling off of us and you could see our breaths. I have walked so far since I have been over here, I don't think I'm ever going to walk anywhere when I get back to the world. The only thing I like over here is when we ride on the choppers. It is really neat riding on them. You can sit right on the edge of the

Photo: Larry Petersen

seat so your legs are hanging outside and when the pilot turns your way it feels like you are going to fall out, but you can't because the wind holds you in…"

All my love
Your little brother
"Tiz"

MORRIS E. (EDDIE) WILLIAMS of Boise, Idaho joined the Army during his junior year at Capital High School. He earned his GED in the service before being shipped to Vietnam in September 1969.

The only son wrote to his family on December 8, 1969 of the holiday dinner the troops had just enjoyed. Lobster, steak and chicken were cooked over open grills and a trailer loaded with pop and beer completed the feast. Bob Hope was visiting troops in the area but hadn't put on any shows yet. His letter concluded:

" I'm sorry I won't be home for Christmas…but wait until next year. That Christmas will have to be one of the best I'll ever have."

Eddie died in a helicopter crash two months later, on February 6, 1970. He was eighteen years old.

"Some people come into our lives, make footprints on our hearts, and we are never the same."

FOREVER IN OUR HEARTS

The rural community of Bancroft, Idaho lost one of its favored sons when enemy mortar fragments took the life of L. Cpl. **JAY D. (DARWIN) MC LAIN** in Vietnam. The young Marine loved the clean air and beauty of his secluded mountain valley, and especially enjoyed riding horses with the Caribou County Mounted Posse. But first and foremost, the 'man' in the lives of his young daughter and three sisters, is remembered for his compassion and devotion to family and friends.

When Darwin's younger sister's fiancé was stationed in Japan he generously saved his money for three weeks, bought her a corsage, and proudly escorted the teenager to her own senior prom. A distressed phone call in the night from another sister, faraway from home and homesick at college, brought counsel and encouragement only a big brother could lend. The following morning, Darwin drove 5 hours to surprise the lonely coed in Salt Lake City, armed with a dozen roses and reassurance she would never forget. His willing five hour return trip that evening to begin work at midnight, was characteristic of his generous nature and willingness to give.

On May 28, 1967, alone and far away from the family and land he loved, Darwin's duty as a defender of freedom, required of him the ultimate gift of sacrifice and devotion. He was twenty-five.

Front Page release of the Twin Falls "Times News" Thursday, April 28, 1996:

Local Soldier Is Missing After Ambush in Vietnam

"**BRENT BAUMERT**, son of Mr. and Mrs. H.O. Baumert…is missing in action in Vietnam, after a boat in which he was riding was ambushed earlier this week. Maj. Harlan M. Meyer, commanding officer, 10th U.S. Army Corps, Twin Falls, said it was reported to him that Baumert was last seen about 200 meters from base camp.

Baumert is with Detachment A, 425 Special Forces Group. Information as to the location of the base camp is not available, but it was reported that Baumert's group was a small detachment based a good many miles from other American forces.

Baumert was originally drafted into the Army after graduation from the University of Idaho and re-enlisted in order to go into Special Forces… After a completion of duty in Germany Baumert came home for a 30-day leave and departed for Viet Nam during the month of January."

Sgt. Baumert was 26 years old at the time of his death.

Custer County Casualty:

Sp4 **JERRY B. WILSON** was known to friends and family in Mackay, Idaho as "Big Red." The 1963 Mackay High School graduate's trademark was his friendly smile, red hair and enthusiasm for life. Jerry loved sports and a favorite pastime was skiing down White Knob Hill with one of his sisters on the back of his skis. Tubing and swimming in the Big Lost River filled summer afternoons, and the happy teenager never lacked for fun or friends.

Jerry joined the Army in March 1965 and was trained in heavy artillery. The young Idaho soldier was shipped to Vietnam on March 25, 1966 and was seriously wounded the following November. While exiting a UH-ID helicopter, fragments from U.S. short artillery hit Jerry's body. Jerry was recovering from his injuries at 3rd Field Hospital when he contracted malaria. Complications from the disease and battle wounds took his life on December 14, 1966. Jerry was twenty years old.

Pfc. **JAMES WALKER**, a native of Blackfoot, Idaho died in Vietnam one month prior to his 20th birthday. Growing up years were filled with 4-H, Future Farmers of America and Boy Scout activities. As a youth James loved the out-of-doors, spending much of his time on the family's ranch in the mountains. The active teenager preferred the cattle operation to the necessary farming to keep the ranch operating, and even tried his hand in the meat packing industry for one year. When James' sister became ill with cancer, he returned to the family home in Blackfoot, and soon after decided to enlist in the Army to finish his schooling.

During this time James met the love of his life, and a daughter Jamie was born to the couple following her father's death. James died October 30, 1966 when the helicopter he was co-piloting was shot down near the Cambodian border. He had been in country three months.

A 1956 Kimberly High School graduate, 1st Lt. **JACK (BUTCH) DODSON**, was killed in Vietnam on May 26, 1967. The combat assault helicopter he was riding in crashed and burned on a mission five days after he arrived in country. Butch had called his family in Hansen, Idaho on May 21st to tell them he was on his way to Vietnam. The 29-year-old was the father and stepfather of four.

Highly interested in civic affairs, Butch was active in Phi Kappa Tau Fraternity while studying at the University of Idaho and served as President of the Twin Falls Jaycees in 1961-62. He was a member of the Elks Lodge and enjoyed his activities with the Boise Parachute Club. Prior to entering the service he was general manager of the State of Idaho Safeco Nu-Lif. Insurance Branch, in Boise for three years. Stationed at Fort Bragg until his departure to Vietnam, Butch was a member of the U.S. Army 191st Assault Helicopter Company.

21-year-old Boise Marine, **GARY JACK FOSTER** died in Vietnam on June 4, 1966 at the Chu Lai Combat Base. His commanding officer reports:

"Gary had been providing night security for the…base and had returned with his crew and vehicle to the maintenance area about 0730 in the morning. As he was outside his vehicle, cleaning a part of the engine, a recoilless rifle on another ONTOS suddenly fired. The projectile struck the ONTOS Gary was working on, causing an explosion which killed (him) instantly."

Expressing the Battalion's heartfelt sympathy at Gary's untimely death, the Major commented on the young Marine's conscientious and hardworking attitude. Gary learned those things growing up in the central Idaho wilderness with a younger sister and family who loved him very much.

Gary was born in 1945 in Lowman, Idaho where his father owned and operated a sawmill on Five Mile Creek, twelve miles north of town. He attended first grade in Boise at Garfield Elementary, but second grade was spent in the living room of his parent's home with four other students, until his father and his crew could build a one room school house.

Two years later, a schoolhouse was moved to Lowman from Garden Valley, and student enrollment soared to 35. It was here that Gary graduated from 8th grade being the only student his age. Four years later in 1964, he graduated from Boise High School where he was a member of ROTC. Gary's first love was always Lowman, and he returned in the summers to work at the South Fork Lodge where he could enjoy hunting and fishing and working on cars. Following graduation, he joined the Marines and was shipped to Vietnam in April of 1966. After only two months in country, the boy whose heart had always been in Idaho, returned home never to leave again.

DAVID JONES from Fernwood, Idaho graduated from St. Maries High School in 1968. A member of the wrestling and football teams, he was voted as "most school spirit" his senior year. The 20-year-old died in Vietnam on April 4, 1970.

A 1966 graduate of American Falls High School, **JAMES B. ANDERSON** joined the Army in 1966, and after basic training went to Airborne School. A member of the 101st Screaming Eagles (small groups of 5 to 7 men who seek out and engage the enemy), James was serving as a platoon leader in Phuoc Long Province. On Jan. 25, 1968 James and eleven of his men were on patrol when a second platoon, under enemy fire, radioed for help. While responding to the call, James's unit reached a fork in the jungle trail where they were hit by enemy machine guns. James was mortally wounded.

Saint Marie's High School Yearbook
David Jones #21

Twenty-year-old James had been in country eight months. On February 3rd, just nine days after his death, he was scheduled for R&R in Hawaii where his fiancé was meeting him to be married.

Major **ANTHONY (TONY) BELLAMY**, from Boise, Idaho served as a Senior Military Advisor to the South Vietnamese 6th Armored Calvary in the Mekong Delta area. A 1957 graduate of Boise High School and a 1961 graduate of the University of Idaho, he was president of ROTC his senior year. A member of Blue Key Honor Society, he also served as president of his fraternity, Sigma Nu. Tony was commissioned a 2nd Lt. after ROTC graduation, and attended language school in preparation for his assignment in Vietnam. Killed by enemy fire on May 5, 1968 at the age of twenty-eight, Tony left a wife and son.

Idaho Falls "Post Register" death notice:

I.F. SOLDIER KILLED IN VIETNAM

Cpl **JOHN ALEX BOYLE**, 18 died from a wound received in a combat operation when engaged by a hostile force in Vietnam on Jan.26. Born in 1950 at Twin Falls, John spent most of his earlier years in Hailey until moving with his family to Idaho Falls in 1964. In school he was active in track and also worked as a projectionist at a local theatre. He was also involved in the Police Association League. John's mother died in December of his senior year and he graduated from Skyline High School in 1968. He entered the Army July 12, 1968 and left for Vietnam on Dec.7th. In country less than two months before his untimely death, John is survived by his father.

Twenty-two-year-old Sp4 **JAMES E. TOOLEY** from Parma, Idaho is remembered in the following Internet Tribute:

JAMES EDWARD TOOLEY SP4
Sunday, November 14, 1999
Submitted by Carol Collins
SISTER

"Jimmy"

"Jimmy" was a fun-loving little brother. He was always easygoing. I remember him playing with his little trucks in the dirt and making rivers and roads for them. The last time I saw him was when he came by the house to say he was leaving for boot camp. It was a warm spring day. We stood outside in the yard under our big elm tree and talked for a few minutes, and then he was gone..."

The Twin Falls "Times News" September 30, 1969 reports:

Wounds Kill T.F. Marine in Vietnam

"A 19-year-old Twin Falls Marine died Saturday of fragmentation wounds while maintaining a defensive position north of First Support Base Elliott in Quang Tri Province, Vietnam.

Mr. and Mrs. Wendel T. Aslett were notified by telegram of the death of their son, Pfc. **ALLEN T. ASLETT** who had been in the Marine Corps for one year.

He had enlisted in the Marines last October and had been in Vietnam since July. He was born July 25, 1950 in Twin Falls and had graduated from Twin Falls High School in 1968.

He was a member of the Boy Scouts of America and the Civil Air Patrol."

An only son from McCall, Idaho, A2C **THOMAS WILLIS** joined the Air Force shortly after graduating from Donnelly High School in 1964. The seventeen-year-old's greatest love was hunting and fishing in the mountains, and he hoped to become a fish and game biologist. He was stationed in California, the year following basic training, where he made Airman 2nd Class in the Strategic Air Command.

Tom went to Vietnam in May 1966, stationed at Da Nang with "The Tiger Flight." Critically wounded, he was sent to the hospital ship, USS Repose off the coast of South Vietnam, where he was treated for three weeks before his death on June 5, 1967. The young soldier was 20 years old.

From the upper valley of the Teton Basin, Pfc **MARK G. O'BRIEN** answered the call to duty in May 1968 when he was drafted into the Marines. Mark left for Vietnam November 1968 and died one month later on January 12, 1968.

A graduate of Teton High School in Driggs, Idaho, Mark was known in the area for his horse breaking abilities and his love for the out of doors. Two summers were spent in the mountains as a sheepherder and Mark's horses and cows regularly took ribbons at the country fairs. After high school he attended the Wyoming Technical School to study mechanics before leaving for the service. Mark was 20 years old when he died from small arms fire in Quang Nam Province, Vietnam.

Vietnam was a long way from the cattle ranch **JOHNNY LEE WARD** grew up on in Cambridge, Idaho. During his junior year of high school, Johnny opted for a logging job near Mc Call and worked in the Idaho forests until being drafted into the Army in 1968. The 21-year-old was shipped overseas on September 9, 1968 and quickly proved his abilities in the jungles of Vietnam.

On May 25, 1969 the capable Idaho Sergeant received the Bronze Star for saving many lives in a fiery ground battle. As U.S. forces were attempting to withdraw from an over-powering enemy attack, Johnny remained behind in a dangerous and exposed location. Manning a M-60 machine gun, he provided protective cover until his men could reach safe positions.

On September 11, 1969 within days of completing his tour of duty, Johnny was serving as a Reconnaissance Sergeant in a forward observer party. A nearby soldier accidentally detonated a Viet Cong mine, hidden in the branches of a tree, and Johnny was fatally wounded. Adding to his recognition for valor and courage, the Purple Heart citation was awarded posthumously.

"Boys will be boys…"

DEVERN PROBART'S zest for life enabled him to find some good in almost every situation. A practical joker and tease, the Pocatello lad had a ready laugh whenever circumstances called for it. During his freshman year in college, he and some fun-loving classmates pulled an elaborate prank that made Paul Harvey's radio program, with the "rest" of the story. Easy going DeVern could also be very serious and had unusual common sense for his young age. Quick to learn, he was bold enough to try almost anything.

On the family farm in Montpelier Idaho, the teenager was an accomplished horseman and had a special quiet way of communicating with animals. His four younger sisters frequently struggled to get an 800 lb. sow back in her pen, but

DeVern could walk up and say, "Com'on Duchess. Let's go back to your house," and the pig would trot down the road behind him, grunting happily.

While working summers in Yellowstone Park during college years, he supplied the guard stationed at the lookout tower at Pelican Point. With packhorses trailing behind, DeVern kept his fishing gear nearby and ready to fish the streams along the trail. By journey's end, he would have enough fish for supper for himself and the guard—without ever leaving the horse's back. Calm and capable beyond his years, adults frequently complimented the parents of the young man. A hero to his four younger sisters, every male suitor suffered by comparison.

A friend, brother, and only son, DeVern proved his valiancy and trust in a far oft corner of the world. His death in a helicopter crash on July 17, 1969 near Xuan Loc was mourned by comrades and troops, American and South Vietnamese alike. At a Memorial Service in Vietnam, his commander stated:

"Captain Probart gave all that any man can give as he gave his life in a spirit of dedication and duty to God and country."

A classroom was named at Idaho State University in honor of DeVern's sacrifice and accomplishment as a distinguished university and ROTC graduate. He was 26 years old at the time of his death.

Paul Harvey reports the "Rest of the Story":

Freshman At ISU Loses All Appetite For Chicken

Larry Irvine, a freshman student at Idaho State University, crept into a darkened chicken yard with five companions on what was planned to be a chicken-stealing escapade.

Suddenly, the roar of a shotgun rent the darkness and Mike Misel, one of the would-be adventurers, collapsed as red gore spread over his clothing.

Terrified, Irvine and the others fled, helping Misel to their nearby car. Speeding away, the other four youths, De Vern Probart, Bob Chandler, Tony Favero and Bruce Welchmann, warned Irvine not to report the incident, and stopped to leave Misel's apparently lifeless body in a snowbank.

Irvine, from St. Maries in northern Idaho was too unnerved. He soon called the sheriff's office.

When deputy Shirley Gameson went to Colonial Hall, a men's

dormitory at ISU, to investigate, he found six sheepish young men-including the supposed shooting victim, clothing still covered with red.

It was all a hoax, the students said, with Irvine as the goat. Chandler's father had been alerted to fire the shotgun in the air on signal, and another youth then tossed the "blood" on Misel, whose "body" was picked up from the snow-bank soon after he was left there.

The six got off with a lecture on pranks.

★★★

PROFILES OF COURAGE

INTERNET TRIBUTE

SP4 **CECIL R. MILLSPAUGH**
Submitted by Gary Wanner
Fought beside him 3-26-68

THANKS BRAVE SOLDIER

I've thought about you 19 brave soldiers every day for the past 32 years and will do so til the day I die. Thanks for your supreme sacrifice.

REST IN PEACE.
June 22, 2000

(23-year-old Cecil Millspaugh, from Declo, Idaho
is remembered by a comrade and friend.)

★★★

19-year-old **LEWIS C (CRAIG) EMERY**, of Parma, Idaho was killed in action March 16, 1979 while on a rescue operation near Nui Ba Den Mountain in Vietnam. Under a hail of enemy fire, young Emery opened the hatch of his armored personnel carrier, with complete disregard for his own safety, to determine the location of comrades in distress.

A 1968 graduate of Parma High School, Craig was an outstanding athlete involved in football, wrestling and track. He was a State Champion Wrestler and attended Boise State College until entering the Army in February 1969. He was awarded the Bronze Star for Valor.

The Marine Corp League of Nampa, Idaho honorably bears the name of a 21-year-old farm laborer from Parma, Idaho. Cpl **FRANCISCO JOHN FLORES**, a true American hero attended elementary schools in Nyssa, Oregon. But when it came time for high school young Flores worked in the fields with his father instead.

In December 1965, the 21-year-old joined the Marine Corps and was shipped to Vietnam in April 1966. There he distinguished himself as a squad leader and diligent defender of the oppressed. Wounded twice, Francisco returned to the battlefield receiving the Purple Heart citation for valor.

In his last letter home dated April 8, 1967 he wrote:

"You sit down and start thinking of back home and then that's when you see what a good thing it was."

Expressing concern over the hardships of the troops he added,

"But…it's not for me to say what's right and wrong."

On May 21, 1967 Francisco was performing his duty again. While leading his squad on patrol, he stepped into a clearing near a hedgerow, and enemy machine gun fire cut him down. He had one month of duty left in Vietnam.

THE FOLLOWING INTERNET TRIBUTE TO A POST FALLS, IDAHO CASUALTY WAS POSTED APRIL 13, 2000

DAVID EDWARD CINKOSKY CAPT
Submitted by Dale Bennett
I witnessed his KIA

A TOAST
Every August 5—I say a number of toasts to David. But I am always alone, as I was that day when David died and I did not. The NVA (40 To 50) didn't get to celebrate their victory because they also died that day. We were 0-1 bird dog pilots, 4th Plt. 219th Av. Co. flying 2 aircraft visual and photo recon missions for MACVSOG CCS.

David volunteered, as did all, for these missions and died the 8th day of his second one year tour. HERE'S TO YOU DAVID!

CALDWELL CASUALTY

19-year-old **TERRY HUSTON** left for Vietnam on May 2, 1966. He died, in country, one month later on June 7, 1966. The 1965 Caldwell High School graduate wrote the following letter home on 101st Airborne stationery:

"Dear Mom and Dad and Girls,

Sorry I haven't written for awhile, but I've been out in the jungle for the last week and didn't have much time to write as we were on the move most of the time. Right now I'm at a place called Qui Nhon for a little rest before we start on the next operation. The last one was a real big one. You'll probably hear about it on the news or in the newspaper. I haven't seen any action yet and actually I hope I don't, but that's just wishful thinking. It rains a lot of the time and at night it gets pretty cold, and you have to have a cover in order to stay warm. Its different back at Phan Rang though, its real hot and seldom rains there. On the last operation we were up near the Cambodian border and the jungle is real thick and at times you can't see ten feet on either side of you. The mountains are the steepest I've ever seen, they almost go straight up, and boy were they hard climbing…to make it even worse the trails were muddy and slick…for every one step forward you would slide back five, it was real rough going… If you want to send a package send Kool Aid (pre-sweetened) and fruit. It's real hard to get fruit over her and everybody is trying to get it. Well, I've got to go now… I've got a lot to do for the next operation…" Love, Terry

Soon after the letter, the nineteen-year-old graduate of Caldwell High School saw combat firsthand, distinguishing himself as a courageous defender and friend.

On June 7, 1966 Private First Class Huston was on a combat mission near Dak To. When the left flank of his company began to withdraw from a large Viet Cong force, Terry remained behind to provide fire cover for his comrades. Left in an open exposed position, he placed suppressive fire against the approaching Viet Cong, killing five. As the enemy gained ground, the nineteen-year-old bravely held off enemy fire until all of his unit had successfully withdrawn to safe defensive positions. As he was making his way back to his company he was hit by enemy fire and fell mortally wounded. For "gallantry in action" and saving many lives against a numerically superior hostile force, Terry Huston, an only son, was posthumously awarded the Silver Star.

★★★

Bingham County Marine, **SHELDON D. HOSKINS** graduated from Snake River High School in 1966. An outstanding athlete and keen competitor he was named co-captain of the football team his senior year. He also took State Wrestling Championships (168 pound class) both his junior and senior year. After graduation Sheldon was offered a 4-year scholarship to Weber State College in Ogden, Utah. Declining the offer, he chose instead to join the Marine Corps on September 6, 1966.

While stationed in the Philippines for 5 months with his older brother, Sheldon determined he would volunteer for Vietnam, so his brother could return home to his wife and family. (The military required only one son per family to serve in Vietnam). He left for Vietnam in March of 1968.

Assigned as a squad leader in Vietnam, Sheldon wrote the following in his last letter home to his family:

> "War is nothing, some live, some don't. My troopers love me and I them, we are the best of a group of experts. I want to live…but I will die for (the) freedom of these people and our great country.
>
> I have a family I love very much to live for, but if I die in Vietnam remember, "I love you all!" You must understand and live as I do, from day to day. When I get home I'll be the same old me…Don't worry about me cause what happens to me is to help my troopers and 'Not for glory.' "

On October 7, 1968, Sheldon's squad engaged the enemy again and was being attacked by automatic weapons and grenades. When the team's forward machine gunners became wounded and disabled, Sheldon left his covered position and maneuvered across 20 meters of fire-swept terrain to reach the guns. He fearlessly commenced firing on the enemy until he ran out of ammunition. While re-loading, the 20-year-old Marine was mortally wounded.

Among Sheldon's posthumous citations for 'courage under fire' were the Silver Star and Purple Heart.

Decades following his death, his family recalls:

> "…as with all heroes, (Sheldon's) real distinction is expressed not in medals, but in the memory of his deed."

★★★

American Falls soldier, 19-year-old Sp4 **John E.S. Mitchell**, Jr. is remembered:

JOHN E S MITCHELL JR SP4
Submitted by
Richard Claywell
FRIEND
Wednesday, April 05, 2000

BRAVE VOLUNTEER
Scott Mitchell volunteered to go into the field with F Troop 17th Cavalry as a medic. He was a 'newbee' and was stationed at the 23rd Medical Battalion, Fire Support Base Hawk Hill. F Troop had run into a NVA unit and the three medics attached to F troop were all killed. The medics had to be replaced. Scott volunteered to go out into the field when others would have nothing to do with going into the field and risking their life for someone else.

Scott was riding on a Armored Personnel Carrier that hit a 500 pound land mine that killed 13 of the 14 people. Scott knew the risks and volunteered for hazardous duty while others were safe and secure. I am proud to know people like Scott. I was the medic that saw the APC hit the land mine.

"What if you don't come back?"

A recipient of the Bronze Star for heroism, **Gerald Baldwin** of Nampa, Idaho was serving in the 25th Infantry Division in the Republic of Vietnam. While on a night ambush patrol, Gerald and his comrades were moving toward their ambush sight when they came in contact with a large enemy force.

The citation for heroism reads:

"Immediately, Private Baldwin, with complete disregard for his own safety, exposed himself to the hail of fire as he engaged the enemy with devastating small arms fire. As the battle progressed, Private Baldwin moved from position to position in order to distribute vital ammunition until he was fatally wounded. Private Baldwin's bravery, aggressiveness, and devotion to duty are in keeping with the highest traditions of the military service and reflect credit upon himself, his unit, the 25th Infantry Division, and even the United States Army."

Gerald graduated from Payette High School in 1967 and was drafted in 1969, spending his 20th birthday at boot camp at Ford Ord in California.

The morning Gerald's mother took him to the airport to leave for Vietnam, she overheard a conversation with his younger brother. When the younger sibling asked, "What if you don't come back?" Gerald replied thoughtfully, "Well, death is just a separation and even if I don't get killed I'll have to leave—get away from everyone to get over everything I've been through, and that will take a long time." Then he added, "So it won't be much different either way."

For his acts of heroism and valor, Gerald was posthumously awarded the Bronze Star and Purple Heart as well as other honorable citations. He died December 12, 1969.

In 1993 Gerald's mother shared:

"Even though it has been more than 20 years since I lost my son, it hasn't been easy to dig out the documentation and memorabilia I had stored away. However, this may promote a healing I didn't allow back then."

Wednesday, December 29, 1999 the following Internet Message was posted:

GERALD LEE BALDWN CPL
Submitted by Dana Martin

Knew him in college and served with him in Vietnam. Gary was a good soldier and friend. He used to like listening to Bob Dylan. So we called him "Dylan."

PROFILES OF HONOR

"Such character is not built here—Larry brought it with him."
(Tribute by Catholic Father at Gonzaga University)

An Endowment Scholarship listed in "Names That Live" at Gonzaga University in Spokane, Washington stands as a continuous remembrance of one of our country's finest, Major **LAWRENCE ACRE** of Coeur d'Alene, Idaho.

A 1951 graduate of Coeur d'Alene High School, Lawrence sacrificed and worked his way through four years of college at Gonzaga University in Spokane, Washington. There he received a Bachelors Degree in Arts and Sciences and also completed four years of ROTC with honors. Upon graduation Lawrence was commissioned as a 2nd Lieutenant in the U.S. Army Infantry Branch.

The highly decorated and respected officer served 7 tours of duty in Vietnam, 3 one-year terms and 4 specific missions of shorter duration. On October 9, 1969 Lawrence was leading a classified helicopter mission. Details of the fateful day are still unknown, but it appears the helicopter crashed as a result of enemy ground fire. All aboard were lost.

In his will, the thirty-four-year-old Major listed Gonzaga University as his main beneficiary. Years earlier he had been known to say, "...if he ever made anything of himself, he would do what he could to give other young people financial help to get through Gonzaga without struggling."

Lawrence's legacy of honor, duty and selfless service has continued for more than three decades, as deserving young people have been beneficiaries of his financial and personal contributions to America's future.

"I've been many places, met many people—Shoshone is the place I want to be."

1964 Shoshone High School graduate, CWO **HENRY J.W. TEWS**, distinguished himself and his small Idaho community with outstanding courage and bravery during his 13 months service in Vietnam. Henry attended the University of Idaho before enlisting in the Army in 1965 and was ranked number one in a class of 42 maintenance students. After completing his first 12-month tour of duty in November 1968, he opted to extend for another 6 months where he served as a maintenance tech and test pilot.

Henry Tews

On December 29, 1968 a helicopter in Henry's unit was forced to land and he was called into the battle zone to assess the damage. The helicopter had taken several enemy hits and the extent of the malfunction was not known. Unwilling to risk the lives of the crew, Henry elected to fly the aircraft out of the area alone. Two armed helicopter escorts were called in to provide protective cover, but shortly after lift off the damaged helicopter lost power and made a quick descent. The crash near the Special Forces Camp at Minh Long claimed Henry's life; the entire crew being saved by his courage and keen sense of duty.

For 13 months of outstanding service and dedication, Henry received: the 24 Oak Leaf Cluster for meritorious achievement in aerial flight; two air medals Oct. '67 and May '68 for Heroism in ground combat; the Bronze Star in May '68; and posthumously, the Distinguished Flying Cross and Purple Heart. He was twenty-one.

Captain **DONALD V. MCGREGOR** died in Vietnam on August 13, 1963. A 1952 graduate of Paul High School, Donald served as Student Body President his senior year. He joined the Idaho National Guard in 1951, and following graduation from The University Of Utah and ROTC in 1956, enlisted in the Army. Stationed at Quang

Naigh at the time of his death, Donald was the father of three sons. He died in the service of his country on August 13, 1963. He was 29 years old.

Thirty-seven years later, one of Donald's sons visited the Wall in Washington, D.C. to pay tribute to his father. Soon after, a tribute was posted on the Internet honoring the continuing legacy of the young Army Captain from southeastern Idaho.

Submitted Wednesday, June 21, 2000

So Proud of Your Son

I didn't know you Sir, but I had the privilege of meeting your son this past week at a gathering in Washington, D.C. at the Vietnam Memorial Wall for Fathers Day, and just thought you should know that you would have been so very proud of this very nice young man.

With Respect, Lil Abrams

★★★

"The Boise Statesman" reports:

Star Soldier
"Meridian high school grad dies of wounds in Vietnam"

"Another valley servicemen has been reported killed in action while fighting for his country in Vietnam. Pfc. **ELMER G. IRELAND**, 21, of Star, the son of Mr. and Mrs. Delwin D. Ireland, was killed July 1, according … to the defense department in Washington. No details of his death were received."

Described as a person everyone liked, Elmer graduated from Meridian High School in 1967. He entered the Army in January 1968 and served with the Scout Dog Platoon, attached to the 101st Airborne Division. Elmer was 21 at the time of his death. Service awards include the Bronze Star, Purple Heart, Good Conduct Medal, Expert Rifleman medal and Vietnam Service Medal.

★★★

"On my honor I will do my duty, to God and my Country"

The familiar words of the Scout Oath were repeated many times in the life and actions of **JAMES CLAYBAUGH**, an Eagle Scout from Huston, Idaho eight miles west of Caldwell.

Jim attended Jr. High and High School at Caldwell where he graduated in 1962. Active in track and DeMolay, he was also an active member of the Elks Lodge and St. John's Catholic Church in Boise. After two years of college, Jim enlisted in the army graduating from Officer Candidate School at Fort Benning, GA in February 1968. While performing his duty in Vietnam, Jim was promoted to 1st Lieutenant, dying a short time later after being in country only 2 months.

Sgt. **Jon D. Peterson** from Shelley, Idaho is honored in poem by Janet Matthews:

The Boy Next Door

Our neighbor has been saddened this week,
We've had a taste of the war.
An honored soldier came home today,
When he left, he was the boy next door.

He fought in battle long and hard,
As so many others have done;
And though I'm saddened by all soldiers
who die,
I especially mourn this one.

I've thought of war, as a distant thing,
Something far removed from me.
But the boy next door came home today,
And now I begin so see.

What is this war?
What is the cause that takes so many lives?
Do we believe in what we're fighting for?
Or is patriotism something that "once was."

I for one am against this war,
I don't agree with what's being done.
But be there a cause or not, our men
are still there.
And we know they will fight till they've
won.

This to me is what patriotism is.
All the boys next door.
Parents who have taught them to be honorable
men,
Willing to fight in a war.

If the "cause" isn't there, the soldier
still is.
And it's this fact that is important to me.
I'm proud to have known the boy next door,
He fought and died for his country.

I feel sad to think this young man is gone,
I've known him all of my life.
I feel so deeply for his mom, his dad,
His brothers and his wife.

But having war hit so close to home,
Has perhaps been a good lesson to me.
Could I teach a son to be such a man
Would I encourage him to fight, if need be.

I realize now what a soldier is,
Courage, strength, and much more.
And whether I believe in the cause or not,
Our country is upheld by the boy next door.

"The Morning News" writer Emily Hone of Blackfoot, Idaho reports June 25, 2001:

"VFW post named in honor of local man who died in Vietnam."

"A young Blackfoot soldier who died when the helicopter he was riding in [was shot down], had the Blackfoot post of the Veterans of Foreign Wars named in his honor, and the post flag will be dedicated in his memory..."

"The **JOHN L. POWERS** VFW Post No. 9443 is the second VFW post in Blackfoot. According to Post Commander Hero Shiosake, the first post was named after Hugh Martin, a Blackfoot sailor who was killed on board the the USS Arizona when the Japanese bombed Pearl Harbor. Shiosaki said the post eventually lost its charter due to inactivity. A new post was chartered and named after Powers.

The 21-year-old Army mechanic was killed Feb. 15. 1971 when the fuel-laden Chinook helicopter he was riding in took a direct hit over Laos."

John Powers is remembered by his family as a young man of skills and maturity well beyond his years—almost as if he knew that his life would be short and he had to make the most of every minute. As a youth he displayed an uncanny aptitude for mechanics and built several inventions. While in Vietnam, his father reported, John didn't have to be on the helicopter, he just loved to fly.

John graduated from Mackay High School in 1967 and joined the army in 1969. He went to Vietnam in September 1970 where he served as a helicopter crew chief.

"I'll be one of them."

Born at Fort Jackson, S.C., **JOHNNY CHAPMAN** attended grade schools in Richland, WA and Pocatello, Idaho. The family moved to Boise when Johnny was in Jr. High and he graduated from Borah High School in 1970. Active in sports in school, he also enjoyed Idaho's great hunting and fishing seasons.

After joining the Army in September 1970, he attended airborne training and was assigned to Fort Bragg, N.C. When Johnny's father returned from Vietnam, he requested duty there also. Arriving in country on July 19, 1971, he died 33 days later. Once again, Johnny had volunteered for duty. This time to serve on a rescue unit to aid a Ranger Team pinned down by enemy fire. The men were lifted in by helicopter and as Johnny rushed in to help the downed Rangers, he was cut down by enemy fire.

Upon his arrival in Vietnam, Johnny learned he was going to be in the "Rangers." Out of 400 men who wanted to get in the company, there were only three picked: a buck Sergeant and two PFC (private first class). Johnny was one of the PFC's. There were 22,000 men in the 101st Division and only 120 Rangers, and "I'll be one of them," he happily reported. After a 30-day trial period Johnny would wear the "Black Beret."

Letters home describe the experience of the 19-year-old corporal:

July 25th He wrote he was stationed at Camp Eagle near Hue and that Vietnam smelled like dog.

July 31st Johnny wrote he had lost six of his buddies. "I don't like trust these gooks one bit and will be glad when I leave this hell hole."

August 11, 1971 was Johnny's last letter home. He had been in (Ranger) training for a week and had been rapelled out of a helicopter that day. "It was scary at first but turned out to be fun." He mentioned the men in his group were the only ones doing PT (physical training) every morning and he would be in great shape by the time he came home. Johnny was happy to hear his dad had retired from the Army.

★★★

"ABOVE AND BEYOND THE CALL OF DUTY"

Unlike most young men his age, 19-year-old **ERIC HARSHBARGER** had already seen much of the 'world' before he arrived in Southeast Asia. Born November 1949 in Pretoria, Union of South Africa, fourteen-month-old Eric was adopted by Colonel and Mrs. Elma Harshbarger, who at the time was Assistant U.S. Air Attache with the American Embassy. Moving with his parents and an adopted sister back to the States at age three, Eric's younger years were spent on Air Force Bases in Ohio, Louisiana, Nebraska and California. In 1962, when Colonel Harshbarger retired from the Air Force, the family moved to Filer, Idaho where Eric graduated from high school in 1968. He immediately enlisted in the Army for specific training as a helicopter-gunner.

Early years were filled with sports, scouting and a special love for hunting. At age thirteen, Eric bagged his first deer and at fifteen shot a black bear while hunting in the White Cloud mountains of central Idaho. When his horse fell on him a week before elk season and broke his ankle, the determined teenager still mounted up and rode for ten days in the mountains, bagging a deer in the process.

At nineteen, Eric took the same indelible spirit with him to the jungles and mountains of Vietnam. Eleven months and 60 combat operations later, the young soldier's life ended in a valiant attempt to provide fire cover for troops being inserted below.

Among the many medals and meritorious citations Eric received was the Distinguished Flying Cross in combat action. Dated November 1, 1969 it reads: "For heroism while participating in aerial flight evidenced by voluntary action above and beyond the call of duty."

While serving as a Crew Chief on a helicopter gunship five miles west of Lai Khe, Eric was placing suppressive fire in a wooded area surrounding the landing zone as a rifle platoon was being inserted. As the lead helicopter touched down, a ground mine detonated disabling the crew. At the same time Eric's machine-gun jammed. Unable to provide cover to the men below, the young Idahoan unflinchingly put his own life in peril by climbing outside his gunship to clear his weapon. While working on the machine gun another mine detonated and Eric was mortally wounded.

Shown seated on right, helicopter Crew Chief and gunner-mechanic, Spec. 4th Eric Harshbarger, in his assigned Huey helicopter at Phu Loi base camp, about thirty five miles northeast of Siagon, South Vietnam, July 1969.

In a letter accompanying the Bronze Star for meritorious service, the commanding officer reviewed Eric's outstanding eleven-month service record in Vietnam. He reported to Colonel Harshbarger that combat aircrew members were allowed to participate in patrol, search and strike operations against the enemy when they were not on air alert duty. Eric had volunteered for every ground combat opportunity that was offered. His personal daring and cool-headed skill in jungle fire fights against Viet Cong and North Vietnamese combat forces were a constant inspiration to fellow soldiers in his unit.

Full military honors and solemn graveside services at Arlington National Cemetery on Eric's 20th birthday closed the final chapter of his short and courageous life.

PROFILES OF DUTY:

THOMAS ALHBERG, Idaho Falls ID

"He was a boy of 19 thrust into the most difficult environment imaginable. Forced to draw strength from deep down, from whatever limited experience his young years had given him. His thoughts were of home and family. His trust was in his God."

"How could I ask that his life be spared if the cost was betrayal of himself."

Signed
A Very Proud Mother
Darlene Pittser

THE CEMETERY ON THE HILL

Today I went to Memorial services
In the cemetery on the hill.
It was to pay tribute to those who had died,
And now in their graves so still.

The speaker spoke of the different battles
Each fought for freedom and peace,
Each life that was given in hope,
That after this one, the fighting would cease.

But today the battle goes on
In a land across the sea,
Where people are fighting that
Their homes and country may be free.

My sons have gone to join them,
These people they do not know,
But have a kindred cause
Against their common foe.

Not very long ago we said goodbye
To another one of my sons.
He was joining those who already know
The horror of war and guns.

I remember the trip to the airport,
The morning was early and bright.
"Get the ticket, check your bags,
Now don't forget to write."

I cried a little when he kissed me
And said, "Don't worry Mom, I'll be O.K."
We watched until the plane was out of sight.
"Go with him God," I prayed.

We thought of him often,
Especially on holidays and such.
"Where is he now, what is he doing,
What did he have for lunch?"

To his brothers and sisters still at home,
He would often give advice.
"Work for a goal, make things count,
I want you to have a better life."

His letters did not come often.
But each was read and reread.
"You kids do your best in school, and be good.
I've had a hard day, so I'm going to bed."

Then came a letter different,
He had moved and was flying more.
"I've had some close calls,
The fighting is rough, we are right in the war."

It was not long after that,
A week or so I'd say.
A knock came at the door,
A strange car stood in the driveway.

Two men in uniforms familiar,
I ask to sit down with dread.
"We are sorry to inform you,
Your Son is missing in action,"
One of them said.

The days go by, some full of hope,
Others dark with fear.
I see his pictures on the shelf,
So many memories I hold dear.

Will he come back
To talk with us again,
To laugh and recall those times
Away back when?

Today I learned he's coming home,
But silent and still.
To join those who went before him,
In the cemetery on the hill.

Written in memory of Thomas O. Ahlberg
Killed in action in Vietnam May 4, 1970
By his mother Darlene Pittser

Eighteen-year-old Pfc. **Robert G Yagues** who enlisted at Mountain Home, Idaho was in Vietnam only one month before he was killed May 3, 1967. The young Rupert native was stationed at Huong Hoa and died during an assault from an enemy bullet. Robert had been home on leave after Christmas to see his family, when he was called back to duty before his furlough was over. He expected to be sent to Korea or Japan when he finished training at San Diego. The last time Robert's parents heard from him, he was on a ship heading to Vietnam. Notice of his death came one month later.

Twenty-one-year-old **Rodney Turner** of Boise, Idaho was another only son. He is remembered by a fellow comrade who witnessed his friend's unfailing courage on November 8, 1969.

> RODNEY CARL TURNER SP4
> Submitted by David McAllister
> SAME PLATOON
> Saturday, October 14, 2000
>
> OUR QUIET FRIEND AND HERO
>
> We had just come in from an 8 day run and some of us were not happy
> to be called out again to help another company in trouble. Not Rodney,
> in fact he took the lead to find the pocket of enemy that had caused the
> damage earlier. While maneuvering to pinpoint the enemy location for
> an air strike he was mortally wounded.
>
> The men of his unit lost a buddy and hero that day and think of him often.
> Truly wishing he could still be with us—and thanking him for his sacrifice.

CALDWELL OFFICER MEETS DEATH IN VIETNAM:
February 9, 1968 Staff Sgt. **Donald Haile**, the son of Canyon Country Sheriff Dale Haile, met death with the same undaunted courage and devotion that he exhibited throughout his military career. While leading the men of Company A, Don's unit came under intense enemy fire from North Vietnamese army regulars. Pinned down by forces of an undetermined size, he quickly tried to regroup the men for a lead assault against the enemy line to no avail. Then with complete disregard to his own safety, Sgt. Haile personally assaulted an enemy machine gun position, killing four enemy soldiers and successfully eliminating the emplacement. Providing an open-

ing in the enemy perimeter, the sergeant held his position until falling mortally wounded. Inspired by their platoon leader's heroic actions, Don's men were able to defeat the remaining enemy force.

Stationed near Da Nang and Chu Lai, Don had written his family weeks earlier that the fighting continued "every day and every night." In addition to two years of service in Germany and assignments in the Panama Canal Zone, Don had filled a 13-month infantry tour in Korea. Prior to leaving for Vietnam in November 1967, he was an instructor at Ford Ord. The 29-year-old father of two was posthumously awarded the Silver Star for valor in gallantly leading his men against hostile forces in intense combat operations.

Born November 1, 1943 in a Relocation Center at Poston, Arizona, 1st Lt. **KAY KIMURA'S** family moved to Caldwell for several years and then to Nampa, Idaho. He graduated from Nampa High School in 1962 and received a football scholarship to Idaho State University and Treasure Valley Community College. Kay joined the Marines in November of 1968. After basic training, he attended Officers Candidate School and helicopter training. He went to Vietnam January 8, 1970.

Serving as a co-pilot of a CH46D Sea Knight helicopter, Kay provided support to the 1st Marine Infantry Division. Following a crash at sea, he was listed as missing in action for three weeks until his parents in Nampa received the following telegram:

> "I deeply regret to inform you that a determination of death has been made in the case of your son, First Lieutenant Kay K. Kimura, USMCC.... Information received from Vietnam reveals your son's aircraft crashed in coastal waters of Thua Thien Province, approximately five miles from land. Indications are that the aircraft impacted the water with no advance warning, with extreme force, and broke up. It is believed your son could not have escaped the impact and that he perished at sea. The single survivor was thrown clear upon the impact. Search and rescue operations met with negative results. The official casualty report that will be prepared by this headquarters will show that your son's death occurred on 7 March 1970, and that his remains were not recovered. In behalf of the United States Marine Corps, I wish to assure you of all possible assistance and to extend my heartfelt condolences in your bereavement."

Kay was twenty-six years old and had been married the August before his call to Vietnam.

INTERNET TRIBUTE:

JAMES EDWARD PIVA CPL

Submitted by Gary Bethke, Captain, USN Ret.
Rival Mackay High School Grad

Sunday, May 28, 2000

REMEMBERING 3 CUSTER COUNTY HEROES

After all these years, on Memorial Day 2000, I decided to check... this website for information on the three young men from Custer County, Idaho whom I knew in my youth—**Jerry Wilson** (Mackay), **John Powers** (Mackay), and **Jim Piva** (Challis). Those of us who attended high school in Mackay and Challis in the mid 1960's always discuss these three great guys when [we get] back in the mountains for annual rodeos and BBQs.

I knew Jim from our grade school days in 4-H clubs, and from competing on the athletic field during our high school days. (Mackay, Challis and Arco were the big rivals of those days.) I was shocked to learn how quickly each of these three men gave the ultimate sacrifice after entering Vietnam... I was in the Navy during the same time frame—While they were facing the horrors of Vietnam, I was several hundred feet under the ocean in a nuclear submarine.

Custer County did their part in Vietnam and the Cold War, sadly with the loss of Jim, John and Jerry.

Cpl Daniel Tedrow
1ST Marine Division
Company A, 1st Battalion
26 Marines

Cpl. **DANIEL (BUCK) TEDROW** from Mullan, Idaho was serving his second tour of duty in Vietnam when gunshot wounds ended his life on Thanksgiving Day 1968. Daniel had previously been seriously wounded while on patrol in Quang Tri in December 1967. Recovering from stomach injuries, for which he was awarded the Purple Heart, the young Marine returned to active service and completed his tour of duty in Vietnam. Nearly one year later, he was critically wounded again, this time in Quang Nam Province while on patrol. For his valor and courage in combat, Daniel became one of few soldiers to receive a second Purple Heart citation, this time posthumously when he succumbed to mortal wounds on November 28th.

In his many letters home, Buck did not mention any political views but said he felt sorry for the people of Vietnam. Many, he said did not want the Americans there. While home on leave in September 1968, he had become engaged and was looking forward to getting married and settling down in his hometown of Mullan. He was twenty years old.

Buck's sister Barbara writes of her only brother who joined the Marines his senior year in high school and left for boot camp shortly after graduation in 1966:

"While looking for this information, I had many sad and wonderful memories surface. My sister and I spent an hour or so on the phone reminiscing. … This experience has brought my brother back to me for a short while … along with many tears…"

MEMORIAL PARK IN VIETNAM, IS DEDICATED TO IDAHO SOLDIER:
On 3 July 1968, the 1st Battalion, 11th Artillery conducted a Vietnam Memorial Service in honor of Idaho soldier **COLIN (ED) LAMB**. Later that fall, the area where the service had been held, was turned into a park with a green lawn and several small shade trees.

The dedicatory plaque reads as follows:

LAMB PARK
1st Lt. Colin E. Lamb
1st Battalion, 11th Artillery
Killed in Action July 1968

Twenty-six-year-old Colin (Ed) Lamb graduated from Caldwell High School in 1960 and Texas A & M in 1965. After joining the army in 1966 and completion of Officer Candidate School, he was posted for active duty in Vietnam in November 1967. A letter to Ed's brother from Major Richard K. Holady, describes the 1st Lieutenant's final command and the respect and confidence of his men:

"I write this letter to you because you can better understand what I will say and can be more gentle with your parents than a stranger. It is with pride that I write this letter and also regret in the loss of Colin E. Lamb. I knew Lt. Lamb only a short time and during that time found him to be a dedicated individual who was a soldier 24 hours a day. I was with him at the time of his death and his courage was beyond question. You may take pride in him, as I take pride in having served him.

I will now relate to you the circumstances surrounding his death. He was fire support coordinator... and his mission was to coordinate all air and artillery fires for the battalion, a job he performed in an outstanding manner. He accompanied the Battalion commander on all missions when units...were in contact with the enemy.

On 3 JUL 68, Company A made contact with an estimated platoon [near the Song Vam Co Dong River, 3 miles south of Ben Luc in the Province of Long An]. With air and artillery support, the unit obtained an enemy body count of 24 and 2 prisoners. The enemy then broke contact and all was quiet. The command and control aircraft that we were in, began to make (a) low, slow circle over the battle area in search of any more enemy activity. Lt. Lamb, then sitting in the right door, spotted an enemy soldier hiding in the brush next to the river and the helicopter went even lower to investigate. The enemy soldier, realizing he had been seen, opened up on us with an automatic weapon. The pilot attempted to get out of danger by turning and climbing out of the river. We then began to receive fire from both sides of the river [causing] the aircraft to fall into the river from 100-150 feet altitude.

It all happened very quickly, and it is my belief that both he and LTC Van Duesen must have been knocked unconscious in the crash because neither came to the surface. When I came to the surface I looked for them and could not see them, so I began to swim toward the shore. I was later rescued.

I know the sorrow you must feel, for we in the 2/47th have a special place in our hearts for Lt. Lamb. With young men like Lt. Lamb the United States need have no fear in the future. He was one of the finest officers I have ever known or hope to know. He was always willing to expose himself to danger in the performance of his duties so that others might live. Company A was my company and had it not been for his efforts that day, we could have taken many casualties. May God be with you in this time of sorrow." Ed received the Bronze Star and Purple Heart Posthumously.

PROFILES OF SACRIFICE

"For those who fight for it, freedom has a taste the protected will never know."
(Twin Falls Casualty, Tommy Kearsley)

RALPH GORTON of Boise, Idaho expressed well the challenges of sacrifice in a 1968 letter written to his wife Nancy:

"After being over here one appreciates a lot more what America is and has to offer her citizens. Our country stands today because of the sacrifice of others, both the men who fought our wars and the wives and sweethearts who gave them the courage to carry on through their ordeals. The sacrifices you make at home are no easier to make than ours are. You face day after day of worrying about our welfare, wondering what we are doing and always hoping we are well and nothing will happen.

I think our struggle here is worth these sacrifices; and regardless of what happens to us as individuals, my love for God, Country and People demand that I do what little I can to see that the freedom we enjoy, is guaranteed against the menace of tyranny. [And] all those who desire the same, are given the chance to live as free men and not as slaves or cogs in a machine. Hopefully, I can do this for the space of a short year and then return to enjoy the very thing I have fought for.

However, if I have to make the biggest sacrifice of all, then I do so willingly, so that someday someone else will not have to, and our country will remain free so that others may live in the security that I have lived in so long. I hope this helps you to understand that 'what we are involved in should make us proud of our own actions for the part we play in the defense of America, The Land of Free Men.'"

Ralph Gorton served as a 2nd Lieutenant in Vietnam. As a Rifle Platoon Commander, he led his men through 5 major combat operations, including Operation Kentucky, Job Stuart, and Napoleon / Saline. On May 27, 1968 Ralph's patrol was pinned down by intense enemy fire during an assault on the village of Phu Con. While maneuvering across the fire swept terrain to deploy his men and encourage their fire, he fell mortally wounded by an enemy bullet. Ralph was twenty-six.

"To the world he was just a man. But to his family, he was the world."

CWO **JESSE D (DON) PHELPS** graduated from Boise High School in 1955 and joined the Idaho National Guard Reserves at age 17. The spring of 1956 he joined the regular army and began a military career. Don served next in the Intelligence Division in Japan and Hawaii, and then as a drill sergeant at Ford Ord, California. He was then transferred to Germany with the Intelligence Division. While there, he fulfilled a lifelong dream and learned to fly helicopters, graduating the first in his class. Don was then assigned to Vietnam.

On November 19, 1965 Don volunteered for a hazardous night rescue flight. Landing his helicopter under heavy enemy fire, he courageously stayed on the ground while cargo was unloaded and the seriously wounded picked up. The mission was successful and Don was awarded the Distinguished Flying Cross. The following month, the father of one died in Vietnam on December 29, 1966.

★★★

COUPLE LOSES AN ONLY CHILD IN VIETNAM:
After finishing school in Filer, Idaho **BILLY G. SMITH** was drafted into the Army Oct. 20, 1966. In May of 1967, he was shipped to Vietnam and assigned to Co. C of the 39th Corps of Engineers. For the next seven months he built roads and repaired vehicles with other members of his unit. On November 12, 1967 Billy was on his way to church services when the jeep he was riding in hit a mine. The 21-year-old soldier was an only child.

An excerpt from a letter home shortly after Billy's arrival in Vietnam, reflects the deep bond of love and devotion he felt for his parents in Buhl, Idaho:

Monday night
30.05.1967

"Dear Mom and Dad,

Well I finally made it back again. There's not very much to talk about over here. I received your package today and I was sure was glad to get it. Mom and Dad thank you very much for everything… I'd really like some pictures. Ok? So thank you both Mom and Dad…"

"Well, like I always do, I started too late, so now it is really getting late so I guess I had better quit for now. I'm sorry about this being so slow but I'll try to do better next time Mom and Dad.

Oh yes, I'm OK. Well, I'll go for now. Write every chance you get, because I will even if it isn't very often. OK. Tell_____ that I love her."

Billy Smith and mother

" With all my love, I love you Mom and Dad more than you'll ever know. I love you both,"
Billy

★★★

Dies in Vietnam

PHILIP A. BEASLEY
. . . Boise native

* * *

Funeral Set For Sailor From Boise

Services for Corpsman Philip Arthur Beasley, 22, of 161 North Twenty-third, who was killed Sept. 30, in active duty with the United States Navy at Quang Nam, South Vietnam after serving there for approximately four months, will be conducted at 2:30 p.m. Friday at the Cloverdale Funeral Home with the Rev. A. B. Cowie officiating. Vault interment will follow at Cloverdale Memorial Park, with military honors.

He was born Feb. 2, 1946, in Boise and moved with his family to Miami, Fla., in April, 1946. They then moved to Atlanta, Ga., in 1947 and then back to Boise in November of 1948. He entered grade school in Wrightwood, Calif., and completed the first grade at Lowell Elementary School in Boise. In 1965 he graduated from Boise High School and then enlisted for four years in the United States Navy in October, 1965.

Survivors include his parents, Mr. and Mrs. Arthur N. Beasley, Boise; three brothers, Richard N., Stephen B., and Eric B. Beasley, all of Boise; two sisters, Ann Marie, and Delores J. Beasley, both of Boise; and a grandmother, Mrs. Pearl M. Beasley, Tarrant, Ala.

DELMAR LAWRENCE of Riggins, Idaho died in Vietnam on April 1, 1968. The father of two went to Vietnam in 1967 and served as a sonar operator on a Navy surveillance patrol plane. Intelligence messages from the plane were sent directly to Washington, D.C. A Cambodian naval vessel in the Gulf of Thailand, shot the plane down ten minutes from the crews' home base.

Delmar received the Air Medal with a Bronze Star for serving as an Aviation Anti-submarine Warfare Tech., Third Class. He also was awarded the Purple Heart and National Defense Service and Vietnam Service medals.

His mother wrote of her 22-year-old son:

"My prayer is that never again will young lives be called on to make such a sacrifice."

Sp4 **JOHN (JOHNNY) A. HURST** from Dubois, Idaho had been reassigned to Firebase Colorado just one day prior to his death on January 7, 1970. The 20-year-old left for Vietnam shortly before Christmas on December 11, 1969 and was in country only one month when he lost his life in a mine blast.

A 1968 graduate of Dubois High School, Johnny lettered in basketball and track and enjoyed hunting, fishing and water skiing in the great Idaho outdoors. Born on Halloween in 1949—birthdays were always filled with excitement and sometimes celebrated a day late to fully enjoy the holiday.

As Johnny's remains returned from the ravages of war, to the peaceful little town in central Idaho, a friend penned the words of grateful tribute:

"... We are sad that only your body returns. We shall never forget you and the other men that make it possible for us to live and enjoy life a little longer in such a beautiful place."

HN **PHILIP BEASLEY**

NATIONAL FUNERAL RECORD

Philip Arthur Beasley

22 Years 7 Months 28 Days

Place Of Death Quang Nam, South Vietnam

Length Of Stay 4 Months
Date Enlisted Oct. 1965
Organization U.S. Navy
Rank Hospital Corpsman

Cemetery
Grave No. 2C Section 84 Row No. PH

Philip was born in Boise and graduated from Boise High School in 1965. He enlisted in the Navy in October 1965 and went to Vietnam in June 1968. He was killed four months later on Sept. 30th from a bullet wound.

1st Lt. **WILLIAM (BILL) BEASLEY** — A former Student Body President of Emmett High School (class of 1960), William was active in basketball and baseball. He attended the University of Idaho from 1960 until 1965, graduating with a B.S. in Business Administration. Active in ROTC, Bill attended Cadet Summer Camp after his junior year and became Cadet Brigade Commander of the Army ROTC program his senior year of college. He was commissioned as a 2nd Lt. upon graduation at the U of I and after basic training he attended helicopter school.

Loyalty to his country had always been high on Bill's priority list. When the outstanding young officer and leader left for Vietnam in July 1966, he was married and also the father of two small children. Bill was also an only child.

As all men find "War is Hell." The new adventure for Bill ended very quickly. He died 2 months after his arrival in Vietnam.

FRANKLIN COUNTY
THURSDAY, DEC. 14, 1967

Preston Youth Dies In Vietnam

Pfc. **CLYDE R. COBURN**, 20, of Preston died of gun shot wounds in Vietnam Saturday. His parents, Mr. and Mrs. Cecil L. Coburn, received word of his death the same day they received a Christmas card from their son.

He is the first known casualty of the Vietnam War from Franklin.

According to the telegram to the family, he died of gun shot wounds while engaged in fire fighting. He was stationed at Phan Thiet in Vietnam. Funeral services are pending the arrival of the body.

He was born July 10, 1947 in Preston and graduated from Preston High School in 1965. He attended Utah State University…(and was) inducted on Dec.13. 1966. He had been in Vietnam for two months.

He is survived by ten brothers and sisters.

SP 5 **WILLIAM BURT**, graduated from Boise Jr. College in 1964 and the University of Idaho in 1966. Formerly from New York State, he enjoyed spending his summers on the family's ranch at Deer Creek near Hailey. His schooling also took him to Paris, France and Guadalajara, Mexico.

Drafted in 1967, he went to Vietnam in December 1968, assigned to a heavy self-propelled artillery battery. He once wrote home, "…I can't wait until this farce of a war is over or until people smarten up and get us out of this sick part of the world."

William's last mission was in the Mekong Delta region. He volunteered to fill the assignment because the designated man refused to go. During the mission, William was hit and mortally wounded by a piece of artillery casing from his own battery. He died on July 11, 1969, shortly before his 25th birthday, and only five days before his battery began its removal to Hawaii.

William's mother wrote of her only son, *"It was a tragic useless waste of an all too short life. He was the kind of young man we can ill afford to lose."*

Spec.5 **LYLE DROWN** from Kimberly, Idaho had just finished his first Army tour of duty in Vietnam. After 13 months in the battlefield, Lyle had enjoyed a 30-day leave at home with his family. On April 14, 1969 he returned to duty in Southeast Asia and died the following day. The twenty-one-year-old graduated from Kimberly High School in 1966 and enlisted in the Army February 6, 1967. His parents and two siblings are residents of Kimberly.

A young father from Terreton, Idaho died one month before his twenty-first birthday on May 10, 1968 during the evacuation of Kham Duc Special Forces Camp. **VERLE SKIDMORE**, 1965 graduate of West Jefferson High School, was one of 20 U.S.

casualties, with another 125 soldiers being wounded. Verle's short life was spent in the Terreton area where he enjoyed farming and the outdoors. Being married shortly after joining the Marines in 1966, he was the father of one son. A baby daughter was born in the fall of 1968, after her father's death.

Cpl **THOMAS A FOREMAN** of Caldwell, Idaho was two months short of being twenty-one when he was killed in Vietnam on January 20, 1969. A 1966 graduate of Caldwell High School, young Foreman became a father, one month after his death, when his son was born.

A "FATHER-SON" SACRIFICE

Twenty-two-year-old **JIM C. McNAMER** of Mountain Home, Idaho was a U.S. Navy hospital corpsman with the 3rd Marine Division in Vietnam. The graduate of Mountain Home High School died as result of fragment wounds from enemy fire on April 17, 1968. Jim's brother was also serving in Vietnam at the time. An Internet Tribute in memory of Jim was posted March 9, 2000:

Good Friend
Submitted by Mona Fuell Fierro

I went to school with Jim and ran around with him and his brothers. He was raised by his mother and grandfather (on his dad's side.) His father gave his life to keep us a free country in Korea. (Jim) was a wonderful friend and wonderful man. I know that anyone that knew him felt the same way.

"The loss to our family cannot be expressed in words."

Twenty-two-year-old **JAMES (JIMMY) SMITH** of Blackfoot, Idaho is remembered by friends and neighbors as an adventurous, personable and fun-loving individual with a great sense of humor. James' family owned a local car dealership and service station where he worked as a youth. During high school years, James and his best friend, Bob Brower, started their own business, "B.S. Destruction Co.", tearing down buildings and cleaning and selling salvaged construction materials. James attained the rank of Eagle Scout in his youth and attended several national jamborees and many scouting events. Proficient at many sports, his favorite past time was water and snow skiing.

A 1964 graduate of Blackfoot High School, James attended Boise State College and graduated from Officers Training the summer of 1968. He was sent to Vietnam in early September of the same year, where he was stationed close to the village of Loc Ninh, northwest of Saigon. As a 1st Lt., James served as Platoon Leader of one of three platoons on patrol, September 12, 1968 in a large rubber plantation a few miles from the Cambodian border. Enemy contact was made soon after the mission commenced.

James was initially Platoon Leader of the third platoon, but when the first platoon made contact, he moved his men forward to assist. Sporadic contact was made throughout the morning as the three platoons exchanged the lead position and continued to move forward.

Late in the afternoon, James' platoon was in the lead position when a rocket propelled grenade exploded nearby. After cautiously moving forward another 200 meters, James halted his men and exchanged small arms fire with the enemy as the other platoons moved forward for support. When James moved from behind a tree to fire at hostile emplacements, he suffered a head wound and fell to the ground. Aid men rushed to the well-liked Lieutenant's assistance, but the wound had been fatal. James had been in country only two short weeks, but during that time cherished letters arrived at the home he loved; one to his parents and one to his good friend Bob.

More than three decades have passed since James' death, but the emotional wounds remain deep and painful. As with many families of Vietnam casualties, it was most difficult for James' parents, now grown older to write about or discuss the loss of their treasured son.

Trevor Smith, the young soldier's nephew, was only two years old when his uncle died. He concludes his tribute with a message understood by an entire generation of children who lost uncles and fathers and brothers so long ago.

"…[The information I'm enclosing]… is based on stories and letters rather than personal memories. After talking with family members and Jimmy's close friends, I can only wish he had lived long enough for me to know him better… The loss to our family cannot be expressed in words."

Letter excerpts from Major **EDWIN N. TROXEL** of Boise, Idaho while serving his second tour of duty in Vietnam:

Note: Edwin's first tour in Vietnam (1970) was as a helicopter pilot in the Special Forces. At the time of his death (August 2, 1971), he was stationed at Luang Prabang, Laos, as a civilian advisor (air attaché) for the American

Embassy (State Department) and Director of Operations for the Loatian Air Force. The base Commander in Florida, where Ed's family was living, reported he had been killed in a plane crash.

1971 — "Again, I am in a situation where I can't talk much about what I am doing. However, I am not flying combat. There is a good trade of opium here and who knows who all is involved. One of my jobs is to see they don't use any U.S. aircraft to haul it."

"Life goes on at the same contrasting pace. There are those that are aware of the war and the importance of its outcome, and there are those that cannot see the enemy, and when he is not shooting at them they just don't give a damn. I have to deal with both kinds and get very frustrated."

In a 1992 interview, Mrs. Troxel shared her husband's official record had been "lost" until three years earlier (1989)—some 18 years after the crash. Ed was an only child and when word came of his death, the military immediately relocated Mary Jean and her two children from the air base in Florida to their former home in Boise, Idaho. Ed's body arrived eleven days later.

Due to the 'classified nature' of her husband's assignments, few people understood the widow's frustration and loss, and more importantly the lack of answers. "The Air Force Times" reported Ed had died in Florida, but Mary Jean knew differently. Her husband truly believed in what he was doing, but all that remained of his life now was a missing record and a sealed casket.

Receiving no personal effects and not being permitted to see the body made closure even more difficult. When POWs were released two years later, the Major's children still hoped to see their father walk off the plane. In the back of her mind, Mary Jane also wondered and questioned the purpose and validity of the war that her husband called "a necessary evil." Sympathetic to demonstrations going on around the country, she viewed the protests as "anti-war" not "anti-American" and resented a congress that would carry on a 'police action' without openly declaring war. Her repeated inquiries and requests concerning her husband's plane crash to the State Department and military were always futile. In the couple's earlier debates over the war, the Major had consented, 'there must be some other way, but I don't know what it is.' And now he was gone.

A 1948 graduate of Boise High School, Ed had always loved to 'live on the edge.' A member of the national ski patrol he excelled in every sport and taught swimming and gymnastics while in college. Holding a business degree from the University of Oregon, he graduated from ROTC and was commissioned a 2nd Lt. in the Air Force. Ed received his wings in 1954 and served as an instructor pilot and ROTC instructor in Texas and Hawaii. While stationed for three years in Italy, he served as a NATO Commander and during his first tour in Southeast Asia, inserted Special Forces troops into North Vietnam.

A continual inspiration to family and friends, the sudden and unexplained loss of the 41-year-old husband and father was a difficult burden to bear. The public's image of a Vietnam casualty in the 1960's and 70's was generally a single young man without family responsibilities, making it less likely for others to relate to the loneliness and isolation of a career man's widow and children.

When Major Troxel's official military records were finally released in 1989, Edwin's family received—for the first time—his medals and honorable recognition. Empty places of the heart could begin to heal, and important steps taken in the long-awaited process of lives forever changed by the tragedy of war.

Funeral records report with brief finality the short lifetime of **FRED STEVEN SMART** of Twin Falls, Idaho:

20 years—2 months—2 days

The young Marine graduated from Twin Falls High School in 1969 and was drafted the following October. In country less than two months, he stepped on an undetected landmine and died soon after on the USS Sanctuary Hospital Ship. Fred had been stationed near Da Nang in the Quang Nam Province. His life ended June 19, 1970.

THE NATIONAL FUNERAL RECORD

Date of Call June 19, 19 70

Burial Permit No.

Old Age Assistance No.

P.F.C. Fred Steven Smart
3. (a) (Full Name of Deceased)

Total No. 426
Yearly No. 50
Monthly No. 6

1. PLACE OF DEATH
(a) County
(b) City, town, rural
(c) Name of hospital, institution or location Viet Nam
(d) Length of stay 2 Months
In this community
(e) If foreign born, how long in U.S.A.?

2. USUAL RESIDENCE OF DECEASED
(a) State Idaho (b) County Twin Falls
(c) City, town. Twin Falls
(d) Street and number. Route #1

3. IF VETERAN, NAME WAR
(b) Viet Nam-
Date enlisted Oct. 1969 Serial No.
Date discharged Pension No.
Organization U.S. Marines
Rank P.F.C. 6 (a) Single X Married Widowed Divorced
4. Sex Male 5. Color or race White
6. (b) Name of spouse If alive, age.
Place of marriage Date

(20) DATE OF DEATH 1970 6 19
7. Date of birth 1950 4 27
8. If less than one day: 20 2 2
Hrs. Min. Years Months Days

9. BIRTHPLACE Nampa, Idaho
10. Usual occupation Serviceman
11. Business or employer U.S. Marines
12. Father's name Fredm W. Smart
13. Father's birthplace Colo.
14. Mother's maiden name Eva Messen
15. Mother's birthplace Colo.
16. Informant Mr. Fred W. Smart
Address Route 1 Twin Falls, Idaho
18. Embalmer's signature U. S. Dispenry License No.

CAUSE OF DEATH

Autopsy—Yes No X Doctor
Address Phone
Body received from Viet Nam Via Treasure Island
Funeral director U. S. Naval Dispensary
Escort Cpl. Steven P. Buxton 2387657
Body forwarded to
Funeral director
Escort

CEMETERY
Grave No. 1D Section 81 Row No. 23PH Range No.

RELATIVES

Mr. & Mrs. Fred Smatt	Parents	Twin Falls, Ida.
Mrs. Eva Love	Mother	Seattle, Wash.
Dan Smart	Brother	Meridian, Idaho
Dick Smart	"	Navy in Viet Nam
Darwin Smart	"	Twin Falls
Dean Smart	"	" "
Judy Smart	Sister	Seattle, Wash.
Francis Smart	"	" "
Lisa Smart	"	Twin Falls, Ida.
Tom Bulmer	Step Brother	" "
Mike Bulmer	"	Pocatello, Idaho
Mrs. Stella Smart	Grandmother	Kuna, Idaho
Mr & Mrs Glen Wilmot	Grandparents	Boise, Idaho

Date of funeral Saturday June 27, 1970
Rosary at Time
Services at Cloverdale Chapel Time 3:00 P.
Cemetery or Crematory Cloverdale Memorial Park
Burial XX Cremation Mausoleum Removal
Address Boise, Idaho
Police Escort: Yes No X Number expected in family room
Clergyman or Reader Chaplain Charles Lapp Phone
Church Presbyterian U.S.Navy Reserve
Singers Merrill Womach
Songs The Lord's Prayer
Nearer My God To Thee
Organist Norm Sandberg

CHURCH AND FRATERNAL ORDERS

CASKET BEARERS
1. Bill Moser
2. Rod Schoen
3. Ron Gillespie
4. Charles Anthony
5. Merle Bartlett
6. Wayne McFadden

Style and size of casket
Manufacturer

	CASH ADVANCED	MERCHANDISE	PROFES SERVI
UNIT SALE ($	Services		15
Vault Box Liner Urn			18
Preparation of Body			
Cemetery, crematory or mausoleum	Spade & Opening 23		2
Clothing, cleaning or pressing			
Telephone and telegraph (Family)			
Professional services			
Use of chapel			
Funeral coach			
Extra cars, drivers, police escort			
RR. tickets, Ry. exp., spec. trip			
Newspaper funeral notices			
Death certificates			
Clergyman or reader			
Singers $ Organist $			
Floral pieces			
Gov't Marker Setting 5718 Bronze Vase			2
Totals			

SALES TAX (%) xx x x xx xx x
"CHARGE TO" CLIENT RESPONSIBLE Cash advanced
Fred W. Smart Merchandise
Street Route 1. Professional service.
City Twin Falls, Sales tax.
Zone State Total
Phone No. Discount allowed

DATE	REFERENCE	PAYMENT	BALAN

FORM NO. 1308-948

Published by THE NATIONAL FUNERAL RECORD, 2502 S. E. DIVISION ST. • PORTLAND 2, OREGON

PROFILES OF SERVICE

"When you go home, tell them of us and say,
We gave our tomorrows, for your today."
(Internet Tribute to Daniel Williams, SP4, Army, Hamer, ID 11Apr 69)

"I wish I could have done so much more."

The youngest of six children, **ROBERT WILLEY** from Grangeville, Idaho joined the army in 1966 rather than waiting to be drafted. In a letter home to his family he wrote:

"The history of the earth had been based on men fighting for something. Out of the guys in Vietnam, most all of them have parents and family back home they had to leave behind. Please understand, this is something I have to do."

The young 21-year-old, known to friends as "Robin" had close family ties and in another letter from Vietnam, he expressed:

"A person can't believe how strong his family ties are until he's away from them awhile. Every time I see Mom and Dad, I thank God for making me so lucky. I really haven't decided what I did to deserve them."

A Vietnamese orphanage was located near Robin's base camp and for Christmas of 1968, he organized his unit in a service project for the little children. Friends and family from his hometown of Grangeville joined in the effort and clothing and gifts were sent overseas for the surprise Christmas party. The camp cook prepared a large dinner for the young orphans and after the celebration was over, Robin wrote home:

"Now that it's over, I wish I could have done so much more."

Robin wrote of the little Vietnamese boys who would come to their camp during the day, to cut GI's hair and shine their shoes. At night the same boys would work for Viet Cong, planting land mines in the earth that was being prepared for a road. One of these mines, called a "bouncing Betty", took Rob's life on May 10, 1969.

Jim Jones (r.) with children at Tay Ninh Orphanage.

Thirty-one-year-old Capt. **TROY R. OLIVER, JR.** of Boise, Idaho died in Vietnam on May 19, 1968 after a distinguished military career. The 1954 Boise High School graduate joined the Marines in 1955 and was stationed in the Marshall Islands, Camp Pendleton and Hawaii. As a Sgt.1st Class, he took his platoon to an annual Marine Corps competition in Virginia where they received first place. Following a recommendation to Officers Candidate School, he graduated in June 1960 as a 2nd Lt. and later served in Okinawa as a liaison officer.

In 1963 Troy was stationed at Marine Headquarters in Washington, D.C. During President John F. Kennedy's term, he fulfilled a 3-month assignment at the White House. After receiving his 1st Lt. bars, he went to Cuba as an intelligence officer in 1966. In 1967 Troy was sent to Saigon, Vietnam with the rank of Captain to serve as the Provost Marshall for the Marine Corp on General Westmoreland's staff. While in Saigon the Idaho native asked for an assignment on the DMZ. Serving as a rifle company commander, Troy was leading a unit of 12 men from Khe Sanh to the coast, when all 13 were killed in an enemy ambush. Troy was the father of two children.

L.Cpl. **DAN R. MOORE** from Idaho Falls, Idaho, was known by family and friends as "Danny."

A typical all-American boy, Danny loved baseball, playing first baseman and pitcher on his Little League and Babe Ruth teams. Teenage years were filled with hunting and fishing and all the activities boys liked to do. From Boot Camp, Danny wrote home of the rigors of war games, the long hikes and the loneliness. From Vietnam he wrote of the heat, the rain and mud, and the many friends he made and lost.

One of his greatest concerns was the tragedy of so many homeless children, and he spent much of his free time helping to construct an orphanage near Hue. Sleepless nights from constant shelling were filled with thoughts of home, and days on the calendar were marked off, one by one, in anticipation of the day he would return.

Danny served as a Marine forward observer in the Naval Gunfire Section of the 101st Air Calvary. The 1966 graduate of Idaho Falls High School died in a helicopter crash over the ocean near Hue. He was 20 years old.

"Everything's going to be just fine…"

Korean War veteran **LESTER G (RED) MICHELS** joined the service in May 1946. First stationed in Guam, he was later sent with the 1st Amphibious Battalion to the Inchon Landing. Following the Korean War, Lester re-enlisted in the Marines and served another year overseas. Between 1953 and 1965 he served at various bases stateside, until he received orders to go to Vietnam on February 9, 1966. The 19-year military veteran and father of four died 40 days later in the vicinity of Quang Ngai. The amiable 6 foot 5 inch soldier with auburn hair, was nicknamed "Red" in the military and known as such by family and friends all his life. Lester's children, ages 13 years to 4 months, moved with their mother back to Blackfoot when he left for Vietnam. Red was 37 years old at the time of his death.

In 1992 his widow, Wanda Michels recalls, "Even after all these years, I miss his cheerful smile and outlook on life, everything was always going to be 'Just fine.' "

A TRADITION OF SERVICE:
The family of L. Cpl. **MICHAEL MC MASTER** from Mountain Home, Idaho, understood well the high price of freedom, when word arrived that Michael had died while serving with the Third Marine Division in Vietnam. His father, Lt. Colonel William G. McMasters was on active duty stationed in Guam at the time, and Michael's brother Larry was also serving in Vietnam with the Army.

The family moved to Mountain Home in 1954 when Michael's father was stationed at the Airbase. The 22-year-old Marine died on June 27, 1969. His funeral services were held at the Mountain Home Base and burial was in Cloverdale Cemetery in Boise, Idaho.

"If I must, I'll give my life along with the others to help end this strife."

Nine year Army Veteran **DAVID E. HERBERT** from Rupert, Idaho was mortally wounded on a "search and destroy operation" on July 2, 1966, at Loc Ninh Province near the Cambodian border.

The twenty-six-year-old had left high school the beginning of his senior year when his mother died, and he was needed to help provide for the family, with his father's ill health. Shortly afterwards, he joined the army.

Before going to Vietnam, David explained to his aunt that he had been in the service for nine years and he felt he was better prepared to go to war than the young men who were being drafted. He said he "didn't want to die anymore than the next guy, but he would do his best to help keep our country free."

David's Aunt Alice Schneider wrote:

May we at home now do our best,
so that you and the others
in peace can rest.

Yes, it is for us who here remain,
to resolve that these dead
have not died in vain.

★★★

MARCH 1968
"IDAHO STATE JOURNAL"

Two Pocatello families receive word of their sons' deaths in Vietnam.

GARY FRAZIER, first reported as missing in action, was killed on March 2, 1968. A fellow student at Pocatello High School, **MICHAEL GREEN** died March 10, 1968 in Vietnam.

Gary Frazier graduated from Pocatello High School in 1965 where he was involved in wrestling and Spanish club. He enlisted in the Army July 5, 1967 and went to Vietnam on December 13, 1967. Gary was with the 24th Infantry Regiment of the Ninth Infantry Division. He died from an enemy bullet while on night patrol. Gary was in country three months.

Michael Green graduated from Pocatello High School in 1966. He was active in Key Club, Tri-Hi-Y, football, track and wrestling. He enlisted in the Army February 12, 1967 and went to Vietnam the following November. Michael was a crew chief gunner on an assault helicopter that crashed March 10th. He had been in country four months.

Both boys were born in Pocatello in 1947—Michael Green on Jan. 23rd and Gary Frazier on Nov. 10th. Michael Green was 21 years old at the time of his death, and his high school friend, Gary Frazier was 20.

May 5, 1966

18-year-old Pfc. **Elmo DeFord** of Hansen, Idaho, died from abdominal wounds he received during a Viet Cong assault on his Army base at Pleiku, South Vietnam. Elmo's mother had died when he was only fifteen and he joined the Army Feb.2, 1965. Completing his high school graduation requirements at night school, Elmo was a member of the base band, while stationed in Hawaii for advanced mechanical training. Survived by his father and three siblings, the young boy had been in country only four months.

"Once I was there…but now I'm gone."

Larry D. De Filippis (Dee) attended grade school and Jr. High School in Idaho Falls, Idaho before moving with his family to California. In 1964, the eighteen-year-old returned to his hometown before joining the Marines on Nov. 23rd. Dee went to Vietnam in February 1966 and was stationed in the vicinity of Da Nang. He died nine months later of fragment wounds from an enemy explosive device.

As a young man Dee had a band and enjoyed writing lyrics and composing much of the music they performed. While in Vietnam, the 20-year-old Marine wrote the following poem:

"For a Country So Fine"

Once I was there
But now I'm gone,
Shot to death,
By some Viet Cong.
But I'm a Marine
So I'll never die
My Spirit will live,
to Sound the Battle cry.
"Gung Ho" "Gung Ho"
My Spirit will yell,
till all the V.C. are
dead and in hell.

Then will I rest,
With a satisfied mind,
knowing I died for
A Country So Fine.

Ldd

Cpl **JESS B. BOICOURT, JR. (RUSTY)** from Nampa, Idaho had only two weeks left of his tour of duty in Vietnam. A graduate of Nampa High School, he attended the University of Idaho for two years before leaving for Vietnam on March 26, 1967. Assigned as a FO (forward observer), he was stationed at Khe Sanh in the Thua Thien Province during his entire 11 months of duty in Vietnam. The outstanding 23-year-old graduated "Honor Man" and earned the Marine's highest award for physical fitness. Following his death from mortar fragments on March 11, 1968 he was awarded the Navy Commendation Medal with V for valor and the Purple Heart.

"The Post Register" reports:

BLAST KILLS I.F. SOLDIER

"A young Ririe Army man was killed in an oil tank explosion in Vietnam Saturday, his parents were notified Monday. He was Spec.4 **ARLO F. BROWN**, 22 from Shelton, a community southwest of Ririe.

The Browns said an Army major notified them their son was killed by an explosion of an oil tank at Ben Hall, 17 miles from Saigon. He had only two weeks more to serve in Vietnam. He was a member of the 193rd Engineering Co., 4th Battalion, and entered the Army April 8, 1965.

He was born in Idaho Falls and graduated from Ririe High School in 1962, and attended Ricks College for one semester."

St. Maries' native **WILLIAM E. ANDERSON** joined the National Guard at age 18 and served in the Korean War. Upon re-enlisting into the Army in 1954, he determined the military would be his career. While stationed in Panama, he met his wife and the couple had two sons. In earlier years, William began working for the St. Joe Forestry

Service near Calder, Idaho at age sixteen. By his eighteenth birthday, he was fighting fires and stationed on lookouts during the summer months.

Three months before William's death in Vietnam, he had been seriously wounded and hospitalized for leg injuries from a booby trap. Recovering quickly, the 25-year-old Idahoan returned to duty. On August 1, 1966 he and six of his company were victims of a grenade thrown from an ambush while on patrol. The veteran of two wars, Sgt. Anderson was the recipient of two Purple Hearts, both awarded for heroic and courageous service in Vietnam.

PROFILES
OF FAITH AND CONVICTION

Larry Petersen, Vietnam, 1969.

A man of faith, "who never feared his own mortality," Major **RAYMOND (PAT) TACKE** from Cottonwood, Idaho died on a sortie flight from Taiwan to Vietnam on March 8, 1969.

The native Idahoan served as Student Body President at Cottonwood High School in 1946 before entering the U.S. Naval Academy in Annapolis, MD. After graduation, Pat opted for a career in the Air Force (due to seasickness) and served as an officer for over 37 years. Following a proud military tradition, his four brothers also served in one or more branches of the service.

In 1968, at the age of forty and after a distinguished military career, Pat volunteered for duty in Vietnam. As a navigator on a C-130, he and his crew flew sorties from Ching Chaun Kang Airbase in Taiwan to Vietnam. In his almost daily letters home to family, Pat described the beauty of the land and his great sympathy for the Vietnamese people. A man of conviction and faith, he practiced his religion with daily rosaries and Mass as circumstances would allow. After eight months of service in Southeast Asia, Major Tacke's plane crashed on a return flight from Vietnam.

In 1999, his daughter Christine recalls: "Our family was notified of my father's death about 24 hours after he was killed. It is a night that has been etched in my memory. He left a wife…and daughters…ages 13, 11, and 7. There is hardly a day that goes by that I do not recall my father. I have found that my relationship to him has grown, even after his death."

Christine completed a memoir of her father in 1995 (26 years after his death), stating it had greatly helped her come to terms with her feelings of loss.

Proud of his heritage as a Native American Flat-head Indian, Pfc **RAYMOND FINLEY** graduated from St. Maries High School in 1966. Frequently a performer in beautiful native costume, Raymond enjoyed dancing for Indian ceremonies and festivals.

When Raymond was a teenager, the St. Maries area experienced a long and serious drought. Teachers at the local high school decided to approach the youth about doing a "rain dance" to bring moisture. Raymond didn't know any rain dances, but consulted with his father who taught him a song and dance. The following day, Raymond performed the "prayer-dance ceremony" and it rained for a week.

One evening before joining the service, Raymond and his mother were looking up into the night sky at the stars above. Contemplating the future, he confided (or perhaps foresaw), "One day when I'm gone, I will be a bright star in the sky above, to guide and take care of my family."

Following in his brother's footsteps to serve his country, Raymond joined the Marines Nov.16, 1966. He went to Vietnam August 1967 and was in country only 2 months before being killed near Quang Nam. Like many other young American soldiers, Raymond's service and sacrifice was remembered and honored by the U.S. military with the symbolic presentation of the Purple Heart.

"The memory of Raymond Finley, a 20-year-old boy of faith, lives on in the night-time skies of St. Maries."

"You have to believe in your cause…"

Sgt. **THOMAS AHLBERG'S** family had moved to Idaho Falls, Idaho from California when he was still a teenager. Finding it hard to adjust, he left Skyline High School during his senior year and enlisted in the Army March 1969. There he earned his GED, and was assigned to the 101st Aviation Battalion in Vietnam.

In his letters home, Tom always encouraged his younger brothers and sisters to be good—to not make the mistakes he did—and stay in school. "Do your best at everything," he promised, "and you won't go wrong." From the battlefields of Vietnam he wrote:

"I believe that what I am doing over here is right. In order to do a good job, you have to believe in your cause. If the family doesn't agree, please don't write and tell me."

"When you are over here, 9,000 miles from home, you feel like you'll never get back home…it's a long, long way."

In January 1970, Tom wrote he was in North Vietnam and said it was a lot different than being in the South. "The V.C. have all kinds of stuff—tanks, choppers and even hard surfaced roads beneath the jungle canopy."

In his last letter home, in April 1970 Tom said he was "flying most of the time" and he must have had "a guardian angel watching over him with so many close calls." On a recent mission, they had just left a firebase when all hell broke loose. The pad he had been on moments earlier went up in a direct hit as the V.C. attempted to down the choppers.

On the night of May 4, 1970, the helicopter on which Tom served as crew chief collided with another chopper, while dropping flares on the enemy. All seven crewmen in the two helicopters were killed. The 19-year-old Sergeant had given his life for what he believed. He was posthumously awarded the Bronze Star for valor.

★★★

"The Buhl Herald" records:

"The tragedy of war became a reality to West End residents when Pfc. **DAVID FAIRCHILD**, 20-year-old son of Mr. and Mrs. Acel Fairchild, was killed in action in Vietnam."

A 1963 graduate of Buhl High School, David had worked on farms in the Buhl and Oakley areas as a youth growing up. After graduation he took a job as a press operator for a mining company in Gabbs, Nevada. Active in his church's youth group at home, David took his love for friends and fun times with him to Nevada, where he organized and supervised a teen club for young people in the area. Drafted into the army the summer of 1965, he arrived at An Khe in SouthVietnam the following December.

Two months later the young twenty-year-old was hit by enemy fire while on a routine patrol. David succumbed to his wounds the following day.

Eight weeks and a life cut short, but not before the inexperienced and devoted Idaho farm boy had proven himself valiant and true to the ideals he cherished.

Two Purple Hearts and a simple granite marker in the west end of the Buhl Cemetery—bear silent record of a sacrifice given and a life well lived.

FIRST WEST END CASUALTY — The war in Vietnam first became a reality to West End residents when Pfc. David Fairchild, 20-year-old son of Mr. and Mrs. Acel Fairchild, was killed in action in Vietnam. He was wounded on February 1, 1966, and died one day later. Final rites for Fairchild were held in Buhl on February 14, 1966, and this marker identifies his final resting place in the West End cemetery.

★★★

INTERNET TRIBUTE TO:

1st Lt. JOHN SHIEFER

Submitted by Rich Miller
Friend

"Just to let you know we haven't forgotten you. You were a great officer and pilot." From Your fellow Condors

John went to Vietnam May 30, 1970 as a Huey Pilot—Aircraft Commander. He and four other men were killed on August 29, 1970, when their helicopter was shot down while inserting troops into a landing zone. The 30-year-old Boise native was stationed at Phu Bhy and was the father of one son.

His wife shares: *"John felt very strongly about serving his country in Asia. It is my wish that people remember, with respect, all of those soldiers who served, regardless of their personal feelings towards our involvement in Vietnam."*

★★★

Sgt. **CHAD CARSON** from Boise, Idaho died December 10, 1969, four days before his twentieth birthday in a military hospital in Japan. Hospitalized for more than three weeks from "a fever of unknown origin" in Soc Trang, Vietnam, Chad was transferred to Japan three days before he succumbed to the unknown illness. He had enlisted in the Army in Sept.1968 and after basic training attended helicopter training. Arriving in Vietnam in June 1969, he served as crew chief of repairs, flying many Huey test flights and some combat missions.

In earlier years, Chad lived and traveled extensively in Latin America, as his father served in the U.S. Diplomatic Corp. While attending school in the Dominican Republic and Bolivia, Chad became fluent in Spanish. When the family moved to Boise during Chad's eighth grade, he took the entrance exams to become a Catholic Priest, but was not accepted.

The young soldier's faith and conviction was reflected in his mother's 1993 tribute and assurance that this record of honor and courage would come forth; a timeless memorial to all those who answered the call of duty, in the far oft land of Vietnam. In a letter to the "Freedom Bird" Veteran group who built the Idaho Vietnam Memorial in Idaho Falls, Chad's mother writes:

"Our sincere thanks... Information on [the] Idaho Falls memorial to our boys is very comforting, and speaks well of the community and especially the three veterans who pushed the idea to include the whole state. I fully understand the effort on the book...

"In God's good time it will appear—a treasure for all generations to come."

Gratefully,
Mary E. Carson

"War brings out the best and worst of men."

PROFILES OF BROTHERHOOD

Pfc **KENNETH SMALL**, a Marine from Salmon, Idaho joined the Marines in July 1968 and died eleven months later in Vietnam. The 19-year-old attended schools in Dubois for eleven years and prior to his senior year, the family moved to Salmon. Graduation and enlistment into the Marine Corps opened an entire new world to a young Idaho boy.

In Vietnam Kenny Moody, a Marine from Middletown, Connecticut, soon became Kenneth Small's closest comrade. Although the two initially had very little in common, including the color of their skin, they formed a close bond and friendship that continued for decades after young Kenneth's death.

Kenny Moody had written home to his father in Connecticut about his Idaho buddy and said, "He is my best friend over here. Even though he is white—I consider him as my brother."

Hearing about Kenny from her own son, Mrs. Small corresponded with Moody's father, expressing her pride in all of the boys. She was 'glad the two were men enough to be brothers and friends, and felt certain their friendship would last forever.'

The soldier's special friendship was pre-empted on June 7, 1969 when their twelve-man squad came under heavy enemy gunfire. Mrs. Small's son Kenneth, was one of seven Marines that died that day, leaving only Moody and four others alive in the unit.

The war had ended for young Kenneth, but the pair's battlefield pledge and relationship continued on. For many years the Idaho Marine's "best friend and brother", from the far off jungles of Vietnam, has kept in touch with the small community of Salmon, Idaho and the mother of his beloved comrade and friend.

Lt. **ROBERT L. TAYLOR** from Fruitvale, Idaho joined the Army in 1954 at the age of seventeen. His early school days were spent in Payette and Caldwell in the Crystal School District. Soon after enlisting, Robert went to Officers Training at Fort Benning, Georgia where he earned the rank of 1st Lieutenant. In August of 1967, at the age of thirty-one, Robert gave up the rank of 1st Lt. to go to Vietnam, where he was affectionately known by his men as "The Bear." While patrolling on a hill near Khe Sanh, another soldier near Robert stepped on a landmine and he was fatally wounded.

A childhood friend from home, Larry Boise was also serving in Vietnam at the time and later shared with Robert's family that he had met his 6 foot 230 pound buddy twice on the battlefield. Both times after "Bob's" death. The first experience happened shortly after a bombing raid when Larry and several others were discussing the size of the hole in the ground. Larry looked up momentarily and into the eyes of "The Bear," his lifelong friend. In another unexpected and hallowed moment, Larry was comforted again by the presence of a special comrade watching over him.

MESSAGES OF BROTHERHOOD:

Capt. **GARY L. STEELE** of Bliss, Idaho died in Vietnam on April 19, 1965 at the age of twenty-six. A member of the helicopter crew pays tribute to the young Idaho officer in the following Internet Tribute:

GARY L. STEELE CAPT.
Submitted by John Hal Barfield
HELICOPTER CREW

"It has been over 30 years and I still think of him. He was my hero."

An Internet Tribute posted by a flight school roommate on October 12, 2000 reads:

JON MICHAEL SPARKS CWO
Submitted by Mel Sheldon

Jon: Today I salute you. I will always remember and treasure our time at Fort Wolters. The early mornings standing in formation at what seemed like 0400, always wondering if (the) war would end. When it came time for us we did not hesitate to go. For many years I have thought about you and what…was going on up north with LamSon 19. While you were flying Guns in Laos, I was flying Scouts, going into Cambodia.

My brother, you will always be with me and when I go to the Wall,
I will always say hello to you.

A POEM OF TRIBUTE:

GRANT MOTTISHAW, a 1963 Pocatello High School Graduate, and 1967 Vietnam Casualty, is remembered by a close schoolmate and friend:

TO HAWKEYE

A friend there never was so dear
A sportsman not as keen
We spent out time together then
We lived our lives as one.
And now alone I sit and wait,
And wonder why you're gone.

Many a day will come to pass
Many a stag will fall.
Our hearts are one until the time
The wild goose no longer flies
And the out-of-doors will weep, my friend
Before your memory dies.

With every chevron flight I see
With every arrow sent,
The thought of you will fill my mind,
My joy is yours to share.
From now until forever, Grant,
I'll be wishing you were there.

Blair A. Petersen

*"A boy's life is not described on a piece of paper, nor by the best
words of a gifted speaker…"*
(From the Life Sketch of Douglas Wade)

"Brotherhood knows not the color of a man's skin…" 18-year-old **DOUGLAS WADE** wrote home from Vietnam in 1966. The inexperienced but compassionate boy from Idaho Falls, Idaho enlisted into the Army right after high school graduation in 1965 and was sent to Vietnam the following December.

Douglas was young in years, but carried an unusual ability and sense of maturity with him to the battlefield. Fellow soldiers immediately recognized the good qualities and judgement of the youngster, and the Private First Class quickly grew to appreciate his fellow comrades of different races and backgrounds. Letters home described his sympathy for the "young underfed boys who represented the ranks of the enemy", and Doug wondered if he could find it in his heart to fire upon them.

The boy-soldier who never reached his nineteenth birthday, had a rich and full childhood while growing up in Southeastern Idaho. A part-time job at a local grocery store, secured at the age of 13, stayed with him until he left home for the service. A talented musician, Doug willingly shared his guitar and music on many occasions, and developed a special kindness and sensitivity through helping his little sister with a difficult handicap. Just fifteen when his father was seriously injured in a fall, the teenager willingly stepped forward with financial as well as emotional assistance to help his family.

During his senior year at Idaho Falls High School, the idealistic youth committed extensive time and research to a report on governmental process. As his open mind processed the principles and foundation of freedom, he became filled with the ideal of 'freedom for all humanity.' Knowing his father had willingly served this cause, he determined he also wanted to serve his country. Demonstrations throughout the U.S. represented a betrayal of everything the 18-year-old held dear. He loved God, country, and his fellowman—taking all those things with him, to a place called Vietnam.

Two months before his nineteenth birthday, an enemy bullet from small arms fire ended the young soldier's life. In a special ceremony in his Idaho hometown, Douglas' parents accepted the posthumous Military Merit Medal of the Republic of Vietnam and the Gallantry Cross With Palm (comparable to the American Silver Star). In part the citation reads:

> The posthumous award is given to Pfc. Douglas J. Wade for "courageous combat," and for "assisting the Republic of Vietnam's Armed Forces in blocking the Red Wave of aggression from engulfing South Vietnam and Southeast Asia."

> "With his enthusiasm and exemplary devoted manner Private Wade willingly executed all of his entrusted missions and set a brilliant example for his comrades-in-arms. He died in the performance of his mission. His loss has been greatly mourned by both American and Vietnamese comrades-in-arms."

INTERNET TRIBUTE:

Submitted by Cherry Adkins
Sister
Wednesday, January 13, 1999

To My Brother

EVERETT W. BRAUBURGER CPL

Everett William "Billy" Brauburger was one of the most exceptional I have ever been honored to know. I'm not only honored, but proud to have him as a brother. He was 8 years older than myself and helped raise me and my younger brother.

One memory I have of Billy was when I was five years old. I had polio and could not walk correctly, he would place me on his shoulders and carry me anywhere I wanted to go. He even let me tag along with him and his friends. I give my heart and my thanks to Billy and all the men and women who carried all of us through the war in Vietnam and fought for freedom. Thank you all. Billy, I love you and miss you.

Everett W. (Billy) Brauburger attended school at Soda Springs High School. He died while serving in the Army in Vietnam on July 24, 1969. A treasured brother and friend, Billy was 20 years old at the time of his death.

"Bob, you did not die alone—a part of us went with you."

ROBERT NELSON wrote the Senior Class Poem at Rigby High School in 1969, entitled The Game of Life. The young soldier's own life ended at the age of nineteen in the jungles of Vietnam.

Robert's brother Brad, was on active duty in Germany, when he received a Compassionate leave to attend his younger brother's funeral. On the flight home, Brad was sitting next to another enlisted man also traveling to Idaho. The two soldiers struck up a conversation and Brad learned the young soldier next to him was escorting his brother's body home. When the plane landed in Idaho Falls, the boys' widowed mother discovered for the first time that both her sons were on board.

Robert was only fifteen years old when his father died, and the young boy became an indispensable part of his mother's life. During high school years Bob played guitar and enjoyed playing his favorite Beatles music with his friends. An avid snow skier, he spent as much time as possible on nearby mountain slopes. Bob joined the army shortly after graduating from Rigby High School and after basic training, he received advanced helicopter training.

The Christmas holiday and New Year's were spent at home with his family before his departure to Vietnam in January 1970. Letters home seldom mentioned any aspect of the war and were always upbeat and cheerful. The last letter arrived to the family home in mid-September. Bob had been in country nine months and was looking forward to R&R in Bangkok, Thailand in early October.

On September 29, 1970—only days before his scheduled departure—Bob was serving as a door gunner on a visual reconnaissance OH6A helicopter. Receiving ground to air fire from the enemy, the helicopter crashed and burned—killing all on board. The young Idaho soldier was awarded posthumously: The Distinguished Flying Cross, Bronze Star, Purple Heart, Good Conduct, National Defense, Vietnam Service, Vietnam Campaign, Aircraft Crewman Badge and Sharpshooters Badge with rifle bars.

"I think about him everyday," Mrs. Nelson shares, *" But I try not to think about what he could have been."*

Thirty years after Bob's death a comrade and fellow soldier posted the following Internet Tribute:

ROBERT WILLIAM NELSON SP4
Tuesday, March 21, 2000
Submitted by Clyde Hinderliter
Friend

God Bless Dr. Robert

I served in Vung Tau with SP4 Nelson (we called him Dr. Robert, or Hey Nelson!) prior to his volunteering to be a door-gunner with the First Cav. He was friendly, wise, calm and humorous. In 1970, the U.S. was withdrawing troops, not sending in replacements. Those of us remaining "in country" were subjected to subtle and blatant harassment designed to motivate us to volunteer to go to the "combat units."

During off-duty hours, Vung Tau was a tropical paradise: Five minutes from the beach on the South China Sea, hot during the day, cool at night. Maid service. Free meals. Friendly natives. We were rich. After work we would hire a Lambertta (6 passenger motorcycle/tricycle), run downtown, have a steam bath, shave and professional massage, then go into town... The sound systems were incredible, stereo was new: Hendrix, Doors, Joplin and the Stones serenaded us. We hired a cab for a full day and toured the peninsula at a cost of $3 each, including meals....

I guess (Dr. Robert) must have left at the end of August to be a door gunner. He made it back to Vung Tau once, about a week later...his light observation helicopter (LOH-Hughes Aricraft Oh-6, shaped like an egg) needed repair. (He) said it wasn't bad, all he did was refuel the LOH and shoot the M-60. ...I don't know how, but we knew when he went down...These LOH's (pronounced Loaches) would go down and try to draw fire. If any fool shot at them, two gunships would come in and defoliate the area with miniguns... and rockets...Dr. Robert was at work and they dropped down into a likely looking clearing...(and) were caught in a crossfire of three 50 cal. machine guns... I'll hear (Dr. Robert's) version soon enough, cause between his Vietnam and my alcoholism, we spent our time in Hell, and will surely meet in Heaven. May God have mercy on our souls.

A farm boy from St. Anthony, Idaho **LARRY D. GREENHALGH** was one of nine brothers to serve his country in armed forces. Larry had returned from serving a two-year mission for his church when he was drafted during a semester off at Ricks College. Born at the Rexburg Maternity Home on Sept.13, 1944, he arrived with an identical twin brother, Terry. Six sisters and nine brothers welcomed the tenth son of Alma and Ethel Greenhalgh.

Larry started school in a four-room schoolhouse at Wilford, about half about mile from the family farm. In the winter he would ice skate down the canal, hang his skates on a nail under the bridge, and then walk the rest of the way. The routine was reversed at lunch-time and repeated again each afternoon. With a large family to feed, there was always work on the farm for everyone, and Larry did his share of chores—milking cows, feeding pigs, planting, hoeing and harvesting all kinds of crops.

At age fourteen, Larry began his freshman year at South Freemont High School in St. Anthony. As a teen he experienced several close calls with death. Once when he was thrown from a run away horse into a tree and another time when the pickup he was riding in, was hit by a tractor. In his early life he learned to love music and spent many hours playing guitar and singing with his brother Terry.

When Larry's college education was interrupted by a draft call to Vietnam, he took his compassion and goodwill with him to the far off corner of the world. Letters home mentioned his love for the Vietnamese people, his pleasure in sharing his rations with the children and delighting them with his magic tricks. He had an abiding faith in his purposes there and many times asked his family to not worry, knowing all was in God's hands.

On March 21, 1969, Larry's family learned he had been killed in action on March 17th. His body was escorted home and on March 26th, the 25-year-old was buried in the Wilford Cemetery with full military rites. As a final tribute and gesture of love, Larry's twin brother Terry dug the grave.

"Part of me is still missing."

Death Notice of another Idaho twin who died in Vietnam on May 21, 1968:

Firth Man Killed In Vietnam

"A Bingham County man, **BRENT R. JONES**, the son of Mrs. Eva Jones of Firth died late last week while serving with B Battery, 140th Artillery. The Jones family was first notified that he was missing following an ammunition dump explosion at Dong Ha. Sunday, the family received a telegram which said he had been killed but details of the incident were unknown.

His family last saw Corporal Jones in February when he was home on leave and en route from Fort Sill, Oklahoma, to Fort Lewis. He would have been 21 years old next month. Funeral services are pending. In addition to his mother, Brent is survived by a twin brother, Blaine; a young daughter Rebecca, and six additional brothers and two sisters."

Nearly one month after Brent's funeral in Firth, his mother received a letter from his commanding officer explaining the events of May 21, 1968:

AGPB—Jones, Brent R.
US 56 628 377 (21 May 68)

Dear Mrs. Jones:

"It is difficult for me to express the sorrow felt by the soldiers of this battery over the recent death of your son, PFC Brent R. Jones, United States Army. Please accept our deepest sympathy in your bereavement.

Your son was critically wounded during the late afternoon of May 21st by an explosion, which occurred within a reinforced protective shelter. Brent was a radio operator for a forward observer team located at a battalion forward combat outpost. This position was on a sandy hill 4 miles south of Ben Hai River, which separates North Vietnam and the Republic of Vietnam and 2 miles inland from the Gulf of Tonkin. Your son's team was occupying the outpost to block an enemy infiltration route into the Republic of Vietnam. I am certain Brent suffered no pain and that he died immediately when the explosion occurred.

On May 25th at 1 o'clock in the afternoon a memorial service was held in the battery area where your son served with skill and courage. Pictures were taken during the service and I will forward them to you upon completion of the processing.

Brent was a fine soldier and he was particularly enthusiastic about his assignment to the forward observer team. His quick understanding of the tasks to be performed and his ability to adapt to quickly changing situations made him a man of great value and won for him the respect of all whom knew him. While I realize that my words cannot lesson the deep sorrow that I know you feel at this time, I do hope you will gain some comfort from the knowledge that your son gave his life in defense of the freedom enjoyed by all of us today."

Sincerely yours,

Michael B. Allen
Captain, Artillery
Commanding

As a youth Brent enjoyed playing on the American Legion All Stars baseball team, proudly claiming the batting title for the region. He completed his high school graduation requirements while in the military and left a loss his twin brother Blaine describes as "an emptiness that can never go away."

The August following Brent's death, little Becky received a letter from the Adjutant General at Army Headquarters, expressing his sympathy and informing her of Corporal Jones' medals and honorable commendations. Cherished tokens of remembrance and sacrifice earned by the young father she would never know.

MIA POW
"All we have are memories"

CWO **JON M. SPARKS** of Carey, Idaho was drafted in August of 1969 after attending one semester at Utah State University in Logan, Utah. The twenty-one-year-old was a graduate of Carey High School and served as a helicopter pilot in Vietnam. Jon had flown combat missions nearly 6 months in Vietnam when he was shot down over Laos on March 19, 1970.

The helicopter crew consisted of four men; two pilots and two gunners, and all on board escaped the crash without serious injuries. One gunner escaped, but the enemy captured Jon and two other crewmembers. There has been no word of them since that fateful day. Jon was married shortly before leaving for Vietnam.

Parents Notified Pocatello Officer Missing in Action

"Capt. **CURTIS R. "DICK" BOHLSCHEID** … has been reported missing in action in Vietnam. A career officer in the Marine Corps, Captain Bohlschied, 30, is a helicopter pilot on his second tour of duty in Vietnam. His parents were notified Tuesday that he is missing. A Marine since 1960 Capt. Bohlscheid served in Vietnam in 1963 and 1964. Returning to the U.S., he was a helicopter flight instructor at Pensacola, Fla. and El Toro, Calif. Marine bases. He was reassigned to Vietnam last Dec.28."

On June 11, 1967 a Marine CH46 helicopter crashed and burned near the southern border of the DMZ, in the vicinity of Quang Tri Province. The crash site was checked by aerial reconnaissance, which revealed the helicopter was completely disintegrated by fire. On June 12, 1967, a ground search-party attempted to reach the crash site, but were driven back by small arms fire. Eleven U.S. Marines, including Captain Bohlscheid were onboard at the time of the crash.

Survived by a wife and two children, the Pocatello native was a graduate of Pocatello High School and the University of Idaho in 1959. Dick was widely known as an accomplished skier.

"[We] see him in our nation's colors. He and thousands who gave their lives."

MISSING AT SEA

January 16, 1966, ENS **HAL T. HOLLINGSWORTH** of Grace, Idaho was on a routine night photographic reconnaissance mission, when the plane he was in missed the arresting cable and plunged into the ocean. Stationed aboard the USS Ranger—an attack aircraft carrier—Hal and the pilot's bodies were never recovered.

A 1961 graduate of Grace High School, Hal was active in football and basketball. He also enjoyed golf and hunting in the mountains near his home. He enlisted in the Navy on January 13, 1964 and trained as a RASC Vigilante jet reconnaissance officer. Left at the Idaho Vietnam Memorial dedication was the following note to Hal:

You are missed by us, the survivors.
You are remembered by us, forever.
Your friend,
Henry "Madman" Mortar
Rangers Team Leader Vietnam

ALSO MISSING AT SEA

December 14, 1971, Captain **GREGG HOLLINGER** from Paul, Idaho was a logistics officer with the South Vietnamese Army. He was presumed lost in a downed aircraft over the China Sea, five minutes from Da Nang. Gregg had filled an earlier tour in Vietnam in 1967-1968 with the 101st Airborne Division. His second tour of duty began October 2, 1971 and he was reported missing two months later. His body was never recovered.
(See Timeline)

The jet stream of an overhead plane arched silently across the fading waves of a distant horizon. Far beneath its lofty rise, a youngster squints against the golden rays of sunlight, and calls for others to see. A familiar ritual—repeatedly rehearsed on the playgrounds and schoolyards of slower paced days long ago. The story of expectation, a legend almost, related by cousins who knew to playmates and friends who believed:

"Uncle Larry"—symbol of a missing friend, forever lost …but always remembered."

It was Christmas Eve 1965, when the foreboding Western Union Telegram arrived at the home of Larry's parents in rural community of Iona, just east of Idaho Falls, Idaho.

"IT IS WITH DEEP REGRET THAT I OFFICIALLY INFORM YOU THAT YOUR SON, TSGT LARRY C THORNTON HAS BEEN MISSING IN FLIGHT SINCE 24 DECEMBER 1965 OVER HOSTILE TERRITORY IN SOUTH VIETNAM. YOUR SON WAS ON A COMBAT STRIKE MISSION OUT OF DANANG AIR BASE AND FAILED TO RETURN.

EXTENSIVE SEARCH IS NOW BEING CONDUCTED. IT IS POSSIBLE YOUR SON COULD HAVE BEEN TAKEN…"

Fun-loving Larry, a tail-gunner on a converted C47 had left for Vietnam only two months earlier. Waiting behind with family and loved ones, a wife and three small sons were counting off the days until his return. Already an experienced and highly decorated officer, Sergeant Thornton fully understood the risks of the dangerous work ahead and was prepared to perform his duty. A two-year veteran of the Korean War, the 33-year-old had joined the Air Force in 1952, choosing the military as his future career.

Initially listed as missing in action, the crew of six had flown their final mission earlier that Christmas Eve. Several days of searching over hostile territory turned up empty with the Air Force finding no evidence of the men or missing plane, and then word arrived:

1965 DEC 27
MR AND MRS CLIFFORD D THORNTON (DLR DON'T PHONE)
RT 1 IDAHO FALLS, IDA

REFERENCE MY PREVIOUS COMMUNICATIONS/S CONCERNING THE MISSING STATUS OF YOUR SON, TSGT **LARRY C THORNTON**. THE ORGANIZED SEARCH HAS NOW BEEN SUSPENDED AS ALL ATTEMPTS TO LOCATE AND RESCUE HIM HAVE THUS FAR BEEN UNSUCCESSFUL EVERY EFFORT WILL CONTINUE TO BE MADE TO DETERMINE HIS STATUS. ANY NEW INFORMATION RECEIVED BY THIS HEADQUARTERS WILL BE FURNISHED YOU IMMEDIATELY.

At first Thorntons believed Larry's plane had gone down in South Vietnam and were advised by the military officials to not release the news immediately because of the nature of the mission. Two years later they learned it was Laos, a "neutral" country at the time. Months of waiting, wondering and praying continued, holding tightly to the hope he might have been captured and still be alive. Every plane overhead a reminder of their missing loved one.

In January 1974 the Department Of Defense officially changed Larry's classification to 'presumed dead.' The investigation ended, with no trace of the plane and Prisoner of War Documents devoid of any record of the crew members' names. Controversy over the possibility of MIAs still being alive and conflicting stories of prisoner sightings made it difficult for families of the missing to put their loved ones to rest. Nine years passed with no word, when the Thornton family finally determined the time had come in 1974 to say goodbye at a Memorial Service in the Iona LDS Chapel.

A flag of remembrance, flown over the nation's capital (March 3, 1983) on what would have been Larry's 61st birthday, was donated to the city of Iona by Larry's mother Minnie Thornton. The symbolic red, white and blue yet waves over the Iona City Building and Community center, the converted old brick building that was once the church where the soldier and his sweetheart had been married. In the nearby community cemetery a granite marker bearing Larry's name, stands at the head of an empty grave.

The years come and go. Everything changes, yet stays the same. Perhaps children now grown yet notice the sky—and remember their friend, "Uncle Larry."

NOTICE FROM HILL AIR FORCE BASE IN OGDEN, UTAH:

The (new base) Service Club will be named Thornton Hall in honor of CMSgt Larry G. Thornton... He was officially reported as missing in action 24 December 1965 while assigned at Tan Son Nhut Air Base, Republic of Vietnam. Sergeant Thornton was officially declared dead 22 January 1974. He had served on previous tour in Korea and began his Vietnam Tour 1 November 1965. He was survived by his wife Marlene and three sons Dennis, Ronald, and Bradley.

In a letter to Larry's family, U.S. Airforce Maj. Gen. Bryce Poe II wrote:

"I am sure the unselfish contributions by CM. Sgt. Thornton and his family will provide inspiration to all who presently live and work at Hill Air Force Base and the surrounding community as well as those who pass this way in the future."

AIRFORCE PILOT MAJOR JON BODAHL MISSING OVER LAOS:

A 1955 graduate of Nampa High School and 1960 graduate of the University of Idaho, 31-year-old **JON BODAHL** was the father of one. During a seven-month period, from February 22nd to September 28, 1967, the Idaho native had flown 111 combat missions over the Republic of North Vietnam.

On November 12, 1969 while stationed at Korat Air Base in Thailand, the Major was called on a search and recovery mission over Laos. While in flight the two F-4s were diverted to another area to provide sir support for rescue units attempting to recover two downed crewman, approximately five miles southwest of Ban Phan Hop, Laos.

Enemy helicopters were also in the region searching for the downed pilots. Flying lead, Jon made several passes at the helicopters before leaving to refuel. Quickly returning to the area, he again made three more passes at the enemy aircraft, encountering ground fire each time. While positioning himself for the fourth pass, Jon radioed that he had an enemy helicopter in sight. Ground fire began again and a large explosion and fireball ignited. The FAC (forward air controller) flying above first surmised that the helicopter had been hit, but when John failed to answer radio calls, it was determined his plane had been hit. No parachutes were observed and no electronic signals were received. The two downed pilots were recovered but an organized search for Jon's plane was futile.

Major Bodahl and his co-pilot Captain Smith continued on a missing status at the expiration of the initial 12-month period of absence. No accounting was ever received from the North Vietnamese government or its allies, and their names never appeared in reliable prisoner communication channels. No other information pertaining to them was ever obtained from any other official or unofficial source. The men were declared killed in action on May 30, 1974.

Glimpses into official military evaluations of the Idaho officer reveal an outstanding service record and tradition of honor:

2 October 1967 Captain Bodahl is recommended for promotion as Aircraft Commander.

Facts and Specific Achievements:
"Captain Bodahl is a truly outstanding F4C pilot and professional officer. In this capacity he has completed a full combat tour of 100 missions over North Vietnam. Thirty-four of these missions were flown into the heart of North Vietnam while subjected to the most intense anti-aircraft and surface-to-air missile defenses. Early in his tour, Captain Bodahl was noted as one of the truly outstanding pilots in this Wing. He was usually selected to fly with mission leaders and on targets that because of their sensitive nature required special aircrew consideration. …His talents and experiences were used extensively in the training and indoctrination of new aircrews. Captain Bodahl was selected to perform the additional duty of Wing Top Secret Control Officer…

Suggested Assignments: Because of his invaluable combat experience as a pilot, this officer should be assigned and utilized as an aircraft commander in a tactical unit. In addition, he should be selected for Air Force professional schools to further mold his career and potential… His demonstrated leadership ability and unlimited career potential dictate that he will be promoted well ahead of his contemporaries.

Don. P Rettberg, Major and Flight Commander

DEPARTMENT OF THE AIR FORCE
WASHINGTON, D. C. 20330

REPORT OF CASUALTY — M-109 — Corrects Report Number M-396 (1970) — DATE PREPARED 24 Mar 72

1. SERVICE IDENTIFICATION (Name, Service Number, Grade or Rate, Component, Branch and Organization)
BODAHL, Jon Keith, FR, Major*, Regular, USAF - 34 Tac Ftr Sq, APO San Francisco 96288

FILE IN MASTER PERSONNEL RECORDS
Initials
Office Symbol DPMSC
Date 24 MAR 1972

2. CASUALTY STATUS XX BATTLE [ ] NON-BATTLE
Laos
12 Nov 69

MISSING IN ACTION

3. DATE AND PLACE OF BIRTH, RACE, RELIGIOUS PREFERENCE
18 Dec 37 - Culbertson MT

4. DATE AND PLACE OF LAST ENTRY ON ACTIVE DUTY IN CURRENT STATUS AND HOME OF RECORD AT TIME

5. SOCIAL SECURITY NUMBER, PAY GRADE, LENGTH OF SERVICE FOR PAY, BASIC PAY, INCENTIVE PAY — CHECK IF APPLICABLE
Yes ** [X] CREW [ ] NON-CREW

6. DUTY STATUS
Active - On duty

7. INTERESTED PERSONS (Name, Address, Relationship)
Mrs. Gerry R. Bodahl — 28 Longwood Dr, Shalimar FL 32579 # — wife (4)
Dawn Renee Bodahl — same — dau
Mrs. Eleanor H. Bodahl — 2414 Cherry Lane, Boise ID 83705 — mother

8. REPORT FOR VA TO FOLLOW [ ] YES [X] NO
9. REPORTING COMMAND AND DATE REPORT RECEIVED IN DEPARTMENT
KORAT RTAFB THAILAND - 12 Nov 69

10. SELECTIVE SERVICE NUMBER, LOCAL BOARD, AND LOCATION (If unknown, enter date and place of first entry in Armed Services)

11. PRIOR SERVICE DATA
[X] YES [ ] NO FR 73 572

12. REMARKS
DATE PCS SEA TOUR COMMENCED: 7 May 69 ** Hostile Pay: Yes
* Promoted to temporary Major effective 1 August 1970, Special Order AB-1951, Department of the Air Force, 1 August 1970.
This individual was reported missing in action on 12 Nov 69. A determination under the provisions of Section 555, Title 37, USC, was made to continue him in a missing in action status following the expiration of twelve months' absence, effective 13 Nov 70.

#Indicates change

FOOTNOTES:
1 Adult next of kin. 4. Person to receive allotment if missing, captured, interned.
3 Beneficiary for gratuity pay in event there is no surviving wife or child — as designated on record of emergency data.
3 Beneficiary for unpaid pay and allowances — as designated on record of emergency data.

13. DISTRIBUTION 14. BY ORDER OF THE SECRETARY OF THE AIR FORCE
ROLAND J BURNS, Lt Col, USAF
Directorate of Personnel Services

DD FORM 1300

H6627

V. OVER-ALL EVALUATION (Compare this officer ONLY with officers of the same grade.)

SPECIFIC JUSTIFICATION REQUIRED FOR THESE SECTIONS								SPECIFIC JUSTIFICATION REQUIRED FOR THESE SECTIONS	
☐ UNSATISFACTORY	☐ MARGINAL	☐ BELOW AVERAGE	☐ ☐ EFFECTIVE AND COMPETENT			☐ ☐ VERY FINE		☐ EXCEPTIONALLY FINE	☒ OUTSTANDING

VI. PROMOTION POTENTIAL

1. DOES NOT DEMONSTRATE A CAPABILITY FOR PROMOTION AT THIS TIME.	☐	2. PERFORMING WELL IN PRESENT GRADE. SHOULD BE CONSIDERED FOR PROMOTION ALONG WITH CONTEMPORARIES.	☐
3. DEMONSTRATES CAPABILITIES FOR INCREASED RESPONSIBILITY. CONSIDER FOR ADVANCEMENT AHEAD OF CONTEMPORARIES.	☐	4. OUTSTANDING GROWTH POTENTIAL BASED ON DEMONSTRATED PERFORMANCE. PROMOTE WELL AHEAD OF CONTEMPORARIES.	☒

VII. COMMENTS FACTS AND SPECIFIC ACHIEVEMENTS: Captain Bodahl is a truly outstanding F4C pilot and professional officer. In this capacity he has completed a full combat tour of 100 missions over North Vietnam. Thirty-four of these missions were flown into the heart of North Vietnam while subjected to the most intense anti-aircraft and surface-to-air missile defenses. Early in his tour, Captain Bodahl was noted as one of the truly outstanding pilots in this Wing. He was usually selected to fly with mission leaders and on targets that because of their sensitive nature required special aircrew consideration. His experience, professional approach, and personal application made him an accepted authority on F4C pilot duties and tactics by other pilots and aircraft commanders. His talents and experience were used extensively in the training and indoctrination of new aircrews. Captain Bodahl was selected to perform the additional duty of Wing Top Secret Control Officer, a job that required much additional effort and administrative ability. He established improved management procedures and soon developed a section that was effectively responsive to the heavy classified workload of this Wing. Captain Bodahl has volunteered for upgrading as an F4C aircraft commander and for another combat tour in SEA. STRENGTHS: Professional ability, dedication to mission and unit objectives, and personal drive are among Captain Bodahl's major strengths. His contributions to the combat efforts of this unit have been such as to identify him as an outstanding leader among his contemporaries. SUGGESTED ASSIGNMENTS: Because of his invaluable combat experience as a pilot, this officer should be assigned and utilized as an aircraft commander in a tactical unit. In addition, he should be selected for Air Force professional schools to further mold his career and potential. OTHER COMMENTS: Captain Bodahl has made outstanding personal contributions to the successes of the 8th Tactical Fighter Wing in SEA. His demonstrated leadership ability and unlimited career potential dictate that he be promoted well ahead of his contemporaries.

VIII. REPORTING OFFICIAL

NAME, GRADE, AFSN, AND ORGANIZATION	DUTY TITLE	SIGNATURE
DON F. RETTBERG	Flight Commander	
Major, 433rd Tac Ftr Sq (PACAF)	AERO RATING: Senior Pilot CODE: 1 DATE: 29 September 1967	

IX. REVIEW BY ENDORSING OFFICIAL I concur. Captain Bodahl has consistently demonstrated outstanding performance during this period. His leadership among his contemporaries has been universally recognized and has been based upon bonafide courage and ability. He knows, and has demonstrated for others to emulate, the difference between bravado and professionally enlightened valor. Because of his ability and courage he has been sought for lead position on the big tough missions. This has resulted in his flying many more RPVI (Hanoi Area) missions than other pilots in the squadron. His mature approach to his flying and his ground duties has contributed greatly to this squadron's effectiveness.

NAME, GRADE, AFSN, AND ORGANIZATION	DUTY TITLE	SIGNATURE
CHARLES E. WOODS	Operations Officer	
Lt Colonel, 433rd Tac Ftr Sq (PACAF)	AERO RATING: Command Pilot CODE: 1 DATE: 2 October 1967	

Review by Endorsing Official: "Captain Bodahl has consistently demonstrated outstanding performance during this period. His leadership among his contemporaries has been universally recognized and has been based upon bonafide courage and ability. He knows, and has demonstrated for others to emulate, the difference between bravado and professionally enlightened valor. Because of his ability and courage he has been sought for lead position on the big tough missions. This has resulted in his flying many more RPVI (Hanoi Area) missions than other pilots in the squadron. His mature approach to his flying and his ground duties has contributed greatly to this squadron."

Charles E Woods, Lt. Colonel
Operations Officer
2 October 1967

Jon was promoted to Aircraft Commander in 1968.

Evaluation November 1969

During the period of this report, Captain Bodahl continued to perform in an outstanding manner. He has been resourceful, diligent and imaginative in the performance of all duties… He is keenly aware of his responsibilities as a leader and strives successfully to develop rapport with both peers and contemporaries. Few possess his aggressiveness, loyalty and devotion to duty. His performance in the demanding area of combat tactical flying has been outstanding. I have flown with him on many occasions and can attest to his flying skill, courage and integrity… He constantly volunteered to fly night strike missions, fully aware of the increased hazards and the constant demand for perfection during ordnance delivery at night…. Captain Bodhal's flying ability ranks him in the top five percent of his contemporaries. He has unlimited potential, freely delivers more than is expected of him and consistently achieves results expected of a more experienced crew.

Among the honorable citations presented to Jon's wife and daughter were: The Purple Heart, Silver Star, Distinguished Flying Cross with 4 Oak Clusters, Air Medal with 10 Oak Clusters, Air Force Commendation with 2 Oak Clusters and Presidential Unit Citation.

"TO LIVE IN THE HEARTS WE LEAVE BEHIND, IS NEVER TO HAVE DIED."
(Thomas Campbell, Circa 1888)

MEMORIALS AND TRIBUTES

Sp4 **MAX W. PUGMIRE** from Montpelier, Idaho went to Vietnam on May 11, 1969. Stationed near Pleiku he wrote home to his family on October 9th that he was somewhere between An Khe and Qui Nhon (the coast). He described the steep mountains, with deep gorges and valleys. It rained heavily at least once a day and the mud was always ankle deep. Max's company had just found a large North Vietnamese weapon and ammo cache. It took his platoon two full days to move it to the [landing] pad which was only 100 meters away. "Finding the cache probably stopped plans for innumerable attacks," and saved many American lives.

Max had been assigned a desk job and wrote that he wouldn't be in the field anymore, assuring his family he would almost be as safe as in the States. Shortly thereafter, his unit was climbing a hill in search of snipers when mortar rounds from U.S. artillery support hit their location. A close friend from Blackfoot, Idaho was seriously injured in the shelling, but survived the attack. He was at Max's side when he died on October 24, 1969.

INTERNET POSTING:

MAX WELKER PUGMIRE SP4
Submitted by Steven Pugmire
Brother
MEMORIAL DAY 1999

Thirty years since you left for Vietnam. I was at the SL airport this week; all that remains from 1969 is the map of the world on the floor. It was the last place I saw you alive. Thirty years. You would have been fifty in April, and there are few days that go by that I don't think about what you missed, what we all missed.

I stood at your grave on Memorial Day. The wind was blowing cold rain and I didn't have time to say what I wanted. Now Mom and Dad are there with you, and my own son, named for you. I miss you all, and hope you are together looking over us, watching out for us. I still need you, even after all these years, but to see you here means something, makes you seem closer. Hope others who knew you come here, but I'm glad I was the first.
All my love, Steve
Friday, June 04, 1999

Wednesday, July 05, 2000
Submitted By Stewart Portela
A friend from the same hometown

With Honor

Thank you for your sacrifice. Your picture is still hanging up in the church of your home ward and is entitled, "an eagle scout who gave his life for his country." Many people see this plaque and remember you with great respect.

★★★

A monument stands in the beautiful Hayden Lake area of northern Idaho, dedicated to a young Marine who lost his life while in the service of his country. Pfc **ROBERT J (JERRY) GORDON** attended schools in Hayden Lake and Coeur d' Alene before leaving to serve in the 5th Marine Regiment at Quang Nam Province in Vietnam.

In a letter to his family he shared, "I'm now staying in the rear but we will be moving out again for the brush in two or three days." Jerry thought they would be going up Hill 196. The 19-year-old missed home and cooked meals. If his plans worked out, he wanted to take the entire family out to dinner at a nice restaurant when he returned. Many of the men in Jerry's company were getting malaria but he preferred the problems of the jungle. Flat open spaces were more risky for patrols and they usually saw fewer enemy troops in the brush.

In another letter the young soldier wondered why he was in Vietnam. "Nothing seems to be going on," he wrote. His parents received the letter the day Jerry died, April 15, 1969. While on patrol in a search and clear operation, their son stepped on a mine and was mortally wounded. Word of his premature death hit the small community of Hayden Lake very hard. Expressing the sentiments of neighbors and friends, a fellow resident wrote the following tribute in Jerry's honor:

In Memory Of A Soldier

A Boy-Man is gone
and so are those
future moments of pleasure

Empty spaces swim
in our hearts seeking
past memories to treasure

Robert Jerry Gordon died
like so many sons
for causes some abhor

Let all those still unsure
know that the cause
was Freedom evermore

We neighbors are grieved
deeply by the loss of
a human so near

Though not personally
known by all of us, we
cherish the sacrifice so dear

This Marine-Soldier is to
be remembered by all
and held Proud

He was more, much more
to us than just
another face in the crowd

When asked the cause of death
Answer loud and clear
Freedom and not in vain

Shout it to one and all
doubters to help ease
that creeping agony of pain

He helped his human brothers
To save future sons
for fathers and mothers

God bless you Pfc Bob
we send our thanks
we fathers and mothers

James B. Crowe

V. OVER-ALL EVALUATION (Compare this officer ONLY with officers of the same grade.)

SPECIFIC JUSTIFICATION REQUIRED FOR THESE SECTIONS								SPECIFIC JUSTIFICATION REQUIRED FOR THESE SECTIONS	
☐ UNSATIS-FACTORY	☐ MARGINAL	☐ BELOW AVERAGE	☐	☐ EFFECTIVE AND COMPETENT	☐	☐ VERY FINE	☐	☐ EXCEPTIONALLY FINE	☒ OUTSTANDING

VI. PROMOTION POTENTIAL

1. DOES NOT DEMONSTRATE A CAPABILITY FOR PROMOTION AT THIS TIME.	☐	2. PERFORMING WELL IN PRESENT GRADE. SHOULD BE CONSIDERED FOR PROMOTION ALONG WITH CONTEMPORARIES.	☐
3. DEMONSTRATES CAPABILITIES FOR INCREASED RESPONSIBILITY. CONSIDER FOR ADVANCEMENT AHEAD OF CONTEMPORARIES.	☐	4. OUTSTANDING GROWTH POTENTIAL BASED ON DEMONSTRATED PERFORMANCE. PROMOTE WELL AHEAD OF CONTEMPORARIES.	☒

VII. COMMENTS FACTS AND SPECIFIC ACHIEVEMENTS: Captain Bodahl is a truly outstanding F4C pilot and professional officer. In this capacity he has completed a full combat tour of 100 missions over North Vietnam. Thirty-four of these missions were flown into the heart of North Vietnam while subjected to the most intense anti-aircraft and surface-to-air missile defenses. Early in his tour, Captain Bodahl was noted as one of the truly outstanding pilots in this Wing. He was usually selected to fly with mission leaders and on targets that because of their sensitive nature required special aircrew consideration. His experience, professional approach, and personal application made him an accepted authority on F4C pilot duties and tactics by other pilots and aircraft commanders. His talents and experience were used extensively in the training and indoctrination of new aircrews. Captain Bodahl was selected to perform the additional duty of Wing Top Secret Control Officer, a job that required much additional effort and administrative ability. He established improved management procedures and soon developed a section that was effectively responsive to the heavy classified workload of this Wing. Captain Bodahl has volunteered for upgrading as an F4C aircraft commander and for another combat tour in SEA. **STRENGTHS:** Professional ability, dedication to mission and unit objectives, and personal drive are among Captain Bodahl's major strengths. His contributions to the combat efforts of this unit have been such as to identify him as an outstanding leader among his contemporaries. **SUGGESTED ASSIGNMENTS:** Because of his invaluable combat experience as a pilot, this officer should be assigned and utilized as an aircraft commander in a tactical unit. In addition, he should be selected for Air Force professional schools to further mold his career and potential. **OTHER COMMENTS:** Captain Bodahl has made outstanding personal contributions to the successes of the 8th Tactical Fighter Wing in SEA. His demonstrated leadership ability and unlimited career potential dictate that he be promoted well ahead of his contemporaries.

VIII. REPORTING OFFICIAL

NAME, GRADE, AFSN, AND ORGANIZATION	DUTY TITLE	SIGNATURE	
DON F. RETTBERG Major, 433rd Tac Ftr Sq (PACAF)	Flight Commander		
	AERO RATING Senior Pilot	CODE 1	DATE 29 September 1967

IX. REVIEW BY ENDORSING OFFICIAL I concur. Captain Bodahl has consistently demonstrated outstanding performance during this period. His leadership among his contemporaries has been universally recognized and has been based upon bonafide courage and ability. He knows, and has demonstrated for others to emulate, the difference between bravado and professionally enlightened valor. Because of his ability and courage he has been sought for lead position on the big tough missions. This has resulted in his flying many more RPVI (Hanoi Area) missions than other pilots in the squadron. His mature approach to his flying and his ground duties has contributed greatly to this squadron's effectiveness.

NAME, GRADE, AFSN, AND ORGANIZATION	DUTY TITLE	SIGNATURE	
CHARLES E. WOODS Lt Colonel, 433rd Tac Ftr Sq (PACAF)	Operations Officer		
	AERO RATING Command Pilot	CODE 1	DATE 2 October 1967

1st Lt. **JOHNNY W. BENTON**, Jerome, Idaho

A 1965 graduate of Jerome High School, Johnny enjoyed tennis and skiing and earned many trophies in competition. After one year of college at Idaho State University, he left for Vietnam. The 21-year-old died after being in Vietnam only one month and five days.

✮✮✮

An Athletic Memorial Fund established at Cascade High School in 1968 honors former Cascade student **JESS WM. (BILLY) CREASON** who graduated in 1965. The American Legion and Auxiliary Post 60 of Cascade, Idaho also erected a memorial in his honor.

Billy joined the Army in August 1966 and was sent to Vietnam in November 1967. He first served as a helicopter mechanic, before requesting duty as a machine-gunner (one of the most dangerous assignments in Vietnam) aboard a helicopter. Initially reported as missing in action for ten days, the 20-year-old Cascade resident was confirmed dead when the helicopter he was riding in was located on May 5, 1968. The crash claimed the lives of the entire crew.

Born and raised in Boise, Idaho **MICHAEL WASSERMAN** graduated from Borah High School in 1966. An avid and talented athlete, Michael's first love was baseball. Playing on both the Borah High School team and representing the American Legion in city league competition after graduation, one of his favorite projects was uniting the community to build a fence and needed improvements at the ball field. Many enjoyable hours were spent with teammates and friends on the ball diamond near his home, playing the game he loved.

Michael attended Boise State College from 1966-68 before joining the Marines at age twenty. He went to Vietnam in August of 1968 where he was a machine gunner for the 2nd Squad, 2nd Platoon.

Three months after his arrival, the Private First Class and his unit were defending a strategic hill in northern Vietnam that blocked the escape route of the 144th North Vietnamese Regiment. As the enemy orchestrated a massive retreat from the lower foothills of the Que Son Mountain range, Mike bravely manned his machine gun as U.S. casualties quickly began to mount. Holding his own against overwhelming odds, Mike continued suppressive fire as four positions to his left and six positions were all overrun and the occupants killed. Courageously facing certain death, the 20-year-old's battle continued until he fell to the ground mortally wounded.

As the battle continued, Michael's close friend Pat Lish, from Madison, Wisconsin worked his way to his comrade's side. Seeing he was too late, Pat shouldered his buddy's lifeless frame and in the midst of enemy fire, carried his friend up the muddy hill. Only a handful of men survived the carnage of that fateful day. Years later, Pat would tell the story of Michael's and others sacrifice in the book entitled "My Time In Hell."

Michael and Pat had exchanged letters prior to the battle and promised to send them to their respective families, in the event of their death. One of Michael's written requests included a quote the young soldier wanted inscribed on his headstone. Puzzled by the inscription Michael's family decided to honor his wishes. Visitors to the Rose Hill Cemetery yet ponder its meaning today:

> "For all whose envious eyes here rest upon,
> I owe it all to Vietnam."

Michael was not a sarcastic person, but genuine and sincere. Unable to hear his own interpretation and explanation of the seemingly ironic statement; his loved ones chose to believe he was proud to have died while serving his country in the face of great odds—and what many felt was a terrible frustrating war that nobody won.

When Michael's personal effects returned to Boise, his gracious mother created her own 'back porch memorial' by adding a seasonal touch of beauty to her son's cherished memory. Growing profusely from the symbolic and simple container of Michael's combat boots, brightly colored petunias bring solace and memories of bright sunny mornings—cheers from the baseball field—and magical moments of a long ago.

"If love could have saved you… you never would have died."

In remembrance of Pfc. **CRAIG H. HANSEN** of Soda Springs, Idaho, his commanding officer wrote:

> "Craig was to all of us a remembrance from which to draw strength and courage."

Born in Montpelier, Idaho Craig graduated from Fielding High School in Paris, Idaho. During school days he was a member of Honor Society and earned the Bausch Science Award. As talented musician he enjoyed playing classical guitar. After graduation Craig attended Brigham Young University on a scholarship. With only one semester left before completing his degree, he was drafted into the Army and left for Vietnam on May 10, 1969. One month later (June 20, 1969) he died during an attack against his Fire Base Ike. Craig would have celebrated his 25th birthday the following August.

In 1990, parents who could never forget the loss and unfulfilled life of a choice son offered this touching tribute:

In Loving Memory of Our Son
Craig H. Hansen
Who Was Killed in Vietnam 21 Years Ago.

When evening shadows
are falling,
and we are sitting all alone,
In our hearts come a longing,
If you could only come home.
We think of you in silence
and also repeat your name,
and all that is left to answer,
is a picture in a frame;
A million times
we needed you,
A million times we cried,
If love could have saved you,
You never would have died;
As the golden gates did open
God saw you needed rest;
His garden must be beautiful,
As he only takes the best.

Mr. and Mrs. Lloyd Hansen

IN MEMORY OF RANDY K. BRONSON:

A boy: so typical, with the breeze blowing in his blonde hair,
full of pranks and laughter.
A man: of such character that he left us a model to emulate.
A memory: so sweet we can still see the mischief in his eyes
     and smile—as we remember him.

"Nearly twenty years have passed now…and in setting down our thoughts and remembrances on paper, we the family of Randy K. Bronson, have been graciously reminded of the love, the laughter, and the happiness that he brought to each of us…and also a sad reminder of how much we love and miss him. Even though so many years have past, the memory of a young Randy, happily home on leave, enjoying the last rainy camping trip with the family is how we picture him in our minds.

Randy was a responsible and loving son. He was not only a brother, but also a good and trusted friend and confidant. He was true and supportive of his friends.

This is an expression of our love and is not intended to make Randy seem like a saint. This is our effort to keep a promise to never let him be forgotten. It is a confession that it really is very difficult to remember his faults. It is our chance to share our sweetest memories with others who suffered such a loss."

Randy joined the army in April of his senior year at Meridian High School in 1968. He was sent to Vietnam in October 1968 and stationed at Dong Tam. When enemy forces attacked the Firebase, Randy ran from the bunker to take his position and was mortally wounded by the impact of mortar shells.

Randy's greatest love was hunting and fishing and special family gatherings. The twenty-year-old soldier received several citations for bravery and courage. (In the early 1990's his mother's home burned down, destroying most of the family's keepsakes of Randy.)

"A special prayer for the survivors who are still hurting inside."

Cpl. **ROD KOEFOD** graduated from Moscow High School in 1966. He enjoyed hitch-hiking across the country and singing in his band after school. He died April 24, 1969 in Vietnam.

In his last letter written to his sister on April 14, 1969 he wrote of his base camp in a village with the Bong Son River on one side, and rice paddies on the other. His reconnaissance team had their own hooch, with bananas and coconuts growing nearby. They had been there two weeks and Rod was beginning to get bored with his paradise. The longest he had been in base camp before was 7 days and he hoped it would stay that way because he was getting really short (nearing the end of his tour). The soldier shared that his worst fear was booby traps.

Rod was scheduled to come home on June 21st and wrote he was anxious to leave "this…two faced school for clowns and actors." Rod died ten days later. He was twenty years old.

A 'Letter of Remembrance' dated November 13, 1988 expresses the loss and wishes of Rod's family in Moscow, Idaho:

Dear Rod,
Twenty years have passed since your death in a land called Vietnam. Family and friends agonized and cried over the fact that you spent the last year of your vibrant youth in an environment wracked with confusion, fear and death all around you. We pray for you and all the men that were in Nam. And a special

prayer for the survivors who are still hurting inside. All you guys did the best you could at that time given the circumstances. The nature of war always leaves people drained—physically, mentally, and spiritually. War is war. We pray for healing and peace on our planet so that no more lives are extracted in war. We pray that our world leaders make decisions based on the betterment of mankind—not on its destruction. You're in our thoughts everyday Rod and our love for you compels us to share our thoughts.

We love you and miss you!

Your Family

The Koefods

19 Years... 20 Months ... 16 Days

Pfc **BRUCE R. BENNETT**, a 19-year-old native of Boise, Idaho was killed in action Sept. 5, 1966 near Quang Tin in Vietnam. A 1965 graduate of South High School in Salt Lake City, Bruce entered the Marine Corps the following October. A member of the 5th Marine Regiment, he had been in Vietnam since February 1966.

A letter from Bruce's mother, Mary Bennett in 1992 reads:

"...I have been to the Vietnam Memorial in Washington D.C. many times. It is such a moving experience and gives me a sense of peace just being there."

"The years have gone by so quickly. Bruce would have been 45 years old this year. I remember him as that six foot tall Marine that wanted to do something for his country and more if he had lived."

A letter from Marine Corps Headquarters to Bruce's mother describes his untimely death.

7 September 1966

"Bruce had been engaged in operations against the Viet Cong in the vicinity of Tam Ky, Quang Tri Province...since 4 September. During the night of 5 September, Bruce and the Marines of his company were in their defensive positions when the Viet Cong attempted an attack. In the ensuing fire-fight Bruce was wounded by enemy small arms fire, and although he received immediate medical attention, he died almost instantaneously at 11:39 p.m. Bruce received the last rites of his faith at the First Medical Battalion Aid Station.

A memorial service for Bruce and the other brave men who died in the service of their country will be participated in by the officers and men of this battalion.

Although Bruce had been with us only a short while, his cheerful disposition, uprightness and devotion to duty won the respect of all who knew him. I realize that words can do little to console you, but I hope the knowledge that we share your sorrow will in some measure alleviate the suffering caused by your great loss.

Bruce's personal effects are being forwarded separately. If you feel that I can be of any help to you, please do not hesitate to write."

H.L. Coffman
Lieutenant Colonel, U.S. Marine Corps
Commanding

A MOTHER'S MEMORIAL TO HER ONLY SON:

Soft in my heart
you rest, beloved
Sunlight breaks the shade,
Gilds the dark grass –
Then, once more, I see you
See your smile,
And I live on with you
Soft in my heart.

In 1999 **DeVern Probart's** sister wrote:

"There is so much I want to share, so much I want to say. We miss him each day. It's like a hollow place that can never be filled."

A 1961 graduate of Pocatello High School, DeVern earned a BA in Business at Idaho State University in 1966. While at ISU he was active in the ROTC program and joined the Special Forces reserve unit where he earned parachutist's wings. During the summers DeVern was employed at Yellowstone Park, his last summer as foreman of the Park helicopter crew at Lake. Following completion of ROTC he was commissioned as a 2nd Lieutenant in the Army in 1966.

The 26-year-old was killed in a helicopter crash near Xuan Loc on July 17, 1969. Among his citations and awards were the Army Commendation Medal for outstanding performance to the ARVN 52nd Regiment and meritorious performance as an Air Defense Artillery Battery commander while stationed in Germany.

Memorial services were regularly held in Vietnam for lost comrades and officers. The kind generosity of the Probart family allows us a respectful and somber understanding of memorials attended by fellow soldiers and friends:

A typical Memorial Service in Vietnam.

VIETNAM MEMORIAL SERVICE
OPENING REMARKS
BY
LTC CHARLES M. BOLEN JR.,
18TH DIV DEP SR ADV

WE ARE GATHERED HERE THIS AFTERNOON TO PAY A FINAL TRIBUTE TO AN OUTSTANDING YOUNG OFFICER WHO DEDICATED HIS LIFE TO THE CAUSE OF PEACE FOR GOD AND COUNTRY. CAPTAIN LEWIS D. PROBART MADE THE SUPREME SACRIFICE FOR THIS CAUSE AS HE GAVE HIS LIFE IN A REMOTE JUNGLE AREA SOUTHEAST OF XUAN LOC, VIETNAM.

FOR NEARLY TWO HUNDRED YEARS YOUNG AMERICANS HAVE ANSWERED THE CALL FOR COURAGE AND STEADFASTNESS IN THAT EVER PRESENT STRUGGLE TO STOP AGGRESSION AND PRESERVE PEACE AROUND THE WORLD. AT THIS POINT IN TIME WE ARE FACE TO FACE WITH THE GREATEST AND MOST DANGEROUS CHALLENGE WE HAVE EVER KNOWN. THERE IS NO EASY SOLUTION TO THIS STRUGGLE FOR FREEDOM AND YOU AND I KNOW THAT FREEDOM HAS NEVER BEEN SECURED WITHOUT SACRIFICE. THE AMERICAN SOLDIER IS KNOWN THROUGHOUT THE WORLD FOR HIS DEVOTION TO THE CAUSE OF PEACE AND HIS SELFLESSNESS IN THAT PURSUIT. THERE IS A GREATER NEED NOW THAN EVER BEFORE FOR INSPIRED MEN OF CAPTAIN PROBART'S DEDICATION, INTEGRITY AND PATRIOTISM.

WE DRAW INSPIRATION FROM THE OUTSTANDING EXAMPLE LEFT BY OUR DEPARTED COMRADE, CAPTAIN PROBART, WHO DIED SO THAT OTHERS MAY LIVE IN PEACE AND FREE-

USAAG-IIICTZ

Mr. and Mrs. Lewis L. Probart
RFD #3 South Box 185
Pocatello, Idaho 83201

Dear Mr. and Mrs. Probart,

This booklet contains a record of the memorial service which was conducted in honor of your son, Captain Probart, at Xuan Loc, Vietnam, on 21 July 1969. It is hoped that this small token of our esteem for him will bring you some comfort in your bereavement.

Please accept my deep sympathy and concern. I trust that you may find comfort in the fact that your son gave his life in a noble cause, the defense of our free way of life. Captain Probart and others who have paid the supreme sacrifice in this struggle have earned the eternal gratitude of all Americans.

Sincerely yours,

CARLETON PREER, JR.
Brigadier General, USA
Commanding

```
                IN MEMORY OF

        CAPTAIN LEWIS D. PROBART

        REGIMENTAL STAFF ADVISOR                              IN MEMORY OF

          OF THE 52ND REGIMENT                        CAPTAIN LEWIS DEVERN PROBART

           XUAN LOC,  VIETNAM                 who was killed  in a helicopter crash  on 17 Jul 69.

              21 JULY 1969                    Captain Probart  was born on 27 Mar 43 in Pocatello,
                                              Idaho.  He served  his country  in the Army Enlisted
          .                                   Reserve for  one and one half years  before his com-
        +  +  +  +  +  +  +                    mission on 5 Aug 66.  He attended Idaho State Univ.,
                                              the Air Defense School at Fort Bliss  and the Infan-
                                              try Ranger School.  His eighteen month tour  in Ger-
            ORDER OF SERVICE                  many led  him through the 62nd Artillery  as platoon
                                              leader, XO and Battery Commander.  Upon his arrival
Opening Remarks         LTC Charles M. Bolen Jr.   in Vietnam, he served as Assistant Battalion Advisor
                        18th Div Dep Sr Adv   to the 1st Bn  of the 52nd Regiment, Senior  Advisor
                                              to the 2nd Bn  of the  52nd Regiment and  Regimental
Eulogy                  LTC Dwight A. Davis   Staff Advisor for the 52nd Regiment.
                        52nd Regt Sr Adv
                                              Captain Probart was awarded the following:
Scripture Reading       Psalm 23 in Unison
                                                   ⟩  National Defense Service Medal
Memorial Address        Chaplain (LTC) Willis F. Young   ⟩  Vietnam Service Medal
                        Staff Chaplain, III CTZ   ⟩  Vietnam Campaign Medal
                                                   ⟩  Army Commendation Medal
Prayers                                            ⟩  Combat Infantryman's Badge

Silent Tribute to the Deceased                Surviving Captain Probart  are his parents  Mr. and
                                              Mrs. Lewis L. Probart of Pocatello, Idaho to whom we
Sounding of Taps                              extend our prayers and deepest sympathy.


 "The person who desires to save his own life will
  lose it; but the one who loses his life for my sake
  will save it."
              (Luke 9:24)
```

DOM. CAPTAIN PROBART GAVE ALL THAT ANY MAN CAN GIVE AS HE GAVE HIS LIFE IN A SPIRIT OF DEDICATION TO DUTY AND DEVOTION TO GOD AND COUNTRY.

MAY GOD HAVE MERCY ON HIS SOUL.

✖✖✖

EULOGY
BY
LTC DWIGHT A. DAVIS, 52ND REGT SR ADV

THIS IS INDEED A SAD OCCASION FOR WHICH WE HAVE GATHERED HERE TODAY. WE MEET IN MEMORY OF A BRAVE YOUNG MAN, A MEMBER OF THIS COMMAND, CAPTAIN LEWIS D. PROBART, WHOSE LIFE WAS GIVEN WITHOUT QUESTION WHILE SERVING HIS COUNTRY AND THE FREE WORLD IN OUR FIGHT TO PRESERVE FREEDOM FOR ALL PEOPLE. HIS UNTIMELY DEATH IS A DEEP FELT LOSS TO THIS ADVISORY TEAM AND ESPECIALLY TO THE ADVISORS AND PERSONNEL OF THE 52ND REGI-

MENT, 18TH INFANTRY DIVISION WITH WHOM HE LIVED AND WORKED. HE HAD WORKED WITH THE 52ND REGIMENT SINCE HIS ARRIVAL IN VIETNAM AND HELD THREE POSITIONS DURING THIS PERIOD OF SERVICE. HE ADVANCED FROM ASSISTANT BATTALION SENIOR ADVISOR TO BATTALION SENIOR ADVISOR AND WAS THEN SELECTED AS THE REGIMENTAL STAFF ADVISOR FOR THE 52ND REIGMENT.

HE WAS AN OUTSTANDING OFFICER, A FINE GENTLEMAN, A MAN OF FAITH AND DEEP MORAL CONVICTIONS, WHO DISPLAYED A RESERVED YET STRONG CHARACTER. HIS EXEMPLIFIED QUALITIES OF LEADERSHIP AND COURAGE AIDED HIM GREATLY IN GAINING THE RESPECT OF HIS COMRADES IN ARMS BOTH VIETNAMESE AND AMERICAN ALIKE. HIS QUIET EFFICIENCY QUICKLY WON FOR HIM THE ADMIRATION OF ALL THOSE WHO SERVED WITH HIM. WE HAVE SUFFERED A GREAT LOSS BUT WE MUST CARRY ON IN THE TRADITION HE DIED TO MAINTAIN. OUR HEARTS ARE FILLED WITH SADNESS FOR HIS FAMILY AND FRIENDS IN THEIR BEREAVEMENT. WE PRAY THAT THEY WILL RECEIVE SOME COMFORT AND STRENGTH IN THE KNOWLEDGE THAT HE DIED A PROUD SOLDIER AND A TRIBUTE TO OUR GREAT NATION.

GOD GRANT HIM HIS JUST REWARD IN HEAVEN.

The United States Military Assistance Command (MACV) issued The Bronze Star (Posthumously) with the following citation:

"... For distinguishing himself by meritorious service in connection with military operations against a hostile force during the period 31 January 1969 to 17 July 1969 while serving as Assistant Battalion Advisor and Battalion Senior Advisor... Upon assignment, Captain Probart's tactful application of knowledge contributed to the establishment of outstanding rapport with his counterparts. His outstanding knowledge of communications, tactics, maintenance and supply were invaluable assets in developing the regiment into a unit worthy of emulation... Demonstrating rare abilities as a leader, staff officer and advisor, Captain Probart participated at great personal risk in numerous combat operations against hostile forces. During these operations, his outstanding example of battlefield courage inspired the indigenous forces to viciously assault the enemy forces. His ability to effectively employ supporting fires was instrumental in inflicting numerous casualties on the hostile forces. His devotion to duty, sense of professionalism and cheerful attitude served as an example for the

Vietnamese he advised, as well as other members of the team... He gave freely of his time and made many personal contributions to the success of the United States mission in the Republic of Vietnam."

(Also see 'Letters Home' and 'Forever in Our Hearts' sections.)

★★★

A CHILD REMEMBERS...

"The Idaho Statesman" reports May 26, 1986:
In Washington D.C.
Idaho woman travels to see dad's name on the 'The Wall'

BOISE (AP)—Memorial Day will have special meaning this year for an Idaho woman, who will see her father's name on the Vietnam Veterans Memorial in Washington, D.C.

Denise Griffin Burress of Caldwell, left for Washington on Saturday to attend a memorial service scheduled for Monday at "The Wall" which honors American service personnel who died in the Vietnam War.

The name of Air Force Maj. **WILLIAM J. GRIFFIN** finally was added to the monument two weeks ago, Burress said. Griffin died March 14, 1969, in a plane crash at Taiwan airbase after many missions in Vietnam...

"We always wondered why his name wasn't there," Burress said, "My brother had gone up there a couple of months before and he looked for it and was amazed he couldn't find it." Burress said she will meet her brother Duane, stationed at Charlottesville, Va., in Washington for the memorial service. Another brother, Sean, 21, who lives in Dallas, was unable to make the trip.

Burress found her father's name had been added to the monument after she saw an item in the Idaho Statesman on Wednesday that reported the addition and said the Vietnam Veterans Memorial Family Search was trying to find relatives of Griffin.

"The last letter we got from him was in February 1969," Burress said. "He talked about the men who were flying supplies into all the little isolated airstrips, and he was amazed they were still able to do it." One Memorial Day several years ago, [she] read the letter on a radio talk show that was honoring veterans. "He took his hat off to... (veterans)... [He wrote] 'They can walk proudly when they return home because they more than proved their love for their country.'"

[Senator Steve Symm's office helped solicit contributions for Burress' trip and the Adolph Coors Co. along with the Boise American Legion chapter helped with travel expenses].

Burress said seeing the Wall with her father's name on it is something she never thought she would be able to do.

"Every time I saw the Wall on TV or a picture of it, I'd sit and look to see if I could see his name," Burress said. "Seeing his name on The Wall has been one of my fondest dreams."

"Goodbye and Thanks"

In 1985 Eric Barker of "The Lewiston Morning Tribune" reported on the Vietnam Moving Wall exhibit that brought tokens of love and remembrance from area residents in northern Idaho in a feature article entitled: 'The Wall is for goodbye and thanks.'

"The wall begins with John H. Anderson and ends with Jessie C. Alba. In between are 58,202 (as of 1975) other names of men and women who went to Vietnam but did not return.

Mementos, photographs and notes began to appear just hours after The Wall That Heals, the traveling Vietnam veterans' memorial, opened at Guy Wicks Field at the University of Idaho... Flowers and flags were laid at the base of the wall. Wreaths and pictures of young men sat on the grass.

Items left at the foot of the long black wall tell the stories behind the faceless names. The mementos are part of the healing process, according to John and Linda Anderson, who travel with the wall. The offerings serve as communication between the survivors and their comrades who did not return, between the dead and those who because of age, health or other reasons did not go to Vietnam.

Among the things left in Moscow were a khaki uniform shirt in a sealed bag, and a photocopied picture of a young man in uniform accompanied by a POW MIA card. An note attached reads, "We love you uncle John." Another picture in an ornate frame holds the smiling image of **DUANE CHARLES AKKERMAN**, a private first class in the Army from Lewiston. A note says, "Taken from us as a result of war on 27 Oct. 67."

Many notes from veterans explain the tragedy of going to war with friends who did not return. One tells the story of best friends Joe and Burl. Joe was a point man for his platoon. The note says he traded duty with his best friend one day so he could stay in camp and eat steak. The friend, Burl, was killed as he stepped off a helicopter. The writer mourns for Joe, who must live feeling responsible for his friend's death. "Life can be sad and it is," says the note, signed Dean Richards 68.

Another note... tells of the treatment Vietnam veterans received upon their return. "I hate society for abandoning us; for spitting on us upon our return. "We didn't want to return as heroes. We just wanted to return alive and hopefully in one piece, just to become a small part of society which hated us."

It is not only veterans and loved ones who leave things. A message written in a child's hand thanks those who died for their country. "Thank you for going to war so we as children won't have to..."

The Andersons say the mementos are left as physical gestures to healing and remembering. They recalled some of the things they have seen in their time traveling with the wall. In Charlotte, N.C., a pressed army field shirt was left. When (the couple) packed up and moved on to another town, they discovered a wedding ring in the front pocket. "I guess some widow had finally let go," John said.

At Patriot's Point, S.C., a man left a photograph of four men carrying a wounded soldier. The four men were killed shortly after they gave their wounded comrade to medics. John Anderson said it as the wounded man who had left the photo...

One family planned a reunion around the traveling wall. A man who became the stepfather of a girl who lost her father in the war left a note. It simply said, "Your daughter is in good hands and well taken care of." Many notes are left by veterans who never had a chance to say good-bye. "It's important for the human psyche to be able to say good-bye," John Anderson said.

The Andersons say they encourage local veterans groups who sponsor appearances of the wall to keep the things people leave behind, and put them on display. That way, they can continue to touch people. When local groups do not keep mementos they are brought to Washington, D.C., where they are displayed for one day; then put into archives."

Tribune/Steve Hanks
Photograph of Army Pfc. Duane Charles Akkerman of Lewiston was left with a note that said: "Taken from us as a result of war on 27 Oct, 67"

Army Pfc Duane Akkerman was 21 years old at the time of his death in Vietnam.

AT A GLANCE:

Statewide Memorials and Tributes to Idaho Casualties:

Steven Dee Merrill, Bannock County—Marine League in Pocatello, Idaho named in his memory.

Gary Boushele, Blaine County—American Legion Post 141 in Bellevue, Idaho named after him.

Francisco Flores, Canyon County—Nampa Marine Corp League named in his honor.

Verle Skidmore, Jefferson County—Terreton VFW Post named after him.

Johnny Benton, Jerome County—Jerome County Memorial casualty.

Lawrence Acre, Kootenai County—Gonzaga University Student Scholarship provided by his will.

Le Roy Damiano, Kootenai County—Kootenai High School in Harrison, Idaho established a scholarship in his name.

Jerry Gordon, Kootenai County—Monument at Hayden Lake built in his memory. Upon his death, Governor Don Samuelson flew flags over state capital at half-mast. (May 6, 1969)

Ronald (Lucky) Rueppel, Latah County—Dreary High School scholarship in the former Valedictorian's name.

Ronald McGregor, Minidoka County—Paul, Idaho National Guard Armory named after former Student Body President and one of the first Idaho soldiers to die in Vietnam.

Mark Anderson, Power County—Marsh Valley Monument at the Arimo Cemetery honoring "All Who Have Served" built by money donated to the young soldier's family.

Kenneth Reitz, Payette County—Street named in U.S. in memory of the young soldier who served three tours of duty in Vietnam, and died two months before his son was born.

Jess (Billy) Creason, Valley County—Cascade High School Memorial Athletic fund and American Legion and Auxiliary Memorial flag and plague at Armstrong Park.

Larry Thornton, Bonneville County—Hill Airforce Base Recreation Center in Ogden, named in his memory.

John Powers, Bingham County—VFW Post in Blackfoot, Idaho named in his memory.

Colin (Ed) Lamb, Canyon County—Lamb Memorial Park dedicated in Vietnam.

Lewis DeVern Probart, Bannock County—Classroom at ISU named in memory of ROTC graduate.

MIA William (Bill) Lemmons, Bannock County—ISU Classroom named in honor of former Student Body President and ROTC graduate at Idaho State University.

Raymond P. Finley, Benewah County—A memorial built at Desmet, Idaho in his memory.

Donald S. McGinley, Minidoka County—Minidoka National Guard Armory named in his memory.

Frank S. Reasoner, Shoshone County—Reasoner Hall at Quantico, VA Marine Base is dedicated in his name in 1972.

PART 3

FREEDOM BIRD

and the Idaho Vietnam Veterans Memorial

FREEDOM BIRD

"I see the airline planes coming over, bringing and taking guys home…
Seeing those big birds makes me feel good as hell. I know one of these
days its going to be my turn."

(Written by 21-year-old Terrance Thomas of Hammett, Idaho,
while stationed in a rice paddy outside of Saigon.)

Eleven years after young Terrance's death in 1968, the image of a boy's fondest dream would rise anew from the mists. The "Freedom Bird"—symbol of home and country-once again prepared to take flight, renewing the message of honor, duty, devotion and sacrifice.

THE INCEPTION OF A CAUSE

"It began as a dream, kindled by a desire to find and receive understanding."

In 1979, a handful of men gathered "after-hours" in the cafeteria of an Idaho Falls potato processing plant, and a proud new era of Idaho history began to unfold. United by the conflict that had followed them from the jungles of Southeast Asia to the doorsteps of home, their desire was to help one another and others like them. At first, the group didn't have a name, nor did they need one. The closeness of the rekindled comradeship they felt in Vietnam, now provided the strength and support they needed to survive at home.

For most, more than a decade had passed since the days of combat. But for many an unresolved and hidden battle raged within. Recognizing the time had come to dispel the past and go forward with life, the men's primary purpose was to find understanding and help one another through the painful process of healing. Forty-five thousand Idahoans had served in Vietnam and the vast majority had returned to their state's farms, communities and universities, living productive lives as responsible citizens. In the late 1970's the public's view of the Vietnam Vet was much less positive. Images of social misfits, the psychologically impaired, and those seeking a free handout, overshadowed society's judgement and lessened appreciation for the sacrifices that had been made.

Older veterans from World War II and Korea had enjoyed affiliation with the organizations of the American Legion and Veterans of Foreign Wars. But the majority of Vietnam returnees felt isolated and alone. If the service and experiences of the Vietnam era were to remain unspoken and be remembered only in silence; soon the war and its lessons for future generations would be lost forever.

The only "rule of order" for the cafeteria meetings was informality. Set protocol or strict guidelines were unnecessary, as each man stood on the ground of mutual respect and tolerance. In the day of their return, deafening cries of dissent and negative images had caused many servicemen to take off uniforms and medals, box up memories, and hide, deep in a closet, a "past" they could never forget. But here in the twilight hours of an empty lunchroom, the lack of necessary rules and discipline, gave them the impetus and freedom to discuss the experiences they needed to share.

When two of the original organizers, Idaho native, Ford Burgess and Jim Grimm, of Mckeesport, PA, entered the Marine Corps nearly twenty years earlier, both were anxious to help their country. "If our fathers did it, we should do it!" Jim declared. But now, years later his memories of illustrious service were mostly scenes of death and fleeing children. One of three sons to serve in Vietnam, Ford had signed up in 1965 at the age of seventeen because he thought, "it was the right thing to do." Nearly a continent away, Jim also entered the Marines the same year, with neither knowing anything about Vietnam or one another.

After a few short months of basic training, Jim Grimm found himself "in country" assigned to a Marine Reconnaissance team as a radio field operator—not because he was trained, but because there was an opening. Eighteen-year-old, Corporal Ford Burgess had been assigned to another Marine unit nearby. While on patrol near Chu Lai, just south of Cham Ki, Ford knew there was another small outfit on a nearby mountain range being hit by enemy fire.

Picking up urgent calls for help from the other unit's radioman, Ford found the coordinates on the map and quickly notified the main base who sent heavy artillery support. Ford's mission was subsequently diverted in another direction, and he never considered the incident again—until one night at a meeting when he told Jim of his experience. After breaking out the map and comparing time and dates, the two tearfully realized they had spoken before. Now eighteen years later, the young boys' lives were "connected" again across a lunchroom table. The time had come to connect the Vietnam experience with home and society. A "new light" on a dark time of our nation's history was waiting to be shed.

THE DREAM UNFOLDS

The word veteran comes from the Latin word for "experience" and there were many among the veterans' ranks who felt the experiences of Vietnam were best left untold. They believed Americans would sooner forget than remember the "war we lost", and doubted the group's ability to help other veterans. "Vietnam," they proclaimed, "should lie in rest."

However, membership in the little group continued to grow by word of mouth. Slowly but surely veterans came in. Some came once or twice out of curiosity, but the majority of participants attended regularly. By the end of the year, the group averaged thirty attendees at meetings that were held twice a month in any available location. Basements of churches, homes and social workers' conference rooms became the backdrops for healing and growth.

At each meeting visitors introduced themselves, told where they served and were given the opportunity to share experiences, discuss adjustment problems, and receive support as many struggled with emotional problems. Everyone who joined the support group needed sympathy and understanding, but most of all, they wanted to be recognized for serving their country. Every man needed to be finally welcomed home.

Analyzing their situation, fellow veteran and founder Gary George recalled, "We just wanted to be looked at and thought of no differently than the veterans of Korea and World War II."

With responsibilities to family and society, organizers recognized their members didn't need the shadows of the Vietnam experience hanging over them. It was time for many to face issues, make necessary adjustments and get on with their lives. Members received personal support and encouragement, but the paramount cause of the group was to be accepted and recognized like other veterans. Even though the war they were called to fight was unpopular, they and their fallen comrades had served with honor. Thousands had paid the ultimate cost and their sacrifice needed to be remembered.

With that focus and goal firmly instilled in their minds, the vision began to unfold. In the eyes of America, the memory of a Vietnam veteran would yet be held with honor and respect.

THE INCEPTION OF A CAUSE

With membership steadily growing, the group's president Ford Burgess recognized the need to become formally organized and set up a charter. The first step was to select a name for the organization. Realizing none of the men's experience was the same, and that Vietnam was not one story—but thousands of stories and individual wars—the veterans collectively drew upon an experience common to all that had served in any capacity in the conflict.

Regardless of their branch of service, assignment or location, one and all had waited and marked off the days until their tour of duty was completed, and the big passenger plane, the "Freedom Bird" as they called it, would take them from the devastation of war. Now ready to move forward with their cause, they unanimously proclaimed themselves, "The Freedom Birds" in honor of the flight that brought them home to freedom.

In 1981 the Freedom Bird organization incorporated and focused their efforts on community service, charity events and social projects to help the greater Idaho Falls area. Functioning as a non-profit organization, they met once a month in the early years of the 1980's and their reputation as a positive and vital force grew with their involvement. Joining with the Chamber of Commerce and other service organizations, they became productive contributors in the community and received positive recognition as a group. As membership numbers steadily increased, the organization was instrumental in arranging professional counseling for eastern Idaho veterans and their families. Veterans became involved in helping other veterans and as a result, everyone benefited.

During the controversial years of the 1970's very few veterans had openly spoken of their Vietnam service, but as the decade of the 1980s emerged, more and more stepped forward to claim their patronage. Becoming more public and involved in civic affairs, the Freedom Bird organization's plans to participate in the 1983 fourth of July parade in Idaho Falls became a turning point. Built entirely by volunteer labor, the groups' parade entry included WWII, Korean and Vietnam veterans, and received the judge's award for "Best Military Float."

However, prior to the parade's beginning, a more courageous and risky plan was being formulated. Twelve Freedom Bird members, with banner in hand, had committed to a "personal stand" by publicly identifying their proud allegiance as Vietnam veterans. Planning to follow the veterans' float down the parade route, the men prepared for an uncertain "walk of freedom."

Veterans groups in the surrounding areas had previously received taunting and jeers from local crowds; reliving for some the humiliation they

1987 – Best military float and Sweepstakes winner.

experienced returning to the states amid anti-war protest and debate. Most returnees had experienced some form of silent or spoken rebuke and the type of reception they would receive today was uncertain. Determined, yet anxious, the twelve held their "Banner of Freedom" as concerned wives and friends stationed themselves at the route's midway point to offer cold drinks and words of encouragement.

Prepared for the worst, the parade commenced; and the "walk" in honor of the flag they had pledged their lives to defend, began. Their defense of country took place in a dark and cloudy time, but today the sun shone again as they received enthusiastic applause and salutes from the cheering crowd. The reception was overwhelming and one by one, other veterans stepped from the curbside and joined in their march. Touched by the display and honored to be one of their ranks, Idaho Attorney General, Jim Jones left the comfort and prestige of his convertible car and walked proudly at their side.

Twelve men had begun the walk of conviction and over 80 Vietnam veterans finished the parade route. Designated as last in line of all parade entries, the veterans' efforts were fully rewarded as they received their "first welcome home." America had finally begun to understand.

THE VISION SPREADS ACROSS THE LAND

In the fall of 1984, Ford Burgess, being recognized for his vision and efforts in behalf of veterans, was selected to represent Idaho as part of a twelve-member state delegation to attend the dedication of the National Vietnam Veterans Memorial in Washington, D.C.

Accompanying him on the trip to the nation's capital was fellow "Freedom Bird" member, Del Ray John. * The two men were invited to carry the Idaho State flag, and prepared to participate in an experience that would ultimately effect the lives of Idahoans for years to come. With hundreds of thousands they gathered on the grass of the Capitol Mall for the dedication ceremony on Veteran's Day, November 11, 1984.

The pair's first experience with the monument was in the early morning hours when they walked to the large open area for their first glimpse of the Wall. At first nothing was visible but a massive "V" buried in the ground. "When you got closer you could see your face looking back at you—and all those names... That's when

it first grabs you," Ford recalls with emotion. Engraved upon the black granite panels were 57,000 names and among them were 243 Idaho casualties and 12 MIA/POW's who never returned. **

Freedom Bird Founders, Ford Call (R) and Del Ray John (L), at the dedication of the National Vietnam Veteran's Memorial November 11, 1984.

The evening of the dedication, Ford and Del Ray discussed their overwhelming experience in the hotel room they shared on 14th Street. Completely awed by the events of the day, the two discussed the impact of the Memorial and the tremendous crowd it drew. As the conversation evolved, the men contemplated the idea of building a Vietnam Memorial back home in Idaho. Inspired by the events they had witnessed, they were anxious to return home and propose to the "Freedom Bird" group the possibility of building "One lasting final tribute to our fellow veterans; to remember those who had fallen and honor those who made it back."

At home, the Freedom Birds readily accepted the men's proposal to build a state memorial. In late 1984 they had committed themselves to the completion of a permanent testimonial to Idahoans who served in Vietnam. Monuments to veterans before the Vietnam era seemed to spring up in city parks across the land, but the aftermath of the nation's last war was much different. A state monument would provide a way to tell future generations about the valor of those that fought and died in a war engulfed by debate. The group set a fund raising goal of $125,000 and the project was scheduled for completion on July 4, 1987.

(*Del Ray John, a former Army Ranger was the third Charter Member of Freedom Birds.)

(** The number increases to 251 known Idaho casualties and MIAs by the year 2001.)

THE DREAM BECOMES A REALITY

Group meetings (over the years) had provided friendship, emotional healing and support, and now a united new focus began to emerge. Social images were gradually changing, and the productive roles the group's members fulfilled as citizens fostered understanding and support in the community.

Many from the Vietnam era shared in troubled and confused memories about the war that divided us as a nation, but the Freedom Birds had no desire to sway opinion or influence judgement. As plans for the memorial unfolded, no political statements were intended or addressed by the veterans group. Their only purpose was to create a lasting tribute, not to war, but to those they served with in the war.

United by that goal, the next five years were filled with combined efforts to obtain funding, gain public and political support and see through the construction of a fitting memorial. Ultimately, the vision and dedication of many would culminate in the fulfillment of a dream to honor the memory of those that fell, and celebrate the lives of those who came home.

As members rallied their energy and enthusiasm, committees were organized and a campaign of public awareness began. Now scheduled meetings focused on plans for the future, leaving little time for the conflicts of the past. Freedom Birds were ready to move forward and obtain new heights.

One evening following a discussion on possible memorial sites, several members drove up to a small knoll overlooking the Snake River in Freeman Park. Standing in the peaceful beauty of a quiet sunset, the group unanimously agreed it was the ideal setting. A meeting with the City Fathers a short time later resulted in the City of Idaho Falls donating a strip of land for the future memorial site.

To generate interest regionally, a statewide design contest had been initiated the summer of 1984, with the deadline slated for December 24, 1984. Over twenty entries were subsequently submitted, and a panel of judges selected a unique design by Tom Chriswell of Idaho Falls. The winning proposal was unveiled on January 23, 1985. A Vietnam veteran and Freedom Bird member, Tom had served as a captain with the 116th Engineers Reserve Battalion 'called up' from Idaho in 1968 and 69. Convinced that the memorial would play an important part in Idaho's past as well as the future, Tom wanted the design to hold different meanings for everyone who viewed it.

AN IMAGE OF HONOR

In its overall concept, the memorial would stand as a large inverted V—the traditional sign of victory turned upside down. Its creator believed that virtually everyone who participated in the war, in whatever capacity, felt his or her "personal private war" was a victory. By inverting the V, designer and engineer Tom Chriswell recognized "the controversy [and disagreement] surrounding the war... and its shattering effect on the heart of American society." The unusual design for the memorial came to Tom one evening when a lamp cast the shadow of an inverted "V" on an open book.

The memorial design featured a 24-foot carbon steel framework overlaid with polished stainless steel on which the names of Idaho fatalities and those missing would be displayed. A relief sculpture was designed for the vertical leg of the structure, and the reverse side of the memorial would bear a copper-etched map of

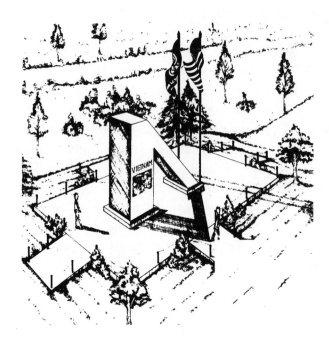

Southeast Asia. Flanked on the right side by two flag poles bearing the United States flag and the State of Idaho flag, the memorial was designed to face north and be centered on a base of ebony obsidian chips.

As the originator had envisioned, when the sun makes its way across the sky, a V-shaped shadow is cast across the park. The shape may represent Vietnam or the failed victory of the Southeast Asia conflict, but when visitors look at their reflection in the stainless steel structure, the designer hopes they will see more than just their image. He desires that they will sense "their place in history."

Freedom Birds recognized most adults had vivid memories and impressions from the era, either from military service or from watching the war's coverage on TV. But Idaho youth received their information only secondhand. The group wanted to convey to future generations our nation's deep sense of gratitude and appreciation for all the men and women who served during a difficult time. The memorial Tom had designed would allow them the opportunity to understand for themselves and be personally touched for the sacrifice.

When visiting the memorial, young and old look into the faces of three figures on a bronzed relief statue. The three images represent a soldier; a woman draped in the folds of the U.S. flag, and a POW (prisoner of war) beneath the furled wings of a powerful eagle, the symbol of freedom. Thousands of women served in Vietnam with the Red Cross and other civilian organizations. Military nurses working in Saigon and in field hospitals throughout the country cared for the wounded and dying. From among their ranks there were eight casualties. Idaho would be the first State Memorial to recognize the service of women in Vietnam. Tom used the mental likeness of his wife Joyce as an image for the contributions of women "in country", as well as the hundreds of thousands of sweethearts, wives and mothers who also made a very real sacrifice.

Working as a mechanical designer and engineer for over twenty years, this was Tom's first attempt at sculpting. With the wet clay laid out on the couple's kitchen table, he worked mostly through the quiet hours of the night. Week after week, month after month, his fingers released the details and images of Vietnam held vividly in his mind. Choosing to not use any models or pictures, he depended on the creative force and expression from within. With no formal training in art or sculpture, Tom says he doubts if his work is technically correct. "But, art isn't art unless it stirs the emotions," he shares. "Molding the clay has been an emotional experience for me."

At one point, the face of the Prisoner of War became so real and life-like, the emotional strain and intensity forced the sculptor to erase the image, and leave a wet towel covering the clay for several days until he could resume his work. Tom described an almost spiritual experience, as he recreated scenes of the past that would now live forever. Nearly two years later, the images he had ultimately created in the 600-lb. clay form were ready to be molded and overlaid for casting in bronze.

The Idaho memorial would also hold the distinction of being the first state memorial to be designed by a Vietnam veteran. From personal experience, Tom Chriswell understood that the "Vietnam War lives in million of memories and stories; participation and protest, joy and grieving, pride and guilt, (and) the entire range of human emotions." His artistic goal was to not tell one story, but "capture imaginations and memories, in order to commemorate our nation's brave, but troubled time."

WINDS OF CHANGE

Work on the memorial signaled the end of close groups and a new focus emerged as former discussion times were replaced with planning and organizational meetings. Despite obstacles and discouraging times, Freedom Bird members knew the work and sacrifice of building the memorial would help fellow veterans heal and restore pride in all who served. From the onset, the group sought no government aid or funding, intending instead, for it to be built from private donations and truly become a "people's memorial."

In 1985 the Freedom Bird organization sponsored the "Moving Wall", a life-size replica of the national Vietnam Veteran's memorial, to be displayed in their local community for several days. Many friends and family members of veterans visited the replica, leaving behind mementos of respect and love. The display also brought added interest to the veteran's project and introduced many local citizens, including a former World Airways flight attendant and civilian volunteer, Nancy Shamel to the group. A close bond was immediately formed as Nancy had served as a stewardess on the actual "Freedom Bird" flights the group had been named for.

(Nancy was invited to join the group's efforts and later served as president of the organization. See Tribute section.)

In 1985 the Freedom Bird organization joined the Veterans of Foreign Wars (VFW) for a brief time and became part of a national membership. This union helped the group receive formal veteran's recognition and allowed them a permanent place to meet. Both groups initially benefited as the VFW enjoyed the strength of new membership, but soon members began to recognize differences.

Being primarily of different generations, the veterans philosophies and focus varied. Unification as a group was difficult with many of the younger men feeling the older veterans had been received home by their country on "the shoulders of victory." For them, there had been no victory or feelings of welcome and acceptance. Younger members often found it difficult to give the dedicated time to attend meetings and fill responsibilities the veterans of WWII and Korea considered a high priority. Other Vietnam veterans considered the protocol and requirements of the VFW too restrictive and felt more comfortable in a relaxed situation where they could focus more intently on their "own mission."

As differences became more apparent, Freedom Bird members decided to separate from the VFW. In 1986, they formed their own charter and working through the state offices in Boise, established themselves as an independent veterans group within the state. Becoming Freedom Bird Post 7257, they maintained open and good relations with the VFW and retained an office in their building. The VFW generously and willingly continued to assist the new organization in building and completion of the memorial.

MONUMENTAL MILESTONES

On July 4, 1986 the dream began to take shape. More than 200 spectators, veterans and well wishers were on hand for the groundbreaking ceremony in Freeman Park. Among the dignitaries present were Mayor Tom Campbell, Idaho Attorney General Jim Jones, Congressman Richard Stallings and State Senator Ann Rydalch. Representatives

JOHN V. EVANS
GOVERNOR

OFFICE OF THE GOVERNOR
STATE CAPITOL
BOISE 83720

April 29, 1986

A MESSAGE FROM THE GOVERNOR

As the Honorary State Chairman for the Idaho Vietnam Veteran's Memorial it is my pleasure to send greetings and best wishes to all those involved in building a memorial to all Idaho Vietnam Veterans.

I strongly support all the efforts on behalf of those Idahoans who served in Vietnam, and want all members to know that I am behind them in their project. I am sure that we will have a tremendous response from the people of Idaho and look forward to the day when the monument is completed.

Again, my best wishes and a tremendous vote of confidence on this very worthwhile endeavor. Together we will soon see this monument become a reality.

Sincerely,

John V. Evans
Governor of Idaho

JVE:cp

from the offices of the Governor and Lieutenant Governor were also present for the long awaited ceremony.

Soon rank and distinction quickly vanished, as quiet onlookers watched twelve dignitaries with gold shovels and the daughter of a Vietnam soldier, yet "Missing in Action", dig into the hallowed earth of the dry hillside. Directly behind them, the shining image of the 'future memorial' glistened in the sun. Standing sentinel, the silver model from the veteran's parade entry earlier that morning, waited in silence as the hallowed earth was parted and then dedicated in thoughtful remembrance.

The following months were filled with fundraisers and community programs to help raise the needed $125,000 to begin construction. A statewide letter campaign organized through the VFW and Attorney General's office solicited much needed help and support. Determined to press forward, in the face of overwhelming financial odds, the group began pouring the cement foundation for the 24-foot memorial.

Meanwhile, opposition to the project began to build, as interests in the Boise area wanted the state memorial to be more centrally located in the western side of the state. In January of 1987 the conflict was settled permanently when Senate-House Resolution 101 was passed.

SENATE CONCURRENT RESOLUTION NO. 101
BY STATE AFFAIRS COMMITTEE

A concurrent resolution recognizing and declaring the Vietnam Veteran's Memorial in Freeman Park in the City of Idaho Falls to be the Official Vietnam Veteran's Memorial of the State of Idaho: Whereas, the United States owes much to veterans from all wars for their physical and mental sacrifice fighting for the protection of our country; and Whereas, of the approximately 33 million veterans in the United States, Idaho is home to more than 122,000 veterans, of which more than 45,000 are Vietnam era veterans; and Whereas, the Legislature of the State of Idaho believes that the contributions and sacrifices of the Idaho Vietnam Veteran should be officially recognized by the people of the State of Idaho, and that the Vietnam Veteran must never be forgotten.

Now, Therefore, be it resolved by the members of the First Regular Session of the Forty-ninth Idaho Legislature, the Senate and the House of Representatives concurring therein, that the Legislature of the State of Idaho hereby recognizes and declares the Vietnam Veteran's Memorial located in Freeman Park in the City of Idaho Falls to be the official Vietnam Veteran's Memorial within the State of Idaho.

"If your dreams are in the clouds—that's where they should be.
Now put legs on them."

In remembrance of the anniversary of Constitution Day on September 18, 1987 the veterans sponsored a "Bell Ringing Ceremony" and a parade and balloon launch at the Bonneville County Museum. First Security Bank joined the effort by donating $2500 and Mountain Bell Telephone Company followed through with a previous pledge of $10,000 by donating two equipment trucks to be raffled off with $100 tickets purchased by area residents. In the late fall the veterans made plans for a holiday lighting contest and the spirit of giving spread to community organizations and individuals alike.

"God stretches your dollars if you help people," was the advice of an 85-year-old widow, Frances Wood. Instead of sponsoring her usual Christmas "charity boutique" in her daughter's garage, she organized a craft sale at the public library, and donated all of her crocheted and knitted items to help the Freedom Bird cause. Family donation cards submitted "in memory" of lost brothers, sons and fathers arrived regularly in the mail. In an effort to honor the loss of others, recently bereaved families graciously suggested money could be sent to the Memorial Fund in lieu of funeral flowers.

Enthusiasm for the project picked up momentum and began to grow statewide. A raffle sponsored by the Disabled Veterans, the VFW, and American Legion in Priest River, Idaho raised $772.00. When Dennis Greenlaugh, (whose older sibling died in Vietnam in 1969) received the 1987 Mountain Bell Volunteer Award, the company donated an additional $1,000 in his brother Larry's name. The chairman of the company adequately expressed the feelings of many. " When people who participated in Vietnam came home, there really wasn't any recognition. It's really fitting we get behind this (effort)."

Freedom Bird members and their families did everything from 'flipping hamburgers' to helping with mail campaigns, and dispersing decorated gallon cans to area businesses for public donations. In addition to generous donations of time and money, the group helped with projects for needy families in the community and kept up with civic responsibilities through the Chamber of Commerce.

In October 1987, the finishing touches were taking place in Tom Chriswell's kitchen where he had been sculpting since January 1986. Sitting on a mahogany easel, the 4-foot high, 7-foot wide concrete frame held the 600 lbs. of molded and carefully formulated clay. Casting experts from the Wasatch Bronze company in Lehi, Utah were prepared to make a rubber and plaster of paris mold of the work that would be transported to

final sculpture

STATE APPROVES VIETNAM VETERANS MEMORIAL

Utah and cast in bronze. The bronzed 'relief statue' would then be bolted onto a vertical leg of the stainless steel memorial.

Determined to see the project to the finish, the Freedom Bird organization met for a Candlelight Ceremony at the future monument sight on November 11, 1987, as names of the dead and missing were read in remembrance. The 5th Anniversary of "The Wall" in Washington, D.C. stood as an ever-present reminder of their goal and purpose.

Proposals had been made as early as 1986 to appropriate the first $200,000 from the pending State Lottery towards the completion of the Vietnam Memorial. As a group, the Freedom Birds had "no feeling one way or the other about the lottery", but many members were adamantly against the funding proposal. They had intended to fund the memorial entirely from private donations and did not want the government or other bureaucracy involved. In March of 1988, the Legislature completed the lottery action in a 48 to 36 House, and 26 to 14 Senate vote. The following November, a constitutional amendment to legalize the state lottery would appear on the ballot, allowing Idaho voters to determine the final outcome.

By spring of 1988, Freedom Birds, with the help of statewide support, had raised about half of the funds needed to see the project through. With secured pledges of donated labor and building materials in place, an additional $60,000 would be needed to complete the construction. Not wanting the 'government to supply a memorial, but the people to supply a memorial', a veteran's spokesman reported, "we aren't looking for state funding from any source. We just want to recognize the service and sacrifice of Americans who went to Vietnam."

In May, the Idaho Falls Police Association donated $1000 towards the cause, and later in the summer the veterans group joined with the Chamber of Commerce to sponsor a "Downwind Chile Cook-off" at the McDermitt Baseball field. Contestants arrived at 8 a.m. and began cooking at 9:00. The festivities included a "Miss Chile Pepper" and "Mr. Hot Sauce" contest, live music, craft booths, an antique car show, hot air balloon rides and lots of food. Chile cook-off winners received a cash prize and advanced to the state finals. But money for the project was still needed.

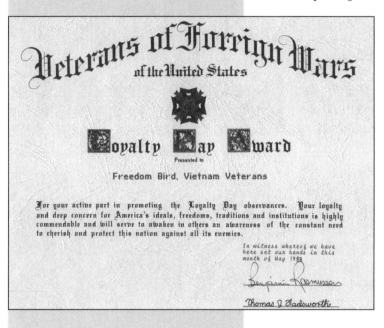

Shortly thereafter, Attorney General Jim Jones (who served in Vietnam 1968-1969) met with county commissioners to ask for help on a supplemental project. In October of 1988, plans were formulated to write a Memorial book and citizens throughout the state were asked to gather information about Idaho's Vietnam War dead.

As the dedicated group joyously reached the milestone of $75,000, (completely through donated funds and money raisers), an unexpected turn of events brought a new dilemma. The state Lottery Amendment, approved by voters in the November election, brought the unexpected offer that funds from the program's first profits had been appropriated to complete the State Memorial.

The group's leaders wondered what to do; continue raising assets in the coming months, or accept the money to insure a timely completion of the project? After long debates and difficult financial considerations, the Freedom Bird organization finally took Idaho up on the offer. Signing the final work over to a state contract, the veterans were granted retention of artistic control.

In November of 1989, Idahoans got their first view of what would become the State Vietnam Veterans Memorial as crews moved the 2-foot metal framework onto the site. Bids were received to finish the stainless structure with Clark and Sons Contractors designated to complete the work. Hopes were high among the veteran's group that the project would be finished for July 4th of Idaho's Centennial year, but unexpected delays moved the dedication to the following month.

August 1990 Regional Newspapers and Media report the story:

"Fifteen years after the nation's most controversial war and six years after the idea first originated, the Idaho Vietnam Veterans Memorial will be dedicated August 4, 1990 in Idaho Falls.

The 28-foot tall inverted "V" of polished stainless steel weighs approximately 5 tons and stands on a black granite base. 110 yards of concrete provide the foundation and a single strand black chain fence will surround the monument and two flagpoles. Finished costs will be approximately $270,000-$75,000 raised by donations and the remaining $200,000 from the Idaho lottery.

700 people have been invited to attend. An open reception begins at 2:00 p.m. followed by the dedication at 3:00 p.m."

Raising a monument JUL 18, 1990

Todd Crosland/Post Register

Dennis Vance of Vern Clark and Sons construction helps guide the main part of the Idaho Vietnam Veterans Memorial onto its foundation Tuesday afternoon at Freeman Park in Idaho Falls. The state memorial honoring those who served in the Vietnam War was commissioned by Freedom Bird, an Idaho Falls-based Vietnam veterans group. The memorial will be dedicated in a public ceremony Aug. 4 at 2:30 p.m.

"To remember, and preserve for generations to come the sacrifice made in the cause of freedom."

(Designer Tom Chriswell)

Freedom Bird Inc.
Cordially invites you to attend
the Dedication of the
Idaho State Vietnam Veterans Memorial
August 4, 1990
Open Reception-2 pm
Dedication-3 pm
Freeman Park Memorial Site
Idaho Falls, Idaho

A MEMORIAL NOT TO WAR, BUT TO THOSE WHO SERVED

Eric Harvego of the "Post Register" reports, "Some things just can't be explained as coincidence. The air was heavy with emotion Saturday in Idaho Falls' Freeman Park as the first of 243 names on the Idaho Vietnam Veterans' Memorial were called out."

"William Ronald Beasley...Anthony Ronald Bellamy... Bruce R. Bennett..."

"As the roll call of the dead and missing started, and friends and families sobbed for their lost ones, two wild swallows came down from the sky and circled the crowd at a low level. After a few minutes, the birds soared to freedom and disappeared into the sky.

The roll call was reminiscent of a high school graduation, but there was little talk of a bright future. This ceremony was mostly about the past, and the soldiers whose bright futures were destroyed."

Visitors from as far away as California attended the ceremony and cars were jammed along the park and side streets as people came in the hot August weather to say goodbye.

Among the nine afternoon speakers were Idaho Attorney General Jim Jones, who delivered the dedicatory address and Nancy Shamel, a former stewardess on the planes that ferried soldiers back and forth from Vietnam. Bill Ray Cammeron, National representative of the VFW spoke of the Wall in Washington, D.C. and commended area residents in saying, " You can be proud that Idaho will also say thank-you to those families who have lost their loved ones in service to their country in Vietnam."

The Idaho Vietnam Veterans' Memorial was the first of its kind to honor the contributions of women, and women at the dedication were grateful and proud of the recognition. Among their ranks were former Red Cross workers, mothers and sweethearts, sisters, daughters and friends. Gold Star Wives, the widows of soldiers who died while serving on active duty, were also recognized at the ceremony. An estimated 20,000 to 50,000 civilian women served "in country" and eight nurses died in Vietnam.

Current Freedom Bird President Gary George officially presented the memorial to Major General Darrel Manning, adjutant general for Idaho, who was representing Governor Cecil Andrus. In his remarks, Gary George confided the mission of Freedom Birds was not yet completed. "A record, a Memorial Book," he informed the group of more than 800, "must be compiled to chronicle this important era in history."

Freedom Bird members referred to the dedication as " a time to remember... a Memorial of an era, a time and event that shaped our country and affected every-one of us." The group's original project proposal read: *"We dedicate this effort to our lost and fallen comrades in the hope that, someday, we may all come home...we may all be free."*

The Ricks College Symphonic Band played the inspiring prelude music, but when it became time to close the emotional ceremony, President Gary George reminded every one the service was not a funeral, but a day to remember and look

forward to the future. He invited guests to come up to the Memorial, to touch it and get close to its meaning.

In lieu of "Taps", program planners had selected a closing song of hope and unification. The familiar chorus of Lee Greenwood's "Proud To Be An American" lifted high above the trees as grateful voices joined in fitting tribute to forever remembered heroes and the land of the free they loved:

> I'm proud to be an American
> where at least I know I'm free,
> And I won't forget the men who died
> who gave that right to me.
> And I'll proudly stand up, next to you
> And defend her still today.
> 'Cause there ain't no doubt I love this land,
> GOD BLESS THE U.S.A.

In the months and years that followed, the Freedom Birds sponsored several Veterans' Day observances and children's programs at the memorial. While organizers turned their attention to plans for a history book, other members began individual quests of remembrance.

One such veteran, Clyde Ricks from Tetonia, Idaho felt especially honored when he was invited to read names of the dead and missing at the 1990 dedication ceremony. Clyde's assigned list contained 26 names—names representing fellow soldiers and lost comrades. Names of men he didn't know, but nonetheless held in deepest respect and esteem.

A philanthropist at heart, though not a man of means; Clyde wished there was something more he could personally do to honor the families left behind. After several days of contemplation, the number "26" prompted a natural response in the mind of the former cross-country runner. It suddenly became clear. He would run a marathon, a "one mile tribute", in memory of each of the 26 men whose names he had read.

Summer ends quickly in the upper Teton Basin, and the 42-year-old farmer knew it would take comprehensive training to be ready for the annual Las Vegas Marathon, the following February. More than three years had passed since his last competition, and as he shared his feelings with a Post Register reporter, he said, "It was an honor for me to read those names… I thought that if there was some other way to pay tribute to them…running a marathon would be a good way to do it."

The following day, the newspaper publicized the plan and printed the names of the 26 men. Two of the casualties' families in Southeastern Idaho contacted Clyde, making the effort to prepare even more meaningful. Averaging 50 miles a week, the determined veteran trained during the final days of summer by running on gravel roads and moving irrigation pipe with his farmhands to get into shape. In mid-October, Clyde increased the pace to 75 miles a week. By early February, he felt ready to face his quest in the parched Nevada desert.

In unseasonably hot weather, nearly two thousand runners lined up at the starting gate to begin the long and grueling course. Clyde kept the pace and things went well for the first half of the race. But with each passing mile, he could feel himself falling farther and farther behind as younger and better-conditioned opponents passed him by. By the time he reached the twenty-mile mark, the fatigued veteran wondered if he could make it at all—yet something in his heart told him he couldn't quit.

Twenty soldiers had been "honored" (as planned), but Clyde had committed himself to twenty-six. He couldn't let them down. With the final six names remaining foremost in his mind, he continued each painful step. Hours later, memories of loyal comrades in Vietnam and the faith of family at home finally carried his exhausted body across the finish line. The timed results of the race revealed Clyde's slowest time ever. But the "unmeasured meaning" of his ultimate finish, yielded his greatest running success.

One man's "quest to remember", beneath a Nevada sky
An offering of selfless tribute, for a cause that could never die.

IN TRIBUTE

In October of 1990, the Idaho Freedom Bird organization, unanimously elected Nancy Shamel, as President of the veterans' group. The unprecedented move aptly reflected the admiration and respect the men held for their valued and trusted friend.

Working tirelessly since 1985, Nancy was instrumental in the planning, construction and final dedication of the Idaho Vietnam Memorial. Donating endless hours of selfless service to "help the guys", she has become a caring extension of a mother's heart, and a friend to the widow and the fatherless. For many years, she has corresponded with family members and cared for the many contributions and entries submitted for this historical project. Without her countless hours of concern and diligence, this record could have never been compiled and preserved for generations to come.

Nancy's story is best told in her own words. On behalf of the Freedom Bird organization, the author wishes to express sincere appreciation to our dear friend and true patriot: Nancy Shamel—loved by many, respected by all.

"We took boys over and brought men home."

May 1967, I was twenty-four years old and my dream of several years had just come true. I became a flight attendant for World Airways, stationed out of Oakland, California. At the time, World Airways was the largest charter airline in the world, and had the largest contract with the military for MAT (Military Air Transport) flights, to and from Vietnam.

My first military flight was to Guam with military personnel and their families. The Flight Attendants figured the flight would be a nightmare, but all fifty-one children were very well behaved and the flight was good. My next experience with the military wasn't as much fun; it was the first of many to Vietnam. We were taking one hundred sixty-eight soldiers to war.

The trips destined for Vietnam were always the worst. The plane was like a tomb. Many of the soldiers slept or wrote letters home, and there was very little talking between themselves or us girls. Most of the soldiers were boys between the ages of eighteen and twenty-two. They had just completed basic training and were headed to a country far away from their homes. Many didn't even know where Vietnam was. They had never heard of such a place until a few years earlier and wondered why they were going there to fight. (I knew) these boys were scared. They had trained with guns and some had limited training in wooded areas to accustom them to jungle conditions, but they had never fought an enemy before. None had any idea what the coming year would bring, or if they would be wounded, or even make it back home.

My first flight to Vietnam was into the DaNang Air Base. After the plane had landed and the door was opened, I had my first smell of Vietnam—a smell that words can't describe. Only those who have been there can understand. There was lots of activity, men, vehicles and machines everywhere; and then I looked across the landing strip and saw unmistakable rows of "body bags" stacked on flatbed vehicles.

Such was my welcome to Vietnam. Making my way to the bottom of the ramp to tell the "passengers" goodbye, I struggled to find the right thing to say. Finally offering a sincere "good luck", I bid each young man farewell with a heartfelt smile.

We did have fun flights, too. Many were R&R (Rest and Relaxation) flights to Australia. When the soldiers had been in Vietnam for six months, they were able to leave for a week. These guys were all smiles and happy to be getting out of the country. The majority of them talked the whole way to Australia. But on the return flights a week later, it was silent again. Most of the men slept, worn out from playing hard on their "break", I suppose. Those that did talk told us some great stories about their week's adventures. Many of the guys fell in love with "Aussie" girls and some even married.

My fourth type of flight was the very best—taking men home. Each return flight meant another 168 had made it through. The tension was always very high as we taxied down the runway. No one spoke until several minutes after we took off, and knew for certain that we were out of enemy firing range. You could physically feel the relief, and the plane instantly became a buzz of conversation, most all the way to the states.

Our return flights were always destined for Travis Air Force Base, in California. Just before landing, the men would always become very quiet again. As the wheels touched the ground they would yell and cheer. I loved being at the bottom of the ramp on these flights. We girls received lots of kisses and hugs. Many of the men would get down on their knees and kiss the ground of the good old United States. They had made it back from a year in hell. I've often said, "I took boys to Vietnam and I brought men home."

In June 1969, I quit flying and married my sweetheart of the past five years. In 1999 we celebrated our 30th anniversary and we enjoy our two grown children and three grandchildren.

In 1985, I had read that a Vietnam Veteran group called "Freedom Bird" was presenting the "Moving Wall" in Idaho Falls. I took a list of several names with me to see if they appeared on the wall. One of the veterans asked me how I knew so many in Vietnam. I told him my story and how I had corresponded with several of the soldiers until I was married. (I was relieved none of their names were on the wall.)

Later, the men in the Freedom Bird group invited me to become an "honorary member." I wasn't a military veteran, but they considered me a "civilian veteran." Their group was actually named for the planes I flew, the "Freedom Bird" that brought them home.

For the next five years the group worked very hard to raise money to help build the State Vietnam Veteran Memorial in Freeman Park, in Idaho Falls. In 1988, Jim Jones (who was at the time State Attorney General) and Tom Chriswell, the memorial designer, decided the group should write a book in honor of all the Vietnam veterans who served from the state. It was a great idea, but no one realized the work involved.

In August 1990, the State Vietnam Veterans Memorial was dedicated. With the primary focus of their work now completed, many members of the group drifted apart. In January 1991, some of the past Freedom Bird members and myself started a support group for Desert Storm families. Sixty families joined the group and we met weekly until the end of war.

Nancy Shamel, 1967
Flight Attendant

As their young sons and daughters arrived home from Saudi Arabia, we met them as a group at the airport to extend a warm welcome home. Soon the word was out, and the phone rang continually as families of other soldiers asked us to meet their loved ones. The next few months we met over two hundred young men and women. It was a deeply rewarding experience. I feel so fortunate to have been able to welcome home soldiers from Vietnam, and now Desert Storm.

Since 1992, Marilyn (author of our book) and myself have been working on this memorial book. This, too, has been a very rewarding project. I have had the pleasure of meeting several family members of the 251 Idaho casualties, and have visited with many on the phone. The historical project has taken much longer than we anticipated, and I am grateful it has finally become a reality. I hope this book may be a healing for us all.

Nancy Shamel

Nancy Shamel, 2002
Freedom Bird President

A SALUTE TO VIETNAM VETERANS

And so, the narrative and story of Idaho's role in the Vietnam War draws to a conclusion, but not to an end. Truly a "new beginning" awaits our proud state as countless "forgotten" stories of veterans unfold, and future generations come to understand and remember the honorable sacrifice of those who went before.

Perhaps, the time has come to open the memories of the past. To view with honor and respect, a time, a place—and a memory called Vietnam.

I salute you of my generation who bravely answered the call of duty, and gave of your all, for the freedoms that we as a people enjoy. Allow us to understand your hidden pain. Enable us to share and offer gratitude for your service, and offer us the chance to say,

"Welcome Home."

—*Marilyn Whyte*

PART 4

ROLL CALL

"We are young, remember us. We have done what we could,
but it is not finished, it is not done.
Our deaths are not ours; they are yours. They will mean what you make them.
We leave you our deaths, give them your meaning."*

October 12, 2000: Once again the lives of young Americans were taken as the USS Cole came under terrorist attack while refueling in the port of Arden, Yemen. Speaking at a Memorial Service for the Cole's injured and lost sailors; President Clinton called upon the inspired words of Archibald McCleese. In tribute to the many valiant who have served our country in the great and costly price of freedom, we were reminded:

"For our tomorrows they gave their today—not for fame or reward, but for simple duty as they understood it. They answered the call to duty, the call to service, and the call to America. 1.3 million have died that we might sleep peacefully under the blanket of freedom.

The young no longer speak, but they have a silence that speaks for them. 'Our deaths are not ours—they are yours. They will mean what you make them. We leave you our deaths, give them your meaning.'*

After all they have given us—we must give them their meaning."

Mr. Clinton continued: "Sleep peacefully under the blanket of freedom. Know them as you did, or remember them, as you will—the first time in uniform, or the last time you said goodbye. All very different Americans—all very different stories, lifelines and goals. But all entered our nation's service."

"History records the triumphs in battle. But no one can write the tears never shed, or the losses that never happened because of those who served. Thank them for a debt we can never repay. After all they have given us, we must give them their meaning."

(*National Cemetery Inscription by Archibald McCleese.)

The following biographical section contains brief sketches of the known 251 men and boys from Idaho who died in the Vietnam War. Comprised from information submitted by family and friends, military records, newspaper accounts, obituaries, high school yearbooks, and Internet listings; it is no doubt incomplete. Only those who loved them can tell the entire story of lives cut short in service to our nation.

In its present form, "Roll Call" represents the lives, hopes and dreams of so many that answered the call of duty and gave the ultimate sacrifice. Please take from this record the timeless message of duty and honor, and add to it an increased understanding and appreciation for their service and dedication.

May these names now hold new meaning and their sacrifice, even greater purpose, as fellow Idahoans and Americans recall with gratitude, so many "Reasons to Remember."

The Author

Major Lawrence Acre
Born 2/2/35
Died 10/9/69
Enlisted from Coeur D'Alene
Army

Went to Vietnam 9/17/69. Graduated from Coeur D'Alene High School in 1951. Graduated from Gonzaga University—Spokane, Washington. Was in the service for fourteen years, completed seven Vietnam Tours—three one year tours & four shorter specific missions. Lawrence was leading a classified mission by helicopter. It was thought that the helicopter was shot down by enemy fire, killing all aboard. Lawrence had named Gonzaga University as his insurance beneficiary to give young people financial assistance.

Cpl. Leo Joe Adakai
Born 5/3/44
Died 8/7/69
Enlisted from Blackfoot
Army
Married

Not Available

Went to Vietnam 3/9/69. Leo died from multiple fragmentation wounds in Khanh Hoa Province.

Sgt. Thomas Oliver Ahlberg
Born 2/3/51
Died 5/4/70.
Enlisted from Idaho Falls
Army—A Co. 101st. Aviation Battalion

Went to Vietnam 11/9/69. Thomas was raised in Montrose, Colorado. Attended Skyline High School in Idaho Falls before quitting school to enlist in the Army where he received his GED. He was from a family of seven children. Three of four sons served in the military in Vietnam. Thomas was a crew chief on a helicopter that crashed into a second helicopter while both were dropping flares in Thua Thien Province. He was mortally wounded.

Private First Class Duane Charles Akkerman
Born 4/17/46
Died 10/27/67
Enlisted from Lewiston
Army—First Cav. Div. (AMBL)
Married

Went to Vietnam 9/27/67. Duane was born in Great Falls, Montana, moving to Weippe, Idaho as a child. A graduate of Lewiston High School, he was a Chippewa Indian from the "Little Shell Tribe." His five brothers all served in the armed forces. Duane's son was two weeks old when he left for Vietnam.

He was killed by small arms fire in Quang Tin Province.

Not Available

Col. Gerald William Alley
MIA/POW
Born 7/28/34
MIA 8/16/78
Enlisted from Pocatello
Air Force
Married

Gerald was in the service for sixteen years. He was reported missing in action when an airplane on which he was a crew member crashed. His remains were returned to the United States in the 90's.

Major James Herbert Allred
Born 9/26/25
Died 12/14/63
Enlisted from Twin Falls
Army
Married

Went to Vietnam in May 1963. Graduated from Twin Falls High School. James was in the armed forces for twenty years. He had participated in aviation in the Navy in WWII and the Army Reserves in Korea. He also served one year as a ground operations officer in Europe. James was a helicopter pilot for Med-Evac, while waiting to leave on R & R a request came in for a Med-Evac. He volunteered for the mission and left in his civilian clothing. The crew had picked up the casualties when they were shot down over the ocean. The co-pilot survived and reported James' last effort was trying to save a crewman who couldn't swim.

Major Harry Arlo Amesbury, Jr.
Born 2/13/32
Died 4/26/72
Enlisted from Caldwell
Married

> Graduated from Clinton High School in Clinton, Idaho. Harry was a pilot and had flown seven years in the Pacific. He had completed one year of ground training before going to Vietnam. An airplane crash in Binh Long Province claimed his life.

2nd Lt. Reese Mark Andersen
Born 7/31/43
Died 4/19/69
Enlisted from Arbon
Marines

> Went to Vietnam 12/11/68. Graduated from Marsh Valley High School, Idaho in 1961. Reese was a platoon leader stationed in Dong Ha, Quang Tri Province. He was killed instantly by a stray bullet that had ricocheted off of a 2 x 4 in his barrack.

Staff Sgt. James Barton Anderson
Born 9/25/47
Died 1/25/68
Enlisted from American Falls
Army—502nd Bat. Parachute Inf. Elite 1st. Brig of 101st. Airborne Div.

> Went to Vietnam 6/12/67. Graduated from American Falls High School in 1966. While serving as platoon leader, he was killed by enemy machine guns while on patrol in Phuoc Long Province. He was scheduled for R & R in February and planned to be married in Hawaii.

Not Available

Sgt. Victor Edward Anderson
Born 4/11/43
Died 1/31/66
Enlisted from Stone
Army—1st. Cav. Div.
Married

> Went to Vietnam 8/15/65. Victor had been in the service for three years. He died from small arms fire.

Sgt. William Edward Anderson
Born 7/22/31
Died 8/1/66
Enlisted from St. Maries
Army—1st. Cav. Div. (AMBL)
Married

> Went to Vietnam 1/27/66. William had served sixteen years in the armed forces. At age 18 he served with the National Guards in Korea and enlisted in the Army in 1954. He and six of his company were victims of a grenade thrown from ambush while on patrol.

Private First Class Allan Theo Aslett
Born 7/25/50
Died 9/27/69
Enlisted from Twin Falls
Marines

> Went to Vietnam 7/6/69. Allan was born in Twin Falls and graduated from Twin Falls High School in 1968. He died from fragmentation wounds while maintaining a defensive position north of support base, Elliott in Quang Tri Province.

Sp.4 Glen Lawrence Atkinson
Born 10/24/46
Died 2/3/69
Enlisted from Caldwell
Army—25th Infantry

> Went to Vietnam 7/12/68. A 1965 graduate of Middleton High School. Glen was stationed in "Hobo Woods" south of Saigon, in the Binh Duong Province. He was serving as a team leader of a gun crew when he was killed while on patrol.

Cpl. Gerald Lee Baldwin
Born 3/18/49
Died 12/12/69
Enlisted from Nampa
Army—Co.D, 2nd Bat. 25th Infantry

Went to Vietnam 8/9/69. Raised in Nampa, Gerald graduated from Payette High School in 1967. He was fatally wounded during a night battle with a large enemy force. He distributed vital ammunition to his company many times before he was hit by gunfire, in the Hua Nghia Province.

LCPL/ E 3 Michael P. Bartelme
Born 8/4/46
Died 5/2/67
Enlisted from Buhl
Marines

Michael had been in the service for two years. He died in Quang Nam Province from small arms fire.

Not Available

Sgt. Brent John Baumert
Born 1/1/40
Died 4/26/66
Enlisted from Twin Falls
Army—A-425 Special Forces Group

Went to Vietnam 1/30/66. Born in Salt Lake City, Utah, he graduated from Twin Falls High School and the University of Idaho.

Brent was originally drafted, but he re-enlisted so he could go into the special forces. He died from hostile gunshot wounds when the boat he was riding in was ambushed on the return trip to base camp.

HN Philip Arthur Beasley
Born 2/2/46
Died 9/30/68
Enlisted from Boise
Navy

Went to Vietnam 5/25/68. A 1965 graduate of Boise High School, Philip enlisted in October 1965. He was killed four months after his arrival in Vietnam in Quang Nam Province.

1st. Lt. William Ronald Beasley
Born 1/16/42
Died 9/25/66
Enlisted from Boise
Army
Married

Went to Vietnam 7/25/66. William was an only child. He graduated from Emmett High School, where he served as student body president his senior year. He was active in the ROTC at the University of Idaho. Serving as a helicopter pilot in Vietnam, he died in a crash two months after his arrival.

Sp. 5 Ross Michael Bee
Born 6/24/46
Died 1/19/67
Enlisted from Georgetown
Army—Co. A, 1st. Bat, 8th Infantry, 4th Inf. Div.

Went to Vietnam 9/15/66. Ross attended high school in Montpelier, Idaho and graduated from Weber County High School in Ogden, Utah in 1964. He had been promoted to Sp5, one day before he was killed leading his patrol in Phu Yen Province.

Major Anthony Rodney Bellamy
Born 1/30/40
Died 5/5/68
Enlisted from Boise
Army
Married

Went to Vietnam 10/26/67. Born in Nampa, Idaho, Anthony graduated from Boise High School in 1957, and the University of Idaho in 1961. He had been in the service for six years, and was serving as a senior military advisor to the South Vietnamese with the 6th Armored Calvary in Mekong Delta. He was killed during the Tet Offensive.

Private First Class Bruce Rolland Bennett
Born 1/29/47
Died 9/5/66
Enlisted from Boise
Marines—1st. Battalion, 5th Marines, 1st. Marine Div.

> Went to Vietnam Feb. 1966. Originally from Boise, Idaho, Bruce graduated from South High School, Salt Lake City, Utah in 1965. He was killed in the vicinity of Tam Ky, Quang Tin Province.

1st. Lt. Johnny William Benton
Born 5/14/47
Died 11/25/68
Enlisted from Jerome
Army

> Went to Vietnam 10/21/68. He graduated from Jerome High School in 1965 and spent one year at Idaho State University. After two years of service in the Army, Johnny was a crewman in a helicopter that crashed in Binh Duong Province.

Capt. Gary W. Bitton
Born 6/28/36
Died 12/6/63
Enlisted from Blackfoot
Air Force

> Went to Vietnam Nov.1963. Gary graduated from Blackfoot High School in 1954 and Brigham Young University in 1958. In Vietnam he was a pilot of a B-26. He and his crew bailed out of their plane after it was hit by enemy fire. Gary died trying to fight the currents of the Mekong River, south of Saigon.
> He had been in the country 21days.

Cpl. William Darwin Blenkinsop
Born 6/26/51
Died 8/29/70
Enlisted from Couer D' Alene
Army—173 Airborne Brigade

> Went to Vietnam 7/16/70. William died from wounds caused by an explosive device in Binh Dinh Province.

Not Available

Major Jon Keith Bodahl
MIA/POW
Born 12/18/37
MIA 9/12/69
Listed as Killed in action 5/30/74
Enlisted from Boise
Air Force—34th Tactical Fighter Squad

Jon graduated from Nampa High School in 1955 and the University of Idaho in 1960. He enlisted in August, 1967, and was an F4 pilot with the 34th Tactical Fighter Squad. Jon was assisting with a rescue mission of two downed crewmen, when his plane was hit by ground fire, approximately five miles southwest of Ban Phan Hop, Laos. He had flown 254 previous missions during a seven month period.

Sgt. Edward James Boggess
Born 6/29/46
Died 12/29/68
Enlisted from Lewiston
Army—A Co. 1st. Bat, 6th Inf. American Div. 11th Light Inf. Brigade

Went to Vietnam 2/9/68. Born in Hermiston, Oregon, Edward attended school in Lewiston, Idaho. He was killed while leading a reconnaissance patrol in the vicinity of Chu Lai, Quang Tin Province. He had five weeks left of his tour of duty in Vietnam.

Capt. Curtis Richard Bohlscheid
MIA/POW
Born 12/9/36
MIA 6/11/67
Enlisted from Pocatello
Marines
Married

Went to Vietnam 6/11/67—Was serving his 2nd tour of duty in Vietnam Curtis graduated from Pocatello High School and University of Idaho in 1959. He had served a total of eight years in the armed forces. Curtis and twelve men aboard a CH46 helicopter crashed and burned near the south border of the DMZ in the vicinity of Quang Tri Province. Aerial reconnaissance revealed the helicopter was disintegrated by fire. U.S. soldiers were not able to reach the crash site because the enemy drove them back.

Cpl. Jess Burton Boicourt, Jr. (Nickname—Rusty)
Born 10/23/45
Died 3/11/68
Enlisted from Nampa
Marines

Went to Vietnam 3/26/67. Rusty graduated from St. Paul North High School and attended the University of Idaho for two years. While serving as a forward observer, he was killed by mortar fragments near Khe Sahn, in Quang Tri Province. He had two weeks left of his duty in Vietnam.

Sp 4 Gary Ray Boushele
Born 9/16/47
Died 10/27/69
Enlisted from Hailey
Army—Co. A, 4th Bat. 21st. Infantry, 11th Infantry Brigade

Went to Vietnam 4/25/69. A graduate of Hailey High School. Gary was a reconnaissance sergeant in Vietnam. According to his Captain, Gary had "unnerving accuracy in the call and adjustments of artillery," which saved the lives of countless men. He was killed during an ambush north of Sa Huynh City, in Quang Ngai Province. American Legion Post 141, Bellevue, Idaho is named in his honor.

Capt. Bruce Gregory Bowles
Born 7/2/41
Died 1/15/69
Enlisted from Boise
Army—1st. Battalion, 14th Artillery
Married

Went to Vietnam 10/24/68. Born in Emmett, Idaho, Bruce graduated from Boise High School in 1960. He also graduated from the Frankfurt Branch of the University of Maryland in Germany and was an Officers Candidate graduate. Bruce was a passenger in a helicopter that crashed and burned after being hit by enemy fire in Quang Ngai Province.

Cpl. John Alex Boyle
Born 2/15/50
Died 1/26/69
Enlisted from Idaho Falls
Army—25th Infantry Div.

Went to Vietnam 12/7/68. John was born in Twin Falls and graduated from Skyline High School in Idaho Falls in 1968. He was an only child and died from small arms fire in Hua Nghia Province.

Ray Eugene Bradley
Born 9/12/36
Died 2/16/67
Enlisted from Boise
Army
Married

Went to Vietnam 8/1/66. Born in Houston, Texas. Ray had served twelve years in the military. He died while serving as a helicopter pilot in Vietnam, when his helicopter struck a power line and crashed.

Cpl. Everett W. (Billy) Brauburger
Born 1/22/49
Died 7/24/69
Enlisted from Soda Springs
Army—Americal Div. Co. A

Went to Vietnam 1/11/69. Born in Wendell, Idaho. Billy attended Soda Springs High School. He was killed near Quang Ngai.

Major Harry Milton Brenn
Born 4/28/33
Died 4/13/67
Enlisted from Moscow
Air Force
Married

A graduate of the University of Idaho. Harry served in the Armed Services for ten years. He was flying a C-131 plane that crashed in the South China Sea. Two men survived, but Harry and six others were killed. He was stationed in the Khanh Hoa Province, and had recently received the Distinguished Flying Cross Medal.

Sgt. Leonard Lee Broenneke
Born 6/21/50
Died 6/14/71
Enlisted from Moscow
Army—Co. D, 2nd Bat. 1st Cavalry Div. Airmobile

Went to Vietnam 7/14/70. Leonard graduated from Moscow High School in 1968. While attempting to drag a wounded companion to safety, he was killed on a reconnaissance mission in Long Khanh Province. He died one month before his tour of duty in Vietnam would have been completed.

Sp 4 Randy K Bronson
Born 1/6/49
Died 5/13/69
Enlisted from Meridian
Army—Co. A, 2nd. Bat. 9th Infantry Div.

Went to Vietnam 9/25/68. Born in Burley, Idaho. Randy graduated from Meridian High School in 1968. He was killed by mortar shells while running from his bunker to take his position at the fire base Dong Tam, in the Dihn Tuong Province.

Sp4 Arlo Frank Brown
Born 5/13/44
Died 1/14/67
Enlisted from Idaho Falls
Army—193rd Engineers Co, 4th Battalion

Went to Vietnam 1/17/66. A 1962 graduate of Ririe High School, Arlo entered the army in April 1965. He was killed in an oil tank explosion at Bien Hoa—seventeen miles from Saigon. His tour of duty in Vietnam would have ended in two weeks.

2nd Lt. Michael Brown
Born 8/25/43
Died 3/7/69
Enlisted from Fremont County
Army—116th Engineers (National Guard Unit)
Married

Went to Vietnam 9/19/68. Michael graduated from South Fremont High School in 1961, When his camp came under heavy fire, the base commander radioed for assistance, U.S. artillery over shot the enemy, hitting Michael's camp and mortally wounding him in Lam Dong Province. His second child was born six weeks after his death.

Not Available

Sgt. Ivan J. Broyles
Born 11/22/38
Died 4/21/66
Enlisted from Blackfoot
Army

Went to Vietnam 1/14/66. Ivan had been living in Long Beach, California before leaving for Vietnam. He had been in the service for eight years.

Capt. Robert Newton Brumet
Born 10/22/27
Died 4/9/64
Enlisted from Plymouth
Air Force
Married

Robert joined the Marines in 1945, and the Air Force in 1947. He had served in the armed forces for fourteen years. He was flying a prop plane, that crashed in Military Reg. 4 in South Vietnam, killing him and a Vietnamese soldier. The cause of the crash was never established.

Sgt. William Bunch
Born 10/13/46
Died 12/28/69
Enlisted from Ahsahka
Marines
Married

Went to Vietnam 3/27/69. William was born in Fairview, New Mexico and graduated from Lancaster High School, Lancaster, California. He joined the service
in Feb. 1966, and served as a jet mechanic. He was killed in a crash of a C117
plane, approximately ten miles from its landing site in the Quang Tin Province
southwest of Chu Lai. He was TDY to the squadron of planes that were used in
the film "Toro,Toro,Toro"

Sp5 William R. Burt, Jr.
Born 9/21/44
Died 7/11/69
Enlisted from Hailey
Army

Went to Vietnam 11/28/68. The only son in his family, William was raised in
Bronxville, New York. He graduated from Bronxville High School in 1962 and
the University of Idaho in 1966. His training also included courses in Paris and
the University of Guadalahara, Mexico. William was killed by a piece of base
plate of an artillery casing from his own battery unit in Long An Province.
He died five days before his unit was being removed to Hawaii

Sgt. Richard Buck Carlson
Born 2/22/44
Died 11/4/66
Enlisted from Twin Falls
Army—25th Infantry
Married

Not Available

Went to Vietnam 1/7/66. Richard was in the armed forces for three years before
being killed by small arms fire.

Not Available

Sgt. Clyde Robert Carrico
Born 8/15/48
Died 12/19/60
Enlisted from Orofino
Army—1st. Infantry Div.
Clyde went to Vietnam 2/4/69 and died in Binh Long Province.

Sgt. Chad Leonard Carson
Born 12/14/49
Died 12/10/69
Enlisted from Boise
Army—164th Aviation Grp. 1st Aviation Bat.121st. Assault Helicopter Co
Went to Vietnam 6/4/69. Born in Denver, Colorado, Chad attended schools in the Dominican Republic of Bolivia. In Vietnam he was a crew chief for repairs on the Huey Helicopter. He became ill of a "fever of unknown origin" and was transferred to the hospital in Japan where he died three days later. He was four days short of being 20 years old.

Private First Class Robert Stanley Chambers
Born 3/24/48
Died 11/24/67
Enlisted from Potlatch
Army—1st. Infantry Div
Went to Vietnam 10/27/67. Robert was killed by small firearm in Binh Long Province.

Cpl. Johnny Howard Chapman
Born 2/15/52
Died 8/20/71
Enlisted from Boise
Army—Co. L, 75th Infantry (Rangers)
Went to Vietnam 7/19/71. Johnny was born at Fort Jackson, South Carolina. There were 120 Rangers stationed in Vietnam, and on Johnny's arrival he was one of three picked to join the group. After a 31-day trial period he would have worn the "Black Beret." Johnny volunteered for a rescue mission of a downed team, and was killed by the enemy as he ran from the helicopter.

AX2 David Roger Chatterton
Born 3/29/38
Died 7/18/67
Enlisted from Twin Falls
Navy

Born in Buhl. David graduated from Twin Falls High School in 1956 and was stationed on board the USS Hornet. On July 18, he volunteered to go inland on a helicopter rescue mission to pick up a downed pilot. The mission was accomplished, but the helicopter was fired upon and David was mortally wounded in the chest. The rescue mission took place in North Vietnam.

Capt. David Edward Cinkosky
Born 9/9/45
Died 8/5/71
Enlisted from Post Falls
Army—4th Platoon, 219 Aviation Co.

David went to Vietnam 5/30/70, and was on his 2nd tour of duty. David was a 0-1 Bird Dog pilot on a visual and photo reconnaissance mission when he was killed in action. The pilot of a second aircraft, witnessed the battle and reported 50 North Vietnam soldiers also lost their lives that day.

Sgt. Conn Kay Clark
Born 12/28/46
Died 7/31/69
Enlisted from Rigby
Army—116th Engineers (National Guard Unit)
Married

Went to Vietnam 9/19/68. Born in Idaho Falls, Idaho. Conn graduated from Rigby High School and was married one month before his deployment to Vietnam. On July 24, 1969, the truck he was riding in hit an enemy land mine in the Lam Dong Province. His brother was also in Vietnam and rushed to his side within an hour. Conn was transferred to a hospital in Japan where he later died. He had one month of his tour of duty left in Vietnam

Cpl. Grant LeRoy Clark
Born 9/21/45
Died 10/30/65
Enlisted from Pocatello
Marines

Went to Vietnam July 1965. Born in Pocatello, the 1963 graduate of Pocatello High School had been in the Marines for two years. Grant was with a ground surveillance radar unit that was sent to remote areas. He was killed by mortar fire while fighting near Da Nang, in Quang Nam Province. He was Pocatello's first war casualty.

1st. Lt. James Bradley Claybaugh
Born 11/20/43
Died 3/29/69
Enlisted from Caldwell
Army—Co. D, 3rd. Bat. 1st Infantry, 11th Infantry Brigade

Went to Vietnam 1/1/69. James graduated from Caldwell High School in 1962 and also attended the University of Idaho and Boise State College. He had served in the Army for two years and also attended Officers Candidate School. James was killed by small arms fire in Quang Ngai Province.

Not Available

Lance Cpl. Larry Dale Coats
Born 8/1/48
Died 9/3/68
Enlisted from Twin Falls
Marines

Went to Vietnam 12/9/67. Born in Wendell, Idaho, Larry graduated from Twin Falls High school in 1966, and also attended College of Southern Idaho. He died from malaria in DaNang, in the Quang Nam Province.

Cpl. Clyde Ralph Coburn
Born 7/10/47
Died 12/9/67
Enlisted from Preston
Army—1st. Cavalry Division

Went to Vietnam 10/6/67. A 1965 graduate of Preston High School , Clyde also attended Utah State University. In Vietnam he was a machine gunner. While on a patrol near Phan Thiet, in Binh Thuan Province, his company came under intense enemy fire. Clyde continually exposed himself, and succeeded in destroying an enemy emplacement. He was moving to draw fire away from his comrades at the time of his death.

Capt. Ralph Brent Cordon
Born 9/27/42
Died 5/2/71
Enlisted from Idaho Falls
Army—188th Engineer Battalion

Went to Vietnam 7/9/70. A native of Idaho Falls, Idaho, Ralph had served with the 116th National Guard unit, before joining the Army. He and seven other soldiers died when a land mine exploded in Quang Nam Province. He had six weeks left of his tour of duty in Vietnam.

Sp 4 Jess William Creason, Jr.
Born 7/23/47
Died 4/26/68
Enlisted from Cascade
Army

Went to Vietnam 10/29/67. Born and raised in Cascade, Jess was a graduate of Cascade High School. In Vietnam he served as a helicopter gunner. Jess was listed as MIA. It was ten days after the crash before the helicopter with the crew still aboard was found. All the men were dead. Cascade High School established an athletic memorial fund in Jess's honor, and a memorial bearing his name was built by the Cascade American Legion.

Not Available

Private First Class Michael Lee Crouson
Born 12/6/44
Died 12/10/66
Enlisted from Pocatello
Marines—Co.C, Marine 3rd Bat. 3rd Marine Div.
Married

> Went to Vietnam Oct. 1966. Michael graduated from Pocatello High School in 1962 and attended Idaho State University. He had two brothers who also served in the Marines. Michael was a machine gun team leader in Vietnam. He was killed from fragmentation wounds that occurred while on patrol near Quang Tri. He had turned 22 years old four days earlier.

S.Sgt. Clyde Arthur Crow
Born 6/23/40
Died 5/19/66
Enlisted from Boise
Air Force

> Clyde had served in the armed forces for eight years. He was killed in a plane crashed just outside Vietnam

Sp4 David Lee Curtis
Born 6/15/51
Died 6/17/71
Enlisted from Weippe
Army—1st. Aviation BDE

> Went to Vietnam 7/4/70. Born in Grangeville. David attended High School in Weippe and Orofino and received his diploma in the service. In Vietnam he was a helicopter electronic maintenance man. He died from drowning in the Quang Nam Province.

BM1 E6 James Marvin Curtis
Born 3/21/35
Died 11/15/68
Enlisted from Hagerman
Navy

> Went to Vietnam 9/28/67. James had been in the armed forces for fourteen years. He was killed by an explosive device in Kien Hoa.

Sp4 LeRoy Edward Damiano
Born 9/30/47
Died 2/12/68
Enlisted from Harrison
Army—25th Infantry Div.

 LeRoy graduated from Kootenai High School in 1965. He died on a reconnaissance mission near the village of Ap Ben Do, in Hua Nghia Province. LeRoy was purposely drawing enemy fire, enabling the rest of his platoon to successfully over run an enemy position. A scholarship fund in his name was established at Kootenai High School.

Private First Class Elmo Lee DeFord
Born 6/1/47
Died 5/2/66
Enlisted from Hansen
Army—3rd Brigade Task Force, 25th Infantry Div.

 Went to Vietnam 12/31/65. Elmo was born in Montpelier and attended schools in Hansen and Wendell. He completed his high school diploma by taking night courses. In Vietnam he was a mechanic on track vehicles. When his base near Pleiku came under attack, Elmo was fatally wounded by hand thrown enemy grenades.

Lance Cpl. Larry D. Defilippis
Born 8/3/46
Died 11/12/66
Enlisted from Idaho Falls
Marines—106mm Recoilless Rifle Platoon, Co. I Battalion

 Went to Vietnam Feb. 1966. He attended school in Idaho Falls before moving to California and moved back to Idaho Falls in 1964. Larry was killed by fragmentation wounds from a hostile explosive device in the vicinity of Da Nang, in Quang Nam Province.

Not Available

SFC Richard Lester Dennis
Born 4/3/29
Died 12/8/67
Enlisted from Smelterville
Army
Married
> Went to Vietnam 12/12/66. Had served in the armed forces for twenty years
> He was killed in a vehicle crash in Binh Dinh Province.

Warrant Officer Thomas LaMont Dives
Born 3/27/48
Died 8/2/69
Enlisted from Malad
Army—101st. Airborne Div.
Married
> Went to Vietnam 5/26/69. Monte was born in Malad and spent most of his life
> there. He graduated from High School in California in 1966.
> In Vietnam he was stationed at at Phu Bai and served as a pilot instructor for
> large twin rotor cargo helicopters. He was killed when his helicopter collided
> with an observation plane near Tam Ky, in the Quang Nam Province.

1st. Lt. Jack LeRoy Dodson (Nickname Butch)
Born 2/14/38
Died 5/26/67
Enlisted from Kimberly
Army—191st. Assault Helicopter Co.
Married
> Went to Vietnam 5/22/67. Born in Twin Falls, Butch graduated from Kimberly
> High School in 1956 and attended the University of Idaho. He served in the
> Army for three years. Butch had been in Vietnam four days when the helicop-
> ter he was riding in crashed and burned on a combat mission.

Sp5 Lyle Eugene Drown
Born 10/21/47
Died 4/15/69
Enlisted from Kimberly
Army—1st. Logic Command

Went to Vietnam 1/22/68

The Twin Falls native graduated from Kimberly High School in 1966 and attended College of Southern Idaho. Lyle had already served thirteen months in Vietnam, and had just returned after a thirty day leave at home. He died from fragmentation wounds in Tay Ninh Province.

Sp4 Michael Lee Earp
Born 1/22/48
Died 6/18/69
Enlisted from Grangeville
Army—116th Engineers (National Guard Unit) Co. D

Went to Vietnam 9/19/68. Michael had been in the service for two years. He was killed by enemy small arms fire, while his company was constructing a 120 mile road from Da Lat to Saigon, in the Lam Dong Province.

Private First Class Donald Lee Eldridge
Born 8/20/47
Died 9/27/68
Enlisted from Emmett
Army—1st. Logic Command

Not Available

Went to Vietnam 6/20/68. The only information available is that Donald drowned in Vinh Long Province.

Sgt. Louis Craig Emery
Born 9/27/50
Died 3/16/70
Enlisted from Parma
Army—Co. C, 4th Bat. 23rd Inf. 25th Inf. Div.

Went to Vietnam 7/9/69. A 1968 graduated of Parma High School, Craig also attended Boise State College. Craig exposed himself to a hail of enemy fire when he got out of the hatch of his armored personnel carrier in order to see where he was driving. He was mortally wounded near Nui Ba Den, Tay Ninh Province.

Private First Class Franklin David Endicott
Born 11/28/46
Died 9/4/67
Enlisted from Boise
Marine

The only information available indicates Franklin was mortally wounded in a ground battle in Quang Nam Province.

Sgt. Steven Glenn England
Born 7/5/51
Died 2/15/71
Enlisted from Pocatello
Army—75th Infantry, 101st. Airborne Div.

Went to Vietnam 8/19/70. Born and raised in Pocatello, Steven graduated from Pocatello High School in 1969. Serving as a medic, Steven volunteered for an evacuation of a wounded soldier of a reconnaissance team. He knew the night extraction would be dangerous due to the location and high winds from a monsoon storm. Steven's crew had successfully picked up the wounded soldier when their helicopter was shot down by enemy fire. All seven on board were killed.

Lance Cpl. Jerry Duane Estes
Born 1/18/45
Died 2/6/66
Enlisted from Boise
Marines—Co. C 1st. Bat, 1st. Marines, 3rd Marine Div.

Born in Kenrich, Idaho, Jerry graduated from Boise High School in 1959.
He joined the Marines in 1963. Jerry was with the first machine gun squad of a weapons platoon. On a night patrol near Da Nang, he was walking in front of the unit when a mine exploded. He was mortally wounded.

Sp4 Gary Gene Evans
Born 12/22/46
Died 6/13/68
Enlisted from Heyburn
Army—1st. Cav. Div. (AMBL)

Went to Vietnam 11/7/67. Gary was born in Twin Falls and attended school at Minico High School. He was the crew chief of a helicopter that was shot down near A Sraun Valley in Thua Thien Province.

Private First Class David Acel Fairchild
Born 5/24/45
Died 2/2/66
Enlisted from Buhl
Army—Co. C 1st. Calvary Co. 4th Platoon of 1st. Calvary Div.

Went to Vietnam 12/19/65. David was born in Twin Falls and graduated from Buhl High School in 1963. In the country only two months, the twenty-year-old was wounded from enemy fire while on patrol near AnKhe. He died the following day.

Private First Class Raymond Patrick Finley
Born 9/15/47
Died 10/1/67
Enlisted from St. Maries
Marine

Went to Vietnam Aug. 1967. Raymond graduated from St. Maries High School in 1966. Following in his brothers' footsetps, he joined the Marines in November of the same year. A full-blood Falthead Indian, he served as a medicine man for the CDA Indian tribe and frequently performed dance ceremonies in full Indian costume. Raymond was killed in Quang Nam Province in Vietnam. A memorial was built in his honor in Desmet, Idaho

Lance Cpl. Winfield Scott Flint
Born 4/18/48
Died 5/14/67
Enlisted from Payette
Marines

Not Available

The only information available is that Winfield died of wounds from an explosive device, in the Quang Tri Province.

Cpl. Francisco John Flores
Born 9/12/45
Died 5/21/67
Enlisted from Parma
Marines

Went to Vietnam April 1966. Francisco attended grade school and junior high school in Nyssa, Oregon. His teenage years were spent working in the fields with his father. In Vietnam Francisco served as a platoon squad leader. He was killed as he stepped into a clearing during a battle with the enemy. Francisco had been wounded two other times. The Nampa, Idaho Marine Corp. League detachment has been named in his honor.

Cpl. Thomas Allen Foreman
Born 3/25/48
Died 1/20/69
Enlisted from Caldwell
Army—1st. Calvary Div. (AMBL)
Married

Went to Vietnam 10/20/68. Thomas graduated from Caldwell High School in 1966 and attended Boise State College for one year. He was killed by small arms firing in Tay Ninh. His wife delivered a son one month after his death.

Cpl. Gary Jack Foster
Born 4/14/45
Died 6/4/66
Enlisted from Boise
Marines—1st. Anti Tank Bat. 1st. Marine Div.

Went to Vietnam April 1966. Gary was born in Boise and graduated from Boise High School in 1964. He was providing night security at Chu Lai Combat Base, in Quang Tin Province, when he was mortally wounded by an explosion.

Private First Class Gary Virgil Frazier
Born 11/10/47
Died 3/2/68
Enlisted from Pocatello
Army—25th Infantry, Reg. of the 9th Inf. Div.

Went to Vietnam 12/9/67. Gary was born in Pocatello and graduated from Pocatello High School in 1965. While on a night patrol in Gia Dinh Providence, he was mortally wounded from enemy fire.

ETN2 Thomas George Funke
Born 3/29/43
Died 11/1/68
Enlisted from Coeur D'Alene
Navy

> Went to Vietnam 9/21/68. Thomas had served in the armed forces for four years and was killed by an explosive device in Go Cong Province.

Private First Class Garry Lee Gabriel
Born 3/3/49
Died 12/27/67
Enlisted from Boise
Marine

> Went to Vietnam 12/19/67. Garry was born in Pocasset, Oklahoma. He died from fragmentation wounds received in Quang Tri Province.

Sp4 Albaro Quezada Garcia
Born 2/19/49
Died 6/24/70
Enlisted from Nampa
Army—Co. C 5th Bat. 3rd Brigade, 9th Inf. Div.

> Went to Vietnam 2/5/70. Albaro was born in Juarez, Mexico and graduated from high school while serving with the Job Corp. in New Jersey. He also attended Boise State College. Albaro was serving as point man when he was seriously wounded while on patrol. Ignoring his wounds, he placed effective enemy fire until reinforcements could arrive. He died the following day.

S.Sgt. Mervin (Dennis) Golden
Born 9/12/44
Died 6/9/68
Enlisted from McCall
Army—Detachment A-246, 5th Special Forces (Airborne) 1st. Special Forces

Went to Vietnam 1/6/67. Dennis was born in Boise and graduated from McCall Donnelly High School in 1962. He attended Brigham Young University and also Boise State College. He had been in the service for four years. Dennis had completed his first tour of duty in Vietnam and extended for another year. Stationed near Pleiku, he was serving as a military advisor to the Montagnards when he was fatally wounded by an accidental detonation of a hand grenade. Dennis' brother Mike was also serving his second tour in Vietnam and he escorted his brothers' body home.

Not Available

S.Sgt. Bruce Lynn Goodsell
Born 5/15/45
Died 1/6/71
Enlisted from Thatcher
Army—1st. Calvary Div. (AMBL)
Married

Went to Vietnam 8/23/70. The only information available is that Bruce was killed in Long Khanh Province.

Private First Class Robert Jerry Gordon
Born 7/25/49
Died 4/15/69
Enlisted from Hayden Lake
Marines—Co. K 3rd.Bat.5th Marine Reg. 1st. Marine Div.

Went to Vietnam 1/28/69. Robert attended schools in Hayden Lake and Coeur D'Alene. He was stationed at Quang Nam Province. Robert was on a search and clear operation, when he stepped on a mine and was fatally wounded. Hayden Lake has a memorial built in his honor.

2nd Lt. Ralph Shoup Gorton III
Born 11/26/42
Died 5/27/68
Enlisted from Boise
Marines—Co. D 1st. Bat. 3rd.Marines, 3rd. Marine Div.

Went to Vietnam 12/28/67. Was born in Soda Springs. Ralph graduated from Boise High School in 1961and attended the University of Idaho from 1961 to 1966. Ralph served as a rifle platoon commander in Quang Tri. His unit was pinned down by intense enemy fire, during an assault on the village of Phu Con. Ralph was maneuvering across the fire swept terrain to deploy his men and point squad, when he was killed by enemy fire.

Sp 4 Michael Frank Green
Born 1/23/47
Died 3/10/68
Enlisted from Pocatello
Army—61st. Assault Helicopter Co. 17th Aviation Bat. 1st. Aviation Brigade

Went to Vietnam 11/2/67. Michael was born in Pocatello and graduated from Pocatello High School in 1966. He enlisted in the Army 2/12/67 and served as a door gunner in Vietnam. He was killed aboard a helicopter that crashed in Khanh Hoa.

Capt. Robert Carrell Green
Born 10/10/43
Died 3/17/71
Enlisted from Donnelly
Army—1st. Aviation Brigade

Went to Vietnam 8/20/70. Born in Boise, Idaho, Robert graduated from McCall Donnelly High School in 1963. The University of Idaho graduate also attended Officers Candidate and Aviation School before going to Vietnam. Robert was returning to the base by helicopter following a mission over enemy territory. He was killed in a midair collision with an airplane.

Not Available

Private First Class Larry Dee Greenhalgh
Born 9/13/44
Died 3/17/69
Enlisted from St. Anthony
Army—199th Light Infantry Brigade

Went to Vietnam 10/18/68. Larry and his twin brother were born in Rexburg and graduated from St. Anthony High School in 1963. Larry was one of seventeen children. Eight of the eleven boys served in the armed forces. Larry was on a patrol when he stepped on a land mine, mortally wounding him at Naum Pen, near San Rang in the Gia Dinh Province.

ATR 3 Charles Clark Gregory
Born 8/20/47
Died 7/29/67
Enlisted from Montpelier
Navy

Went to Vietnam June 1967. Charles was born in Parryton, Texas and graduated from Montpelier High School in 1965. Charles was stationed aboard the USS Forrestal where he served as an aviation radar Tech. He was one of 128 men who died aboard the carrier when it was ravaged by fire in the Gulf of Tonkin, Vietnam.

Major William James Griffin
Born 12/18/34
Died 3/14/69
Enlisted from Homedale
Air Force
Married

William had been in the service for fourteen years. He was killed in an airplane crash in Quang Tri Prov.

S.Sgt. Donald Jack Haile
Born 10/12/38
Died 2/9/68
Enlisted from Caldwell
Army—Co. A 2nd Bat. 1st. Infantry, 196th Lt.Inf. Brigade

Went to Vietnam 11/25/67. Donald graduated from Caldwell High School in 1957 and entered the Army the same year. He was discharged in 1960 and re-enlisted in January 1962. The Sergeant served 13 months in Korea and then went to Vietnam. Donald was a platoon leader on patrol in the Quang Nam Province when his men where pinned down by heavy gunfire. He personally assaulted an enemy machine gun position and eliminated the hostile emplacement. His actions provided an opening into the enemy perimeter, but Donald was mortally wounded.

Private First Class Craig Hayes Hansen
Born 8/8/44
Died 6/20/69
Enlisted from Soda Springs
Army—Co. D 2nd Bat. 1st Calvary Div. (Airmobile)
Married

Went to Vietnam 5/10/69. Craig was born in Montpelier and graduated from Fielding High School in Paris, Idaho. He was attending Brigham Young University when he was drafted prior to his final semester before graduation. Craig was killed a month after his arrival in Vietnam during an attack on his Firebase (IKE) in Tay Ninh Province.

Lance Cpl. Robert Warren Hansen
Born 1/15/47
Died 5/10/69
Enlisted from Naples
Marine

Went to Vietnam 8/18/68. Robert graduated from Bonners Ferry High School in 1966 where he served as vice president of his senior class. He was killed by mortar fire in Vietnam in Quang Tri Province.

Sp.4 Eric Thomas Harshbarger
Born 11/13/49
Died 11/1/69
Enlisted from Filer
Army—D Troop (air) Cavalry, 1st Infantry Division

Went to Vietnam 12/7/68. Eric was born in Pretoria, Republic of South Africa and adopted by a U.S. Colonel and his wife. He graduated from Filer High School in 1968. Eric was a crew chief on a helicopter gun ship that was suppressing fire into a wooded area, in the Hua Nghia Province. When his gun became inoperative, Eric exposed himself outside the aircraft to clear the weapon. A mine below the helicopter detonated and mortally wounded Eric. He had one month of tour of duty left in Vietnam. Eric was buried in Arlington Cemetery on his 20th birthday.

Sp 4 Lonnie Hilton Hendrickson
Born 4/16/48
Died 4/3/69
Enlisted from Orofino
Army—116th Engineers (National Guard Unit)
Married

Went to Vietnam 9/12/68. Born in Rexburg, Idaho, Lonnie graduated from Orofino High School in 1966. He enlisted in the National Guard in 1967. He was killed in Vietnam by a land mine explosion in the Lam Dong Province. His wife was expecting a baby a month after his death.

Lance Cpl. William Barton Hepburn
Born 12/27/47
Died 8/23/66
Enlisted from Lewiston
Marines

Went to Vietnam Oct. 1965. William was born in Omaha, Washington and soon after moved to Lewiston, Idaho with his family. He attended Lewiston High School until he joined the Marines. William died from small arms fire at Da Nang in the Quang Nam Province.

Cpl. David Edwin Herbert
Born 5/16/40
Died 7/2/66
Army—1st. Infantry Div.

Went to Vietnam 3/1/66. David quit school the beginning of his senior year to go to work when his father became seriously ill. He was in the service for eight years before going to Vietnam. David was on a search and destroy operation near Loc Ninh Province, near the Cambodian border, when he was mortally wounded.

Private First Class Craig W. Hirschi
Born 7/29/49
Died 9/15/70
Enlisted from Rexburg
Marines

Went to Vietnam 8/8/70. Craig was born in Rexburg and attended schools in Sugar City, Idaho. He had been in country for one month, when he was fatally wounded by a grenade in Quang Nam Province. He was originally reported missing in action for eleven days before his body was finally recovered.

Private First Class Teddy Merlin Hodges, Jr.
Born 3/19/45
Died 6/6/69
Enlisted from Malta
Marines—Co. H, 2nd Bat. 3rd. Marines, 3rd. Marine Div.

Went to Vietnam 4/6/69. A native of Rexburg, Idaho, Teddy graduated from Raft River High School in Malta in 1964. He served as a radio operator in Vietnam. Teddy was mortally wounded by shrapnel from enemy fire, nine miles northwest of Cam Lo in Quang Tri Province.

Capt. Gregg Neyman Hollinger
MIA/POW
Born 5/9/42
MIA 12/14/71
Enlisted from Paul
Army—MACV Advisors Unit

Went to Vietnam 12/14/71 (second tour of duty). Gregg graduated from Minico High School in 1961 and the University of Idaho in 1965. He enlisted in the Army in 1965 and his first tour of duty in Vietnam was from 1967 to 1968 with 101st. Airborne. At the time of his death, Gregg was a logistic officer working with the South Vietnamese Army. His plane was returning from the DMZ zone when it was presumably lost in the China Sea, five minutes from DaNang. The crews bodies were never recovered.

Ensign Hal T. Hollingsworth
MIA/POW
Born 6/29/42
MIA 1/16/66
Enlisted from Grace
Navy

Hal was born in Preston, Idaho and graduated from Grace High School in 1961. He attended Utah State Agricultural College for two years. In 1964 he enlisted in the Navy and was trained in photographic reconnaissance. Hal was stationed aboard the USS Ranger (an attack aircraft carrier) His RASC Vigilante jet was on a routine night carrier landing flight when it missed an arresting cable on the carrier and plunged into the ocean. Neither the pilot or Hal's bodies were recovered.

Cpl. Sheldon Dale Hoskins
Born 5/12/48
Died 10/7/68
Enlisted from Blackfoot
Marines—Co. G, 2nd Bat. 5th Marines, 1st. Marine Div.

   Went to Vietnam 2/27/68. Sheldon and his twin sister were born in Blackfoot
   and he graduated from Snake River High School in 1966. The state wrestling
   champion was awarded a 4 year scholarship to Weber State College in Ogden,
   Utah, but declined it to enlist in the Marines. Sheldon had served in the
   Philippines with his older brother for five months when he volunteered for
   Vietnam in place of his married brother. In Vietnam Sheldon served as a squad
   leader in Quang Nam Province. While engaged in an enemy battle, he left his
   covered position and maneuvered 20 meters across fire swept terrain to reach
   a wounded comrade. He commenced firing on the enemy until he expended all
   of his ammunition. Sheldon was mortally wounded while reloading.

Cpl. Douglas G. Howes
Born 8/24/49
Died 3/16/70
Army—132nd Aviation Co. 14th Bat. 16th Combat Aviation Group

   Went to Vietnam 1/24/70. Douglas was originally from Roy, Utah. In Vietnam he
   was a crew member on a helicopter, that crashed in Quang Ngai Province. He
   had planned to wait until he had been in eight months to take the customary
   six month R & R, but he lived only three months.

M.Sgt. William Balt Hunt
MIA/POW
Born 7/31/35
MIA 11/4/66
Enlisted from Sandpoint
Army—CTZ Mike Force (Detachment A302) 5th Special Forces
Married

   Went to Vietnam 11/4/66. William originally enlisted in the service in 1953. In
   November of 1966, William was ten miles from Dau Tieng (northeast of Soui
   Da). He voluntarily left his aircraft to help reinforce troops on the ground. As
   the enemy threatened to overrun their dwindling ranks, William sent the patrol
   ahead and stayed behind to provide cover with a Nung (South Vietnamese) soldier.
   The Nung soldier reported William had died, but his body was never found.

Private First Class Jerry Antone Hurianek
Born 6/24/47
Died 6/27/69
Enlisted from Middleton
Marines—3rd. Marine Division

Went to Vietnam 2/23/69. Jerry was born in Ketchican, Alaska and graduated from Middleton High School in 1965. His mother had died when he was one year old and Jerry spent most of his growing up years in the home of a foster family. He attended Treasure Valley Community College in Ontario, Oregon and also Boise State College. Three days after his twenty-second birthday, he died from mortar wounds received at Quang Tri Province.

Sp 4 John Allen Hurst
Born 10/31/49
Died 1/7/70
Enlisted from Dubois
Army—Co.B, 2nd Bat. 18th Infantry, 1st. Inv.Div. (The Big Red One)

Went to Vietnam 12/10/69. Johnny was born in Idaho Falls and graduated from Dubois High School in 1968. He had been in country only one month when he was moved to a new Firebase (Colorado) in Tay Ninh Province. He died the following day in a land mine blast.

Private First Class Terry Floyd Huston
Born 1/2/47
Died 6/7/66
Enlisted from Caldwell
Army—Co. A, 2nd Bat. 502 Infantry, 1st. Brig. 101st Airborne Div.

Went to Vietnam 5/2/66. Terry was born in Nampa and graduated from Caldwell High School in 1965. During a combat mission near Dak To, his company was withdrawing from heavy ground fire. Terry remained behind to provide cover for his comrades while they withdrew to defensive positions. As he moved to join them he was fatally wounded.

Private First Class Elmer Glenn Ireland
Born 6/29/48
Died 7/1/69
Enlisted from Star
Army—Scout Dog Platoon—Attached to the 101st. Airborne

Went to Vietnam 1/13/69. Elmer graduated from Meridian High School in 1967. In Vietnam he served in a highly trained unit in Quang Ngai as a dog handler. Two days after his twenty-first birthday, he died from multiple fragmentation wounds.

Sp4 Lloyd Bruce Jensen
Born 3/14/43
Died 12/12/66
Enlisted from Boise
Army—Headquarter Co. 4th Engineers Bat.
Married

Went to Vietnam 7/7/66. The only information available indicates Lloyd died from an accidental fall from a military vehicle.

A3C/E2 Bob Jewett
Born 10/5/47
Died 4/28/67
Enlisted from Challis
Air Force

Went to Vietnam 3/24/67. Bob was born in Pocatello and graduated from Galt High School in Galt, Montana. He was killed during a mortar attack near DaNang, in the Quang Tri Province.

Private First Class Henry David Johnson
Born 12/8/48
Died 5/23/69
Enlisted from Nez Pierce
Marines

Went to Vietnam 2/27/69. David was a 1967 graduated of Lewiston High School. He was killed while on patrol near DaNang, in the Quang Nam Province. Henry had been wounded six weeks earlier, and had been back on active duty for only one week. His body was escorted home by a long time friend (Norman Eastman) who was also on active duty in Vietnam.

Cpl Brent R. Jones
Born 6/25/47
Died 5/21/68
Enlisted from Firth
Army—B Battery, 140th Artillery

Went to Vietnam 2/14/68. Brent was a twin who attended Firth High School and earned his GED while in the armed services. In Vietnam he served as a radio operator for a forward observation team. At the time of his death, he was stationed four miles south of the Ben Hai River that separated North and South Vietnam. The team was occupying an outpost to block enemy infiltration when Brent died in the explosion of an American ammunition sight.

Lance Cpl. David Samuel Jones
Born 8/29/49
Died 1/4/70
Enlisted from Fernwood
Marines

Went to Vietnam 3/12/69. David graduated from St. Maries High School in 1968 where he was active in wrestling and football, and voted as having the "Most School Spirit." The only information available indicates he was killed by an explosive device in Quang Nam Province.

Lance Cpl. Howard Lemuel Jones, Jr.
Born 3/4/48
Died 2/24/68
Enlisted from Post Falls
Marines—3rd. Marine, Div. 26, LSU Detachment

Went to Vietnam 7/7/67. Howard was killed two weeks before his twentieth birthday by mortar fire in Thua Thien.

CWO Tommy L. Kearsley
Born 7/1/47
Died 5/4/70
Enlisted from Buhl
Army—101st. Airborne (Airmobile)

Went to Vietnam 5/21/69. Tommy was born in Portland, Oregon and graduated from Buhl High School in 1965. Tommy was a helicopter pilot stationed at Phu-Bai. One week before the end of his tour of duty, he was on a night mission dropping flares to help defend American ground troops. During the fateful mission in Thua Thien, Province, a midair collision took his life.

1st. Lt. Kay Kazu Kimura
Born 11/1/43
Died 3/7/70
Enlisted from Nampa
Marines—Support of 1st. Marine Div.

Went to Vietnam 1/8/70. Kay was born in a Relocation Camp in Poston, Arizona during World War II. He graduated from Nampa High School in 1962 and attended Idaho State University and Treasure Valley Community College on a football scholarship. In Vietnam, Kay was a co-pilot of a CH46D Sea Knight helicopter. He was flying in support of the 1st Marine Division when his helicopter crashed in the coastal waters five miles from land in Thua Thien Province.

Cpl. Rodger Magnus Koefod (nickname—Rod)
Born 7/7/48
Died 4/27/69
Enlisted from Moscow
Army—173rd. Airborne Div.

Went to Vietnam 6/23/68. Rod graduated from Moscow High School in 1966. His reconnaissance team base camp was bordered on one side by the Bang Son River and the other side by rice paddies. He died from fragmentation wounds received in Binh Dinh Providence.

1st. Lt. Colin Edward Lamb
Born 2/11/42
Died 7/3/68
Enlisted from Caldwell
Army—1st. bat. 11th Artillery, 9th Inf. Div. at Headquarters and service Battery

Went to Vietnam 12/5/67. Graduated from Caldwell High School in 1960. Colin was flying a helicopter on a command and control mission with the Battalion Commander when it was hit by enemy fire. The aircraft crashed into the Song Vam Co Dong River, three miles from Ben Luc in Long An, Province. A memorial park in Vietnam was named in his memory.

Not Available

Cpl. Robert Wilbur Larison
Born 12/17/48
Died 11/1/67
Enlisted from Pocatello
Army—25th Infantry Div.
Married

Went to Vietnam 8/23/67. The only information available indicates Robert was killed by explosive device in Hua Nghia, Province.

Sgt. Dale K. Larson
Born 10/24/47
Died 11/12/68
Enlisted from Burley
Army—1st. Air Cavalry Div.

Went to Vietnam 7/18/68

The Burley native graduated from Burley High school in 1966 and was attending Ricks College in Rexburg when he was drafted. Stationed in Binh Duong Province in Vietnam, Dale was serving as a helicopter crew chief and door gunner. The helicopter he was riding in collided midair with another huey and crashed into the mine field surrounding the base camp, killing all onboard. During Dale's four months in country, he had been on fifty combat missions.

Private First Class John Gilbert Larson
Born 9/12/47
Died 12/30/66
Enlisted from Blackfoot
Army—Co. C, 1st. Bat (airborne) 1st. Cav. (AMBL)

Went to Vietnam 8/17/66. John was born in Blackfoot, Idaho and grew up in the Moreland Area. He served as a medic in Vietnam. During an air assault on his company he made several trips into heavy gunfire to treat and evacuate the wounded. When the medic from another platoon was killed, John provided assistance to both units. A close friend of John's was hit by enemy fire and John raced forward; shielding his friend with his own body while trying to revive him. He was mortally wounded.

AX3-E4 Delmar Leon Lawrence
Born 1/6/46
Died 4/1/68
Enlisted from Riggins
Navy
Married

Went to Vietnam in 1967. Delmar had served for four years in the armed services and was a sonar operator. While on an aerial surveillance patrol (that sent messages directly to Washington D. C.) his plane was shot down in the Gulf of Thailand by a Cambodian naval vessel. He was the father of two young daughters.

Major William E. Lemmons
Born 1/12/42
POW/MIA
Declared as Killed in Action 6/12/78
Enlisted from Pocatello
Army—196th Lt. Infantry Brig. Brigade Aviation Detachment

Went to Vietnam June 1967. A native of Burley, Idaho, William graduated from Pocatello High School in 1960 and Idaho State University in 1965. In Vietnam, William was an H-23 helicopter pilot. On a return flight to the Chu Lai Base, he radioed that he was ten miles south. William was never heard from again. Officials speculated that the experienced pilot may have hit a strange wind sheer and crashed in the river. The wreckage or Bill's remains were never found. A classroom at Idaho State University is named in his honor.

Not Available

Private First Class Robert R. Lewis
Born 10/14/47
Died 5/31/69
Enlisted from Boise
Army—1st. Infantry Div.

Went to Vietnam 12/13/68. The only available information indicates Robert was originally from Modesto, California. He died from injuries in a vehicle crash in Long Khanh Province.

Sp4 Gilbert Ray Lish
Born 11/30/47
Died 1/2/68
Enlisted from Boise
Army—Co. D 68th Engineers Bat. 20th Eng. Brigade
Married

Went to Vietnam 9/1/67. Ray had been driving dump truck at Vihn Long Airfield, but he volunteered to help defend the base when it came under enemy attack. He was mortally wounded while trying to relieve two soldiers pinned down by enemy fire. Ray had been wounded two other times during his tour of duty in Vietnam.

Sp4 James John Lister
Born 5/13/47
Died 3/21/69
Enlisted from Burley
Army—Co. C 5th Bat. 46th Inf. with 198th Lt. Inf. Brigade Am I Div.

Went to Vietnam 9/23/68. Originally from Burley, Idaho, James graduated from Roosevelt High School in Utah in 1967 where he had moved for work as a teenager. He had just returned to action in Vietnam after a weeks R & R in Australia when he died on a routine patrol in Quang Ngai Province. A booby trap exploded near James, taking the twenty-one-year-old's life.

Sp4 James Alton Lockwood
Born 5/25/46
Died 9/17/66
Enlisted from Sandpoint
Army—1st. Brigade, 101st. Airborne Div.
Married

Went to Vietnam 7/26/66. James graduated from Sandpoint High School in 1964 and served in the armed forces for two years.He died from multiple fragmentation wounds at the age of twenty. James left a wife and daughter.

Cpl. Herman Augusta Lohman, Jr.
Born 1/24/48
Died 4/6/68
Enlisted from Twin Falls
Marines—3rd. Platoon, Golf 2/26

Herman graduated from Twin Falls High School in 1966 and served as a Cadet officer in the Civil Air Patrol. At the time of his death, he was on his second tour of duty in Vietnam and had spent eighteen months in country. While walking point for his squad on Hill 700, just outside the Khe Sanh Combat Base, Herman tripped a land mine and was mortally wounded.

Col. Herlihy Townsend Long
Born 3/15/24
Died 1/27/68
Enlisted from Mt. Home
Army
Married

Not Available

Went to Vietnam 8/7/67. Available information indicates Colonel Long was originally from Macon, Georgia. His military career extended over a twenty six year period before he was killed by artillery fire in Quang Tri Province.

Not Available

Not Available

John E. Lumbry
Enlisted from Caldwell, Idaho
Army
    No additional information is available.

Cpl Neile Cooper MacKay
Born 4/17/45
Died 1/10/70
Enlisted from Weiser
Army—101st. Airborne Div.
    Went to Vietnam 11/16/69. The only available information indicates Neile died of wounds received in small arms fire in Thua Thien Province.

Lance Cpl. Danny Joe Maggard
Born 12/14/49
Died 3/18/69
Enlisted from Parma
Marines
    Went to Vietnam 9/9/68. Danny died of wounds from small arms fire in Quang Nam Province. The twenty-year-old was in country six months.

Sp 4 Eddie D. Mapes
Born 1/18/51
Died 7/12/70
Enlisted from Kootenai
Army—196th Light Infantry Brigade
    Went to Vietnam 5/31/70. The only available information on Eddie indicates he died from an explosive device in Quang Tin Province.

Sp4 Clayton Arthur Martin
Born 1/12/44
Died 10/16/67
Enlisted from Idaho Falls
Army—Co.A, 2nd Bat.(Mech) 25th Infantry Div.
Married

Went to Vietnam 3/20/6. Clayton graduated from Burley High School in 1963 and Idaho State University in 1965. In Vietnam, Clayton was involved in a company sweep at the base of Nui Ba Den Mountain in Tay Ninh Province. When his platoon came under heavy fire, he went back to the armored personnel carrier for more ammunition. On the way he picked up his wounded squad leader. While placing him near the carrier for protection, Clayton was hit by shrapnel from an exploding grenade. He died six weeks later in a hospital in Japan.

Private First Class Richard Peter Massine
Born 11/21/45
Died 11/20/66
Enlisted from Kellogg
Army—Co. B 1st. Bn, 35th Infantry, 3rd Bde Task Force, 25th Inf. Div.
Married

Not Available

Went to Vietnam 7/7/66. Richard was a casualty of an enemy explosive device in South Vietnam.

L.Cdr. Roderick L. Mayer
MIA/POW
Born 3/2/39
MIA 10/17/65
Declared as Killed in Action—10/31/77
Enlisted from Lewiston
Air Force

Rod graduated from Lewiston High School in 1957 and the University of Idaho in 1961. Roderick was an F4 pilot stationed aboard the USS Independence, who had flown more than 70 missions. He was shot down over the Thai Nguyen Bridge near Hanoi and he and his co-pilot ejected and were taken prisoners. His co-pilot, Dave Wheat spent 7 1/2 years in prison and was released in 1973. There has been no word on the fate of Rod. A total of three planes from the carrier were lost at the same time

Sp 4 Steven Michael McArthur
Born 2/8/49
Died 4/28/68
Enlisted from Coeur D'Alene
Army—101st. Airborne

Went to Vietnam 11/17/67. Steven was born and raised in Coeur D'Alene where he boxed on the Jaycee's team and played football in high school. He also boxed while stationed at Fort Gordon, Georgia. In Vietnam, the nineteen-year-old died from multiple fragmentation wounds while serving in Thua Thien, Province near Hue.

Not Available

S.Sgt. Raymond Louis McCaslin
Born 4/8/37
Died 12/26/69
Enlisted from Boise
Marines

Went to Vietnam 12/18/69. Available information indicates Raymond had been in the service for fourteen years. He died from an explosive device in Quang Nam Province.

Private First Class Steven James McDonald
Born 6/20/51
Died 11/28/71
Enlisted from Ketchum
Army

Went to Vietnam 10/19/71. Steven was born in Spokane, Washington. He graduated from Santa Ana High School and attended Saddleback Jr. College in San Juan Capistrano, California. He enjoyed being with his family in Ketchum, Idaho before his deployment to Vietnam. Steven was "in country" only one month when he died with 32 other soldiers in a helicopter crash.

Cpl. Donald Smith McGinley
Born 3/31/28
Died 7/29/68
Enlisted from Rupert
Army—Serv. Bat.of the 6th & 8th Artillery, 1st. Field Force

Went to Vietnam 11/11/67. Donald was born in Albany, Missouri and spent his younger years in Rupert, Idaho. A veteran of the Korean War, he also served a tour of duty in Germany where he contracted tuberculosis. After a two year hospitalization, he worked in the Rupert area before re-enlisting in the Army in 1963. In Vietnam, Donald's battery flew soldiers into heavy battle areas. He succumbed in 1968 to a rare disease while stationed in Binh Dinh Province. He was the father of two.

Not Available

Capt. Donald Vernon McGregor
Born 12/22/33
Died 8/13/63
Enlisted from Paul
Army—51st. Infantry Battalion
Married

Born in Heyburn, Donald graduated from Paul High School in 1952 and the University of Utah in 1956. He joined the Idaho National Guard in 1951and the Army in 1956. He died from small arms fire in Quang Naigh, Province in Vietnam. The National Guard Armory in Minidoka, Idaho is named in his honor

Lance Cpl. Jay Darwin McLain
Born 2/7/42
Died 5/28/67
Enlisted from Bancroft
Marines

A former member of the "Caribou Mounted Posse," Darwin operated heavy equipment in Vietnam. He died from mortar fire in Quang Tin Province at the age of twenty-five.

Not Available

Not Available

Cpl. Michael Lee McMasters
Born 2/24/47
Died 6/27/69
Enlisted from Mt. Home
Marine—3 rd. Marine Div.

 Went to Vietnam 8/20/68. Michael was born in Plainsville, Ohio. He graduated from Mountain Home High School in 1965 and attended University of Utah for 2 1/2 years. He was killed by an explosive device in Quang Tri Province. At the time of his death, he had a brother serving in the Army in Vietnam and his father was in the service stationed on Guam Island.

HN Jim Carl McNamar
Born 9/16/45
Died 4/17/68
Enlisted from Mt. Home
Navy—with 3rd Marine Division

 Jim graduated from Mountain Home High School and attended Navy Hospital Corp. School before leaving for Vietnam. He died of fragmentation wounds to the head and body in Quang Tri Province. At the time of his death, he had a brother in the Army who was also serving in Vietnam. Jim's dad also lost his life while serving his country in the Korean War.

ATCS Franklin DeLano McNary
Born 2/24/34
Died 6/13/67
Enlisted from Coeur D'Alene
Navy
Married

 The only information available indicates Franklin was in the service for sixteen years. He died from a disease, off the shore of Vietnam (most likely on a hospital ship).

Col. Richard Joseph Meechan
Born 1/6/28
Died 6/15/72
Enlisted from Payette
Air Force—417th Tactical Fighter Squadron

Richard graduated from Payette High School in 1945 and the University of Portland, Oregon in 1949. Enlisting in 1950, he had served in the Korean War, and also served three tours in Vietnam. Richard was Squadron Commander of the F4 fighter bomber Squadron. He was on his way back to the US on a civilian aircraft (Cathay Pacific) when a bomb detonated, killing all eighty passengers and crew. The bomb had been placed onboard by the disgruntled lover of a fellow passenger. The crash occurred near Cheo Reo, in the Phu Bon Province. Richard had just been awarded the Distinguished Flying Cross from a dangerous bombing mission on 6/5/72.

Cpl. Steven Dee Merrell
Born 1/28/50
Died 5/15/70
Enlisted from Pocatello
Marines

Went to Vietnam 8/7/69. Steven graduated from Pocatello High School where he was active in National Honor Society. He joined the Marines at age 19 and graduated as "honor man" of the platoon. In Vietnam, her served as a radio man and interpreter. He helped build a school for the children. Steven died at the age of twenty from fragmentation wounds in Thua Thien, Province.

Lester G. Michels
Born 4/18/29
Died 3/21/66
Enlisted from Blackfoot
Marines
Married

Went to Vietnam 2/9/46. Lester was born in Hackensack, New Jersey. A veteran of the Korean War, he had served in the Marines for nineteen years. He moved his family to Blackfoot before leaving for Vietnam. Forty days after arriving in country, he was killed by small arms fire in Quang Ngai.

Not Available

Sp 4 Cecil Ray Millspaugh
Born 10/4/44
Died 3/26/68
Enlisted from Declo
Army—4th Infantry Division
Married

> Went to Vietnam 8/22/67. Cecil died from multiple fragmentation wounds received in Kontum.

Not Available

Sp 4 John E.S. Mitchell, Jr.
Born 2/12/51
Died 7/2/70
Enlisted from American Falls
Army—196th Light Brigade

> Went to Vietnam 5/2/70
> John was a Medic, serving with the 23rd. Medical Bat. At Fire Support Base Hawk Hill in Quang Tin Province. He had volunteered to go into the field with F troop 17th Cavalry, to replace three medics that had just been killed. While riding on an armored personnel carrier that hit a 500 pound land mine, John died with 13 of the 14 soldiers aboard.

Private First Class Lonnie Ray Mitchell
Born 10/5/47
Died 12/6/68
Enlisted from King Hill
Marines

> Went to Vietnam 8/26/68. Lonnie was born in Ontario, Oregon and graduated from Glenns Ferry High School in 1966. The twenty-one-year-old was killed by small arms fire in Quang Nam Province.

Not Available

Sp 4 Gary O Mooer
Born 3/15/45
Died 7/23/67
Army

> Went to Vietnam 9/15/66. The only information available indicates Gary enlisted from Madison County and was originally from Rosebud Montana. He died near Pleiku in Vietnam.

Sp 4 Dean L. Moon
Born 7/12/47
Died 3/19/69
Enlisted from Sterling
Army—Co.D, 3rd. Bat. 506th Infantry, 101st. Airborne Div.

Went to Vietnam 5/31/1968. A 1967 graduate of Aberdeen High School, Dean was stationed at Phan Thiet. As his company was patrolling along a river, he was killed instantly by an enemy sniper's bullet.

Michael James Mooney
Born 2/9/51
Died 8/10/69
Enlisted from Eagle
Marines—3rd Marine Division

Went to Vietnam 6/26/69. Eighteen-year-old Michael was born in Chicago, Illinois. In Vietnam he served as an ammunition man in the 81-millimeter mortar section, attached to E company stationed at Quang Tri. During an enemy attack, Michael was killed by mortar projectiles and grenades, that exploded nearby.

Lance Cpl. Dan Ross Moore
Born 8/31/48
Died 10/17/68
Enlisted from Idaho Falls
Marines

Went to Vietnam 6/12/68. Dan graduated from Idaho Falls High School in 1966 and served as a forward observer with naval gunfire section of the 101st Air Cavalry. He was killed in a helicopter crash in the ocean near Hue. While in country, he helped construct an orphanage for the many homeless children near Hue.

Private First Class William Ralph Morledge
Born 2/24/48
Died 9/20/68
Enlisted from Emmett
Army—1st. Infantry Division

Went to Vietnam 8/18/68. Before his tour of duty , William enjoyed rodeo bareback riding and bull riding. In country only three months, the twenty-year-old died at Bihn Duong.

Not Available

Sgt. Ronald Grant Mottishaw
Born 10/5/45
Died 2/16/67
Enlisted from Pocatello
Army—4th Infantry

Went to Vietnam 9/22/66. Ronald was a native of Pocatello, Idaho and was a 1963 graduate of Pocatello High School. He also attended Idaho State University. In Vietnam, Ronald served as a combat medic who transported the wounded. When his ambulance struck and detonated a land mine, he and his two passengers were mortally wounded.

1st. Lt. Lester Neal Moulton
Born 5/13/42
Died 5/25/70
Enlisted from Victor
Army—173rd Airborne Brigade
Married

Went to Vietnam 8/20/69. A native of Idaho Falls, Idaho, Neal graduated from Teton High School in 1960 and Brigham Young University in 1964. He served as a company commander in Vietnam and had met his father, wife and daughter in Hawaii on R & R. When his patrol came under fire at Bihn Dinh Province, two of Neal's men were wounded. He successfully rescued the first man but when he returned for the second soldier both men were killed by enemy fire.

Private First Class Danny L. Naillon
Born 10/1/46
Died 9/12/66
Enlisted from Payette
Army

Went to Vietnam 1/9/66. Available information indicates Danny had been in the Army for two years. His death in Vietnam was listed as a ground casualty.

Private First Class Jimmy D. Nakayama
Born 11/19/43
Died 11/17/65
Enlisted from Rigby
Army—1st. Cav. Division (AMBL)

Went to Vietnam 8/19/65. Jimmy graduated from Rigby High School and had been in the service for four years. He was one of 234 soldiers that died in three days of fighting at (Landing Zone) Xray and Albany in IaDrang, the "Valley of Death."

Sp 4 Robert William Nelson
Born 2/15/51
Died 9/29/70
Enlisted from Rigby
Army—1st. Cav. Division (AMBL)

Went to Vietnam 1/12/70. Robert was born in Montpelier, Idaho and graduated from Rigby High School in 1969. Serving as a door gunner on a OH6A helicopter, he died in a crash in Binh Duong Province at the age of nineteen.

Cpl. Steven Harold Nipp
Born 8/6/48
Died 2/8/69
Enlisted from Post Falls
Marines

Went to Vietnam 9/30/67. Steven was born in Coeur D'Alene, Idaho and graduated from Post Falls High School in 1966. He died from fragmentation wounds to the head , while on patrol outside of DaNang in Quang Ngai, Province.

Private First Class Mark James O'Brien
Born 9/27/47
Died 12/14/68
Enlisted from Tetonia
Marines

Went to Vietnam 11/9/68. A native of Driggs, Idaho, Mark graduated from Teton High School and studied auto mechanics at the Wyoming Technical Institute. He was drafted one month before completing the course. Mark had been stationed in Quang Nam Province for only one month when he was killed by enemy small arms fire.

Not Available

Not Available

Capt. Troy R. Oliver, Jr.
Born 10/10/36
Died 5/19/68
Enlisted from Boise
Marines
Married

Went to Vietnam 6/20/67. Troy was born in Twin Falls, Idaho and graduated from Boise High School in 1954. He had been in the service for fourteen years and served as the Provost Marshall on Westmoreland's staff. Troy later requested an assignment on the DMZ. While serving as a rifle company commander in Quang Tin Province, he was leading a unit of twelve men from Khe Sahn to the coast. The company was ambushed by the enemy and all thirteen men died.

Sgt. William Whitby Olsen
Born 8/26/47
Died 5/23/69
Enlisted from Pocatello
Army—9th Infantry Division

Went to Vietnam 8/4/68. Available information indicates William died from multiple fragmentation wounds in Kien Hoa, Province.

S.Sgt. Bennett Walfred Olson
Born 10/3/37
Died 1/8/68
Enlisted from Caldwell
Marines
Married

Went to Vietnam 10/27/67. Bennett was listed as a helicopter crewman. The twelve year Marine veteran died in a crash at Thua Thien.

1st. Lt. David King Omstead
Born 5/4/47
Died 6/16/68
Enlisted from Harrison
Married

> Went to Vietnam 3/6/68. David was originally from Costa Mesa, California. He died from small arms fire in Gia Dinh Province.

Not Available

EN 1 Michael Harris Painter
Born 2/28/43
Died 8/8/69
Enlisted from Moscow
Coast Guards
Married

> A four year service veteran, Michael was killed by mortar fire. He was the only coastguardsman from the Pacific Northwest to be killed in action.

Sp 4 Steven J. Perry
Born 7/23/50
Died 12/28/68
Army
Enlisted from Boise

> Went to Vietnam 9/25/68. Steven was originally from Salt Lake City, Utah. He died in Phong Dinh Province.

Not Available

S.Sgt. William Don Petersen
Born 3/6/36
Died 11/15/67
Enlisted from Boise
Army—Co. C, 1st. Battalion, 7th Cavalry
Married

> Went to Vietnam 4/12/67. A native of Phoenix, Arizona, William graduated from Boise High School in 1954. He attended the University of Idaho and also Boise State College. William was a platoon leader in Vietnam with ten years of military service and experience. On a search and destroy mission near Ha Tay, he eliminated an enemy emplacement with a grenade before exposing himself to enemy fire in an effort to rescue a wounded comrade. He died in Quang Nam Province.

Sp 4 Bobby Gene Peterson
Born 7/23/47
Died 7/27/67
Enlisted from Idaho Falls
Army—1st. Bat.(The Big Red One), 1st. Inf.

Went to Vietnam 12/16/66. Bobby was stationed at Phuoc Vin, Bih Duong Province, 35 miles north of Saigon. The base camp was assaulted during the night by Viet Cong rockets and mortar fire. Bobby was mortally wounded, dying four days after his twentieth birthday.

Sgt. Jon Dale Peterson
Born 8/10/47
Died 4/1/69
Enlisted from Shelley
Army—1st. Air Cavalry Division
Married

Went to Vietnam 1/4/69. Jon was a graduate of Shelley High School and attended the Idaho Technical College in Pocatello. The Sergeant was killed while leading his men in battle at Long Khanh Province.

CWO Jesse Donald Phelps
MIA/POW
Born 10/1/37
MIA—12/19/66
Enlisted from Boise
Army—Co.A, 229th Aviation Bat. (Assault Helicopters)
Married

Went to Vietnam 12/28/65. A native of Ogden, Utah, Jesse graduated from Nampa High School in 1955. The twelve year Army veteran had served for nine years in the Intelligence Division. He was a helicopter pilot in Vietnam and died in a crash. The Chief Warrant Officer was awarded the Distinguished Flying Cross for the successful loading of seriously wounded soldiers on 11/19/65.

Sgt. Samuel C. Phillips III
Born 7/7/43
Died 10/2/67
Enlisted from Homedale
Army

Went to Vietnam 5/16/66. Available information indicates Sergeant Phillips had been in the service for three years. He was killed in a plane crash in Lam Dong.

Louis Alphonse Pichon, Jr.
Bjorn 1/7/28
Died 3/26/69
Enlisted from Ketchum
Marines
Married

A native of Slidell, Louisiana, Louis was ready to retire after twenty years in the military when the government requested his services in Vietnam. He was in country only four months when he was killed by small arms fire in Quang Tri Province.

Cpl. James Edward Piva
Born 3/20/48
Died 2/27/70
Enlisted from Challis
Army—Co. D, 3rd. Bat. 25th Infantry Division

Went to Vietnam 12/18/69. Born in Challis, James graduated from Challis High School in 1966 and attended Idaho State University for two years. He also attended flight school in Reno, Neveda. He was killed when his base at Tay Ninh, in Hua Nghia Province, came under hostile mortar fire.

L.Cpl. Michael Lee Poletti
Born 2/12/50
Died 9/10/68
Enlisted from Pocatello
Marines

Went to Vietnam 3/16/68. Michael was born in Pocatello and attended Pocatello High School. He enlisted in the Marines because his older brother, Mario was serving in Vietnam. Mario extended his tour for six months so he could come home with his brother. Both sons were stationed near Da Nang in different branches of the service. Mario escorted Michael's body home.

Private First Class Robert Allan Powell
Born 6/3/48
Died 9/19/66
Enlisted from Boise
Marines—26th Marine Regiment Co.

Went to Vietnam 8/66. A native of Weiser, Idaho. Robert attended Capital High School in Boise. The eighteen-year-old had been in country only one month when he died from small arms fire near Da Nang in the Quang Nam Province.

Sp.4 John Lynn Powers
MIA/POW
Born 10/13/49
MIA 2/15/71
Enlisted from Mackay
Army

Went to Vietnam 9/70. John graduated from Caldwell High in 1967 and joined the Army in September of 1970. In Vietnam he was serving as crew chief on a helicopter loaded with barrels of fuel. The helicopter took a direct enemy hit near Laos and exploded in midair. No remains of the wreckage or crew were ever found.

Private First Class Michael Lloyd Priest
Born 3/31/47
Died 4/8/67
Enlisted from Idaho Falls
Army—1st. Cavalry, Airmobile Unit in the 7th Cav. Division

Went to Vietnam 2/17/67. Michael was born in Idaho Falls and graduated from Shelley High School in 1965. He had been active in 4-H for many years and was named Idaho State Tractor winner in 1963. Michael died from small arms fire in Binh Dinh Province.

Capt. Lewis DeVern Probart
Born 3/27/43
Died 7/17/69
Enlisted from Pocatello
Army—52nd Regiment

Went to Vietnam 1/28/69. A native of Pocatello, DeVern graduated from Pocatello High School in 1961 and Idaho State University in 1965. In Vietnam he held the positions of Assistant Battalion Senior Advisor, Battalion Senior Advisor and Regimental Staff Advisor. He was killed in a helicopter crash near Xuan Loc in the Phuoc Tuy Province.

Sp.4 Max Welker Pugmire
Born 4/10/49
Died 10/24/69
Enlisted from Montpelier
Army—Co. B, 3rd. Bat. 4th Infantry Div. 8th Infantry

Went to Vietnam 5/10/69. Max was stationed near Pleiku in the central highlands. His unit was climbing a hill in search of a sniper when Max was killed by supporting mortar rounds from his own troop. A close friend from Blackfoot, Frank Christensen was at his side and was also seriously wounded.

1st. Lt. Frank Reasoner
Born 9/16/37
Died 7/12/65
Enlisted from Kellogg
Marines—Co. A 3rd Reconnaissance Bat. 3rd. Marine Div.
Married

A native of Spokane, Washington, Frank Reasoner became the SECOND MEDAL OF HONOR RECEIPIENT IN VIETNAM. Serving as commanding officer, Frank was leading a reconnaissance patrol that came under heavy fire from fifty to one hundred Viet Cong. Frank took a point position with five men and repeatedly exposed himself and shouted encouragement to his pinned down troops. Taking out an enemy automatic weapons position, he provided cover power for his comrades. When his radio man was hit, Frank ran to his aid through machine gun fire and was mortally wounded.

Not Available

Cpl. Christopher Ray Reed
Born 12/21/46
Died 6/9/69
Enlisted from Boise
Marines—3rd. Battallion, 5th Marines

Went to Vietnam 9/26/98. Available information indicates Christopher was a three year service veteran. He died from mortar wounds in Quang Nam Province.

E4 Keith H. Reitz
Born 10/25/48
Died 3/9/70
Enlisted from Payette
Army—Co. C 228th AVN BN, 1st. Cavalry Div.
Married

Went to Vietnam 11/19/69. Keith left for his third tour of duty one week after his marriage. A native of Ontario, Oregon, he enlisted as a student at Payette High School and received his GED in the service. In Vietnam, he was stationed at Quan Lai in Binh Long Province. Keith was a flight engineer on a CH47B helicopter that crashed near the base from mechanical failure. The entire crew of four perished.

Sp 4 Michael Hugh Richards
Born 5/10/50
Died 3/15/71
Enlisted from Bonners Ferry
Army—196th Light Infantry Brigade

Went to Vietnam 8/12/70. The only information available indicates twenty-year-old Michael died in Quang Tin Province.

Sp 4 Arturo Recio Rios
Born 2/19/47
Died 4/19/68
Enlisted from Idaho Falls
Army—9th Infantry Division

Went to Vietnam 9/15/67. Arturo was born in Alamo, Texas and attended O.E. Bell Jr. High School in Idaho Falls, Idaho. He was drafted into the Army while he was working and had been in Vietnam for six months. In February of 1968, the young soldier (who had been previously wounded) received serious stomach wounds at Dinh Tuong Province. He died two month later in a hospital in Japan.

HN Samuel Henri Rodriquez
Born 2/21/46
Died 5/19/68
Enlisted from Wendell
Navy

Not Available

Went to Vietnam 4/13/68. The only information available indicates Samuel was in country one month before he died in a mortar attack at Quang Nam Province.

Private First Class Ralph Lee Rotter
Born 4/14/44
Died 1/2/68
Enlisted from Lewiston
Army—25th Infantry Division

Went to Vietnam 10/19/67. A native of Colville, Washington, Ralph joined the Army in April 1967 and was assigned to Vietnam the following October. The twenty-three-year-old died from shrapnel wounds received in Tay Nihn Province.

Not Available

Cpl. Douglas Noel Rowe
Born 11/13/46
Died 3/9/69
Enlisted from Pocatello
Army—Co. B, 2nd Bat. 5th Cav. 1st. Cav. Air Mobile Division

Went to Vietnam 12/17/68. Douglas was born in Rupert, Idaho and graduated from Blackfoot High School in 1965 and attended Idaho State University for two years. Doug was wounded, but he exposed himself to hostile fire to take up a defensive firing position. He defended his position until he fell mortally wounded. The company of 61 soldiers lost 52 casualties at Tay Ninh Province.

1st. Lt. Ronald Benton Rueppel (nickname—"Lucky")
Born 3/30/48
Died 9/27/71
Enlisted from Moscow
Army—Troop B, 1st. Cav. Assigned to Aero-weapon Platoon
Married

Went to Vietnam 9/12/71. The 1966 Dreary High School valedictorian was attending the University of Idaho when he was assigned to Vietnam. Ronald was a Cobra helicopter pilot and had already flown 24 missions in his first 15 days in country. While flying in adverse weather conditions in An Giang Province, his helicopter struck and tree and crashed into the Mekong River.

GSGT-E7 Lynne Harlan Rutter
Born 9/5/31
Died 11/5/70
Enlisted from Jerome
Marines
Married

Went to Vietnam 1/28/70. An eighteen year service veteran, Lynne was originally from Rehway, New Jersey. He died from a heart attack in Quang Nam Province.

Sgt. Vicente Diaz Sandoval
Born 4/10/45
Died 4/8/67
Enlisted from American Falls
Army—1st. Cavalry Division (AMBL)

Went to Vietnam 8/2/66. Vicente died two days before his twenty second birthday in Binh Dinh Province. He suffered mortal fragmentation wounds during an enemy assault.

Sp 4 Floyd Gwen Savell
Born 6/4/46
Died 2/14/67
Enlisted from Boise
Army—Co. A 1st. Bat. 35th Infantry, 25th Infantry Div.

Went to Vietnam 5/5/66. Originally from Greenwood, Mississippi, Floyd was a graduate of Meridian High School. In Vietnam, he served as a platoon squad leader and wrote home that he had been out on patrols for 84 days. On a reconnaissance patrol near Phu Cat in Binh Dinh Province, during intense fighting with the enemy, Floyd set out to find the point man who had become separated from the platoon. Floyd was wounded but continued his search until he was killed.

Private First Class Marshall Gust Schaffner
Born 2/2/47
Died 3/18/68
Enlisted from Cataldo
Marines—Co. H, 2nd Bat. 44th Marines, 9th Marine Amphibious Brigade

Went to Vietnam 6/20/67. Marshall was a graduate of Kootenai High School. In Vietnam his company was defending the village of Vihn Quan Thuong. Marshall was mortally wounded while providing cover for a wounded Marine forward artillery observer. His heroic actions were instrumental in saving many lives.

Private First Class Ronald Dean Shaff
Born 1/28/49
Died 2/19/69
Enlisted from Filer
Marines—Co. M, 3rd.Bat. 9th Marines, 3rd Marine Division

Went to Vietnam 8/29/68. Ronald attended schools in Filer, Idaho and was an ammunition man in Vietnam. During a search and destroy mission in Quang Tri Province, his company came under heavy fire. While maneuvering through hazardous terrain to replace ammunition, he was mortally wounded by automatic weapon fire.

1st. Lt. John Frederick Shiefer
Born 10/14/39
Died 8/29/70
Enlisted from Boise
Army—Co.C, 2nd Squadron, 17th Reg. of the 101st Airborne Division
Married

Went to Vietnam 5/30/70. A native of Boise, Idaho, John graduated from Boise Jr. College in 1969 and attended the University of Idaho for two years. He originally joined the Navy Reserve, and the Army and National Guard Reserve. In 1969, John joined the regular army and served as a Huey helicopter pilot in Vietnam. He and four others were killed when his helicopter was shot down while attempting to insert troops into a landing zone at Thau Thien Province.

WO Glen Emery Shropshire
Born 12/27/46
Died 7/31/67
Enlisted from Sandpoint
Army
Married

Went to Vietnam 5/3/67. As a 1965 senior at Sandpoint High School, Glen wrote the graduating class prophecy. He had served as a helicopter pilot in Vietnam for three months when his helicopter crashed near Pleiku. The young Warrant Officer was twenty years old.

Lance Cpl. Verle Jennings Skidmore
Born 6/4/47
Died 5/10/68
Enlisted from Terreton
Marines—D Battery, 2nd Battalion, 13th Marines
Married

Went to Vietnam 3/3/68. Verle graduated from Jefferson High School in 1965 and was stationed in Da Nang in Vietnam. His company was helping with the evacuation of Kham Duc (a special forces camp near the Cambodian border), when he was killed by the enemy. Nineteen U.S. soldiers were killed in the attack and 125 were wounded.

Private First Class Kenneth Lloyd Small
Born 2/24/50
Died 6/7/69
Enlisted from Salmon
Marines

Went to Vietnam 12/29/68. Kenneth was born in Idaho Falls, Idaho and attended school in Dubois until his junior year. He graduated from Salmon High School. He and six other Marines were killed in a battle in Quang Nam Province. Only five men in his squad survived the attack.

Private First Class Fred Steven Smart
Born 4/27/50
Died 6/19/70
Enlisted from Meridian
Marines—Co. C-1st. Battalion, 7th Marines, 1st. Marine Division

Went to Vietnam 5/15/70. The 1969 graduate of Twin Falls High School was stationed near Da Nang in Quang Nam Province. Fred was critically wounded when he stepped on a landmine. The twenty-year-old died aboard the USS Sanctuary Hospital ship.

Sp 4 Ariel James Smith
Born 12/19/43
Died 11/8/69
Enlisted from Shelley
Army

Went to Vietnam 5/8/69. The 1962 graduate of Shelley High School died from multiple fragment wounds in Binh Duong Province. Two months prior to his death, he was awarded the Purple Heart Medal for wounds he received in battle.

Sp4 Billy Gene Smith
Born 6/9/46
Died 11/12/67
Enlisted from Twin Falls
Army—Co. C 39th Engineers
Married

Went to Vietnam 4/12/67. A native of Gooding, Idaho, Billy attended school in Filer, Idaho. While stationed in Quang Ngai Province, a jeep he was riding in hit a landmine, killing all on board. The men were on their way to church services.

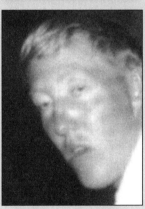

Sp 4 Gary Clarence Smith
Born 11/5/43
Died 10/10/68
Enlisted from Pingree
National Guard—116th Engineers

Went to Vietnam 9/19/68. Gary was with an advance detachment of forty men setting up a base camp near Boa Loc in Lam Dong Province (fifty miles from the Cambodian border). The truck he was on exploded when it took a direct hit from enemy fire. Gary was the first casualty of the 116th Engineer Battalion.

1st. Lt. James Anderson Smith
Born 5/1/46
Died 9/12/68
Enlisted from Blackfoot
Army—Co. D, 1st. Bat. 2nd Infantry, 1st. Infantry Division

Went to Vietnam 8/23/68. James graduated from Blackfoot High School in 1964. He was stationed in the village of Loc Ninh (75 miles northwest of Saigon), near the Cambodian border. James moved his battalion forward to assist during an engagement with the enemy when he was killed by small arms fire in Binh Long Province.

Private First Class Michael Allan Snyder
Born 10/17/42
Died 4/6/68
Enlisted from Lewiston
Army—1st. Cavalry Division (AMBL)
Married

Went to Vietnam 12/3/67. Originally from Tillamook, Oregon, Michael graduated from Enterprise High School in 1959. He was stationed at Utah Beach in Quang Tri Province. He was killed in action near the demilitarized zone (DMZ) four months after arriving in country.

CWO Jon Michael Sparks
MIA/POW Born 2/24/50
MIA 1971
Declared as Killed in Action 3/11/76
Enlisted from Carey
Army—1st. Aviation BDE
Married

Went to Vietnam 3/19/71. A graduate of Carey High School, Jon was attending Utah State University in Logan, Utah when he was drafted. The twenty-one-year-old helicopter pilot's aircraft was shot down over Laos. Both pilots and the two gunners aboard escaped injury. One gunman escaped but the other men were captured and never seen again.

Sp 4 Ronald Lee Stapleman
Born 3/16/45
Died 6/10/67
Enlisted from Paul
Army—628th Maint. Support Co. (A bomb and mine disposal unit)
Married

Went to Vietnam 6/16/66. A 1964 graduate of Minico High School, Ronald attended Boise Jr. College for one year prior to his service in Vietnam. Two days before the end of his tour of duty, he was killed by mortar rounds near Pleiku.

Not Available

Not Available

Capt. Gary Lyn Steele
Born 9/15/38
Died 4/19/65
Enlisted from Bliss
Army

The only information available indicates Gary was a three year Army veteran. He was a crewman on a helicopter that crashed in Vietnam.

Col. Mark Stephensen
MIA/POW
Born 5/1/30
MIA 4/29/67
Remains returned to the US in April 1988
Air Force
Married

Went to Vietnam on his second tour in 1966. A native of Riverton, Utah, Mark had attended Brigham Young University prior to becoming an Air Force pilot. During his seventeen year career, he flew several different aircraft. On his second tour of duty in Vietnam he had flown 94 combat missions and six other support missions. He and his WSO were reported missing when they failed to return from a night mission over the Paul Damieler Bridge. Captain Sigler was captured and held prisoner until 1973. Mark's fate was undetermined until his remains were returned in 1988.

Cdr. Clarence W. Stoddard, Jr.
MIA/POW
Born 1/30/67
MIA 9/14/66
Enlisted from Atlanta
Navy
Married

Clarence was an 18 year service veteran and a pilot of the U.S. Skyraider (a close support aircraft of the Navy). He flew his last mission in Vietnam on 9/14/66. The plane crashed at sea and his body was never recovered.

Major Raymond LeRoy Tacke (Nickname "Pat")
Born 9/22/28
Died 3/8/69
Enlisted from Cottonwood
Air Force
Married

Went to Vietnam 7/68. Pat graduated from Cottonwood High School in 1946 and attended Gonzaga University in Spokane, Washington. He received an Appointment to the U.S. Naval Academy and graduated in 1952. He joined the Air Force because he suffered from sea sickness and became a career officer. Pat was a navigator on a C-130 aircraft with the 50th Tactical Air Command Airlift Squadron. He was stationed at Taiwan and volunteered to fly a sortie to Vietnam. He died returning from the mission.

Sgt. David Arlington Tanner
Born 4/1/48
Died 12/8/67
Enlisted from Boise
Army—101st. Airborne Division
Married

Went to Vietnam 6/24/67. The only information available indicates David died during an enemy attack in Lam Dong Province.

Lt. Robert L. Taylor (Nickname "The Bear")
Born 12/15/37
Died 4/4/68
Enlisted from Fruitland
Army—82nd Airborne Special Forces
Married

Went to Vietnam 9/7/67. Robert was born in Fruitland, Idaho and attended school in Payette and Caldwell. The twelve year service veteran died in Khe Sahn in Quang Tri Province when he or someone near him stepped on a mine.

Cpl. Daniel Cline Tedrow (Nickname "Buck")
Born 2/3/48
Died 11/27/68
Enlisted from Mullan
Marines—1st. Marine Div. Co. A, 1st. Bat. 26th Marines

Went to Vietnam on his second tour of duty 9/2/68. A native of Wallace, Idaho, Daniel graduated from Mullan High School in 1966. On his first tour of duty he had been wounded near Quang Tri. Two months after his second tour began he died from gunshot wounds while on patrol in Quang Nam Province. Daniel died on Thanksgiving Day 1968.

CWO Henry James William Tews
Born 4/11/46
Died 12/29/68
Enlisted from Shoshone
Army—174th Assault Helicopter Co. 14th CAB, 16th Aviation Combat Grp

Went to Vietnam 9/28/67. Henry graduated from Shoshone High School in 1964 and attended the University of Idaho. He had completed his first tour of duty in Vietnam and had just returned from a leave at home. He died the first month of his six month extended tour. While attempting to fly a downed helicopter from a battle zone, the aircraft lost power and crashed in Quang Ngai Province.

Private First Class Terence Pierce Thomas
Born 6/20/46
Died 3/11/68
Enlisted from Hammett
Army—Co. D, 1st. Bat, 2nd Infantry, 1st. Inf. Division

Went to Vietnam 10/27/67. Terence grew up in Hemmett, Idaho and graduated from Glenns Ferry High School in 1964. He had attended one year at Idaho State University. Terence was an assistant gunner leading his platoon on a search and destroy mission when he was mortally wounded.

CMS Larry C. Thornton
MIA/POW
Born 3/3/32
MIA 12/24/65
Declared as Killed in Action 1/27/74
Enlisted from Idaho Falls
Air Force
Married

> Went to Vietnam 11/1/65. Larry graduated from Iona High School and joined the National Guard in 1950. He served active duty in Korea before enlisting in the Air Force in 1953. Serving as a gunner on a FG47 aircraft, he was reported missing in action when his plane failed to return to Ton Son Nhut Air Base in Saigon.

Sp 4 James (Jimmy) Edward Tooley
Born 9/15/46
Died 12/19/66
Enlisted from Parma
Army

> Went to Vietnam 3/5/66. Available information indicates Jimmy graduated from Parma High School in 1966. He died from an illness while in Vietnam.

Major Edwin Newton Troxel
Born 12/29/29
Died 8/2/71
Enlisted from Boise
Air Force
Married

> Went to Vietnam in 1971. A 1948 graduate of Boise High School, Edwin graduated from the University of Oregon in 1953. He served as a helicopter pilot with the Special Forces during his first tour of duty in Vietnam. On his second tour, Edwin served as an air attache to the American Embassy. He was also directing operations of the Laotian Air Force. He died in a plane crash.

Not Available

Not Available

1st. Lt. Kenneth Eugene Turner
Born 5/9/41
Died 4/24/66
Enlisted from Bruneau
Army—Co. B, 2nd Bat. 27th Infantry, 25th Inf. Division

Went to Vietnam 3/23/66. Kenneth attended High School at St. Teresa's Academy in Boise and graduated from Gonzaga Prep School in 1959 and the University of Idaho in 1964. He was leading his platoon on an ambush patrol near CuChi when he was killed by a Viet Cong sniper. Kenneth had been in country one month.

Sp.4 Rodney Carl Turner
Born 7/2/48
Died 11/8/69
Enlisted from Boise
Army—1st. Infantry Division

Went to Vietnam 6/5/69. A native of Nampa, Idaho, Rodney graduated from Boise High School. His platoon had just returned from an eight day patrol when they were called out to help another company. Rodney was mortally wounded while leading the patrol in Binh Duong Province.

Private First Class Wesley William Vermeesch
Born 6/4/47
Died 10/30/69
Enlisted from Pierce
Army—4th Infantry Division
Married

Went to Vietnam 10/13/69. Available information indicates Wesley had been in country only seventeen days when he died from multiple fragmentation wounds in Binh Dinh Province.

Capt. George Francis Volk
Born 12/29/40
Died 4/21/67
Enlisted from Boise
Army

Went to Vietnam 7/15/66. George was a three year service veteran. The only information available indicates he was killed in a vehicle crash.

Private First Class Douglas John Wade
Born 4/9/47
Died 2/19/66
Enlisted from Idaho Falls
Army—1st. Cavalry Division (AMBL)

Went to Vietnam 12/22/65. Douglas graduated from Idaho Falls High School in 1965. He was killed by small arms fire.

M.Sgt. Howard Bert Waldron
Born 5/18/26
Died 3/6/68
Enlisted from Coeur D'Alene
Marines
Married

Went to Vietnam 3/6/98. A native of Declo, Idaho, Howard graduated from Hamilton High School, Hamilton, Montana. He joined the Marines in 1943 and served in WWII and was at Iwo Jima in Korea. He retired after 22 1/2 years of service, but agreed to return in 1966 upon the Marine Corps' request. The C-123 transport plane he was flying on was shot down near the Khe Sahn Air Base. All 47 on board were killed.

Not Available

Private First Class James Lloyd Walker
Born 11/18/46
Died 10/30/66
Enlisted from Blackfoot
Army—101st Airborne, 25th Infantry

Went to Vietnam 7/15/66. James was a native of Blackfoot, Idaho and had been married a short time before joining the Army. He was serving as a co-pilot on a helicopter that was shot down near the Cambodian border. All on board were killed.

Private First Class Jimmy Lee Ward
Born 5/1/47
Died 11/30/67
Enlisted from Nampa
Marines—Co.G, 2nd Bat. 9th Marines, 3 Marine Division

Went to Vietnam 9/15/67. Jeremy was born in Nampa, Idaho and graduated from Vallivue High School in Caldwell. He joined the National Guard in 1965 and the Marines in 1967. While serving as a rifleman of the 2nd platoon, he was killed by small arms fire. He had been in country two months.

Sgt. Johnny Lee Ward
Born 11/28/47
Died 9/11/69
Enlisted from Cambridge
Army—Battalion A, 3rd. Bat. 6th Artillary

Went to Vietnam 9/9/68. Johnny was born in Weiser, Idaho and left school during his junior year to work. In May of 1969, he had been awarded the Bronze Star for saving many lives during a battle. He was serving as a reconnaissance sergeant of a forward observer patrol when an enemy mine detonated in a nearby tree. Johnny was mortally wounded and died in Binh Thuan Province.

Sgt. Dennis Wartchow
Born 7/6/50
Died 9/4/69
Enlisted from Idaho Falls
Army—Co.B, 2nd Bat. (Air Mobile) 8th Cavalry

Went to Vietnam 7/19/69. Dennis attended school in Idaho Falls and graduated from Jackson-Wilson High School in Jackson Hole, Wyoming. He was wounded when his company came under heavy fire in Tay Nihn Province, but continued to lay down defensive fire until his wounded comrades could be evacuated. Dennis was killed as the enemy advanced.

Private First Class Michael Leon Wasserman
Born 7/16/48
Died 10/12/68
Enlisted from Boise
Marines—Co. E,. 2nd Bat. 5th Regiment of the 1st. Marines Div.

Went to Vietnam 7/25/68. A native of Boise, Idaho, Michael graduated from Boise High School in 1966 and attended two years at Boise State College. He served as a machine gunner near the Que Son Mountain Range in Vietnam. As his company was defending a strategic hill to block the escape of the 144th North Vietnamese Regiment, Michael was killed while bravely holding his position. Six Marine positions to his right and four positions to his left were overrun before he fell from an enemy bullet.

S. Sgt. Russel Lee Watson
Born 2/28/42
Died 2/6/67
Enlisted from Post Falls
Army—1st. Infantry Division
Married

Went to Vietnam 10/13/66. Russel joined the army at the age of seventeen. He was in the service eight years before going to Vietnam. Serving as a mortar platoon leader, he was standing at the rear of an armored personnel carrier when it exploded and burned. Russel died on his son's first birthday and a second child was born six weeks after his death.

CWO Edward Joseph Weidenbach
Born 9/30/24
Died 5/5/67
Enlisted from Nampa
Army—HHC 228th AVN Co. 1st. Cavalry Division
Married

Went to Vietnam 2/24/67. Edward served as an Air Force gunner on B17 & B24 aircraft from 1942 to 1945. He was a helicopter mechanic in the Army from 1953 to 1957 and as an army helicopter pilot in Vietnam in 1966 and 1967. While flying aboard a Chinook CH-47, he was killed in action. His unit was known as the "Guns a go-go"

Not Available

Noel Thomas West
Born 12/6/40
Died 6/19/67
Enlisted from Wendell
Army—9th Infantry Division
> Went to Vietnam 1/10/67. Noel was originally from Tacoma, Washington. Available information indicates he died from multiple fragmentation wounds received in Gia Dinh Province.

Not Available

Cpl. Michel T. Wheeler
Born 1/18/49
Died 3/16/68
Enlisted from Emmett
Army—173rd. Airborne Brigade
> Went to Vietnam 10/3/67. Military records indicate Michel died from mortar fire wounds in Quang Tin Province.

Sgt. William Whitney
Born 8/28/47
Died 11/8/67
Enlisted from Pocatello
Army—190th Assault Helicopter Co. 1st. Aviation Brigade
> Went to Vietnam 7/20/67. A native of Pocatello, Idaho, William attended Jr. High School in Pocatello. He graduated from Davis High School in Kaysville, Utah in 1965. Bill was a crew chief and right door gunner on a UH-l0 assault helicopter. His helicopter was shot down while on a night emergency mission to rescue a besieged Special Forces patrol at Hue-Phu Bai. Two other helicopters were also shot down.

Sp 5 Robert Leon Willey (Nickname—"Robin")
Born 7/19/47
Died 5/10/69
Enlisted from Grangeville
Army
> Went to Vietnam 4/26/68. Robin was the youngest of six children and joined the Army rather than waiting to be drafted. In Vietnam, he helped provide a 1968 Christmas celebration for a Vietnamese orphanage. Robin was killed by a land mine (known to soldiers as a "Bouncing Betty") in Phu Yen Province.

Sgt. Bill Gene Williams
Born 3/14/44
Died 6/3/70
Enlisted from Hailey
Army—1st. Cavalry Division (AMBL)
Married

Not Available

Went to Vietnam 8/21/69. A native of Gooding, Idaho, Bill attended school in Gooding and Shoshone. After attending college in California, he transferred to Idaho State University where he graduated in 1968. He completed his practice teaching in Hailey and had signed a contract at Minico High School before his enlistment to the Army. He had two months left of service when he died from injuries received in Cambodia.

Sp 4 Daniel Eugene Williams
Born 3/15/48
Died 4/11/69
Enlisted from Hamer
Army—1st. Infantry

Went to Vietnam 2/15/69. Daniel attended schools in Hamer and West Jefferson and planned to continue his education after the service. He had served two years in the Army and was assigned briefly in Germany before his deployment to Vietnam. Daniel was serving as a medic when he died from multiple fragmentation wounds in Bihn Duong Province.

Sp. 4 Morris Edward Williams
Born 10/9/51
Died 2/6/70
Enlisted from Boise
Army—326th Med. Bat. (Aero-Medical Evacuation Team) 101st. Airborne Div.

Went to Vietnam 10/17/69. Eddie was born in Emmett, Idaho and was a junior at Capital High School when he volunteered to join the Army in 1968. He obtained his GED in the service. He was a crew chief of a medical evacuation helicopter, attempting to evacuate a soldier near the Song Troui River, in Thua Thien Province. The helicopter had engine failure on its final approach to the pick-up site and crashed. All on board were killed.

Airman 2nd Class Thomas Murten Willis
Born 10/3/46
Died 6/5/67
Enlisted from Mc Call
Air Force—Strategic Air Command

Went to Vietnam 5/2/66. Thomas was born in Council, Idaho and graduated from McCall Donnelly High School in 1964. He had been stationed at Da Nang with "The Tiger Flight" before dying aboard the USS Repose, off the coast of South Vietnam.

Sgt. Jerry Barber Wilson (Nickname "Big Red")
Born 6/1/45
Died 12/14/66
Enlisted from Mackay
Army—Spc. 4th, Co. A, 2nd Bat. 18th Inf. 1st. Inf. Div (The Big Red One)

Went to Vietnam 3/25/66. Jerry was born in Caliente, Nevada and graduated from Mackay High School in 1963, He was wounded on 11/15/66 while exiting a UH-ID helicopter and later contracted malaria while recovering from his wounds in the 3rd Field Hospital.

1st. Lt. Robert Evans Wise
Born 11/26/41
Died 3/5/67
Enlisted from Coeur D'Alene
Army—1st. Air Cav. Div. Asst. Operations officer with the assault support helicopter bat.

Went to Vietnam 10/15/66. Robert graduated from Coeur D'Alene High School in 1960 and the University of Idaho in 1965. He was a pilot on the Chinook helicopter, assigned to AnShe, in Binh Dinh Providence. Roberts' helicopter was shot down as he was leaving base early in the morning. The enemy had approached the perimeter of his camp during the night. Robert and fourteen others lost their lives.

L.Cpl. Eugene Eben Wolters
Born 1/30/51
Died 8/30/70
Enlisted from Coeur D'Alene
Marines—Bat. B, 1st. Bat. 11th Marines

Went to Vietnam 10/15/69. Eugene was born in Coeur D'Alene and attended Coeur D' Alene High School. Military records indicate he was stationed near Da Nang, in Quang Nam Province when he was killed.

1st. Lt. Strather Franklin Wood
Born 4/26/44
Died 2/18/71
Enlisted from Boise
Marines

Went to Vietnam 1/11/71. Strather was originally from Eugene, Oregon. Military records indicate he was a crewman on a helicopter that crashed in Thua Thien Province.

Not Available

Private First Class Robert Gene Yagues
Born 5/19/48
Died 5/3/67
Enlisted from Mt. Home
Marines

A native of Rupert, Idaho, Robert attended schools there before moving to Mountain Home. Available information indicates he died of head wounds received in hostile enemy action near Huong Hoa, in the Quang Tri Province. Eighteen-year-old Robert had only been in country one month before his death.

Sp. 4 Kenneth Wilson Young
Born 8/23/45
Died 5/24/69
Enlisted from St. Anthony
Army—116th Engineers National Guard—Co.D

Went to Vietnam 9/19/68. Kenneth was born in St. Anthony, Idaho and graduated from South Fremont High School in 1963. He attended Ricks College and had been in the Nation Guard for two years. Kenneth was killed at Boa Loc when a trip flare was accidentally tripped causing a grassfire to detonate a mine where he was standing. His death occurred at the battalion base camp with Kenneth becoming the second casualty of the 116th.

A LIVING LEGACY

Children of Idaho Vietnam Casualties*

Duane Akkerman . . . . .1 son

James Allred . . . . .3 sons and 2 daughters

Harry Amesbury . . . . .4 sons

William Beasley . . . . .2 children

Anthony Bellamy . . . . .1 son

Gary Bitton . . . . .3 children

Jon Bodahl . . . . .1 daughter

Curtis Bohlscheid . . . . .2 children

Ray Bradley . . . . .2 children

Harry Brenn . . . . .2 sons and 1 daughter

Michael Brown . . . . .1 son and a daughter (born six weeks after his death)

William Bunch . . . . .1 daughter

David Chatterton . . . . .2 sons and 1 daughter

Thomas LaMont Dives . . . . .2 children

Jack (Butch) Dodson . . . . .2 daughters and 2 stepchildren

Thomas Foreman . . . . .A son (born one month after his death)

Robert Green . . . . .1 son

William Griffin . . . . .1 daughter and 2 sons

Donald Haile . . . . .2 children

Lonnie Hendrickson . . .His wife was expecting a child one month after his death

Teddy Merlin Hodges . . . . .3 children

William Hunt . . . . .2 sons

Brent Jones . . . . .1 daughter

Tommy Kearsley . . . . .2 sons

Delmar Lawrence . . . . .2 daughters

William (Bill) Lemmons . . . . .2 children

James Lockwood . . . . .1 daughter

Clayton Martin . . . . .1 son and 1 daughter

Jay (Darwin) McLain . . . . .1 daughter

Donald McGinley . . . . .2 children

Donald McGregor . . . . .3 sons

Lester (Red) Michels . . . . .3 sons and 1 daughter

Lester (Neal) Moulton . . . . .1 daughter

Jimmy Nakayama . . . . .A daughter born shortly before his death

Troy Oliver . . . . .2 daughters

William Peterson . . . . .3 daughters

Keith Reitz .A son (born two months after his death)

Ralph Rotter . . . . .1 daughter

Ronald (Lucky) Rueppel . . . . .A son (who later graduated from West Point)

John Shiefer . . . . .1 son

Glen Shropshire . . . . .1 son

Verle Skidmore . . . . .1 son and a daughter (born after his death)

Ariel James Smith . . . . .1 son

Michael Snyder . . . . .1 daughter

Mark Stephensen . . . . .Father of several children

Raymond Pat Tacke . . . . .3 daughters

Larry Thornton . . . . .3 sons

Edwin Troxel . . . . .1 daughter and 1 son

Howard Waldron . . . . .2 children

James Walker . . . . .A daughter (born after his death)

Russel Watson . . . . .Died on his son's 1st birthday,
a daughter (was born 6 weeks later)

(*This section has been compiled from available obituaries and information submitted by family members and friends. The Freedom Bird organization regrets that additional descendants have not yet been identified, and freely acknowledge this list is incomplete. It is however, an important beginning, as we pay tribute and remembrance to the (known and unknown) posterity, and proud legacy of Idaho husbands and fathers who died in the service of their country.)

MEN'S AGES
AT THE TIME OF DEATH

AGE IN YEARS	NUMBER OF CASUALTIES	
18	13	
19	25	
20	48	
21	39	Total 125
22	22	
9	9	
10	10	
13	13	
11	11	Total 65
27	3	
28	5	
29	6	
30	5	
31	3	
32	1	
33	3	
34	2	
35	1	
36	5	
37	2	
38	1	
39	1	
40	3	
41	3	
42	1	
44	2	
MIA/POW	14	(Exact ages unknown)

251 KNOWN CASUALTIES
(Compiled from Freedom Bird Records)

PART 5

THE
HISTORY, CULTURE,
AND
CONFLICT

*of a place
called Vietnam*

As U.S. ARMY SOLDIERS COMPLETED THEIR 12-MONTH TOUR of duty in the early 1970's, they received an "in-country" military publication entitled, "Tour 365", published by the United States Army, Vietnam. Interestingly, the semi-annual periodical, that described the ethnic, social and political background of the Vietnamese people, was distributed to young servicemen as they left the country and the devastation of war.

Designed to serve as a memento and souvenir (from a place and time) that forever changed young soldiers' lives; its text provides us with an invaluable and unique perspective. In a very real, although miniscule way, we too have experienced the painful conflict of Vietnam, as we "entered" the hearts and lives of those who served. The following section will utilize the insights of the "in-country" publication, and other significant historical and political studies. As we consider our "shared" experience, the concluding pages will allow us to explore the lessons and conflict of a place called Vietnam.

The writings and insight of gifted historians, political analysts and military experts best portray the...

HISTORY, CULTURE AND CONFLICT
OF A PLACE CALLED VIETNAM

As World War II came to an end, and America drew a collective breath of relief and hope for the future, few citizens would have even recognized the name "Vietnam." It was no wonder, the "far off corner" of the world couldn't be found on a map or atlas, and was some 9,000 miles away from our nation's capital.

Located along the coast of the Indo-Chinese peninsula south of China, Vietnam had been stripped of its original name by the French in the late 1800's. Lumped together with its neighbors, Laos and Cambodia, the country became part of French Indochina. Decades of political upheaval and unrest—fueled by the threat of communism—were about to alter the course of history in Southeast Asia and change America's identity forever.

Early Beginnings: History and Culture

A 1970, "Tour 365" publication describes the complex background of a people politically grounded in a strong ethnic and cultural identity:

One of the first important steps in understanding the Vietnam War, is recognizing Vietnam's past, and a people who had been struggling for independence for nearly 2,000 years. After centuries of Chinese domination, the Vietnamese drove invaders from the Red River Delta in 938 AD, and for the next 900 years remained an independent nation. The Lyn Dynasty, established in 1009, was the first great Vietnamese reign that ushered in cultural development, territorial expansion and prosperity. The Lyn rulers gave the government the form it retained until the French conquest in the 19th Century.

The role of the emperor was dominant. Seen as the father of the nation-family, he was the temporal monarch in whom all power of state resided. Honored also as the religious head, the reigning monarch acted as intermediary with heaven, while the "mandarinate," a civil bureaucracy, performed the functions of administering the country.

Threatened by invaders in the mid-13th Century, Dai-Viet (as Vietnam was then called), realized its independence and survival depended on a good relationship with China. Making appropriate gestures to the Chinese, the Vietnamese enjoyed a maximum degree of independence as a tributary state to China for the next one hundred years.

European influence reached Vietnam in 1535, when the Portuguese landed at Da Nang and the first Catholic missionaries entered Vietnam during the 16th Century Confucian-oriented officials had their misgiving about the new religion. Viewing it as the forerunner of conquest, leaders feared its effect upon the traditional order, which had been the foundation of state for centuries. Despite a loosely enforced ban, missionary activities spread quickly and a substantial portion of the Vietnamese population accepted Christianity.

Toward the middle of the 19th Century, pressure mounted in France for the government to establish a valuable position in Vietnam. Envious of the power other European nations were establishing in Asia, France took a stand to protect missionaries who were, at the time, being persecuted. In 1858 the French captured the city of Da Nang and in 1861 they took Saigon. Over the next 30 years the French expanded their control over all of French Indochina, or what today is Vietnam, Laos and Cambodia.

The basic political structure of French Indochina was completed by 1900. Each of Vietnam's three regions was treated separately, although basic policy decisions were made in Paris. The emperor and the mandarinate remained in both central and north Vietnam; while Cochin China (the southern portion of Vietnam) was administered directly by the French. The outward structure of government remained, but French authorities made all major decisions.

French colonialism had profound economic effects that demoralized emperors and encouraged members of the mandarinate to became self-seekers and yes men. Villagers were stripped of their land and absentee ownership developed large-scale agricultural and rubber plantations. While prosperous Vietnamese moved into the cities, more and more of the land was tilled by peasants who did not own it. Huge canal systems were dug in the Mekong Delta to exploit rice production and by the early 20th century the French had managed to produce a rice surplus.

20th Century Southeast Asia

European ideas and culture infused the country, especially among the mandarin classes. Western thought also stimulated another movement—growing Vietnamese allegiance. Early in the 20th century nationalist movements began to develop among affluent urban intellectuals. Loosely organized anti-French "secret societies" developed, although most lacked specific political objectives.

As time progressed, leadership of the covert movement was taken over by the Indochinese Communist Party (Dong Duong Cong San Dang). Founded in Hong Kong in 1930, it combined several independent Communist groups under the leadership of Nguyen Ai Quoc—later known as Ho Chi Minh.

When France fell to Germany in June of 1940, all of French Indochina was ceded to the Japanese. But lucrative agreements with wealthy French interests remained intact. Meanwhile, Ho Chi Minh became the leading national political figure in Vietnam. Developing a policy of collaboration with all non-Communist nationalists, his political party soon broadened its political and social base, becoming known as the "Vietnam Independency League" or the Viet Minh.

One of the first actions of the Viet Minh, under the direction of Vo Nguyen Giap, was the formation of covert guerrilla bands to stage attacks against the Japanese and French. Ho Chi Minh was jailed in 1941. But the activities of the Viet Minh continued under a nationalist guise, as Ho developed and strengthened Communist cells (organizations) throughout Vietnam.

The Indochina War

As World War II approached a climatic end with the bombing of Hiroshima, Vietnamese Emperor Bao Dia feared the French would return once Japan surrendered to American Allied forces. Shortly after he abdicated his throne and handed power over to Ho Chi Minh in 1945, French troops re-entered Vietnam. The Viet Minh and French attempted to negotiate an independence settlement for the country throughout the following year.

Ho and his followers ultimately determined the only way to achieve an independent Vietnam was through a "war of liberation."

France fought the resolute Viet Minh on the battlefield for the next eight years. On May 7, 1954, the French army suffered a decisive and humiliating defeat at Dien Bien Phu.

The following day, the Geneva Conference, called by the Big Four (Britain, France, the United States and Soviet Union) addressed the Indochina War and hostilities in Korea.

At the same time, the groundwork for the South East Asia Treaty Organization (SEATO) was being laid, with South Vietnam being included as a "protocol state." The United States had accepted the obligation, if asked by the government of South Vietnam, to take action in response to an armed attack and consult on appropriate measures. President Eisenhower instituted economic aid to the new country and America's active interest in Vietnam began.

Vietnam is divided

The Geneva Conference agreement reached for Vietnam fixed a "provisional boundary" line along the 17th parallel and required the total evacuation of French military forces, as well as the removal of Viet Minh forces from the South. The French handed over governmental control to non-Communist Vietnamese who established Saigon as the capital in South Vietnam. The Ngo Dinh Diem administration struggled to organize a "pro-Western" government and develop a "non-Communist" society.

In Hanoi, Ho Chi Minh began the total "communization" of the land north of 17th parallel. Despite the cease-fire agreement, a well-organized Viet Minh underground was intentionally left behind in the South. Thousands of selected party members were ordered to hide their weapons and wait for the call. The organization would become the basis of Ho's ultimate dream to establish a unified Communist Vietnam.

Ho Chi Minh erroneously presumed the South would fall by subversion (underhanded corruption), and force would not be necessary. Much to the surprise and dismay of Communist leaders, the South began to strengthen agriculturally and economically. Communist agitators and agents left behind were being exposed and morale in the ranks was falling. The North's food production dropped by 10 per cent as the South's improved by 20 per cent. Despite the North Vietnam's larger industrial base, the South's per capita gross national production was nearly 50 per cent higher. A major revision in overall strategy was soon apparent—military force would be needed to take over the South.

Communist Expansion

In 1959 the pace of terrorism accelerated and Viet Cong recruiting was stepped up.

A massive Communist propaganda campaign claimed the South's government was falling apart and the acts of terrorism were the result of popular dissent. In 1960 "The National Liberation Front" appeared, calling for the overthrow of the 'dictatorial Diem administration' and U.S. imperialists. An estimated 40,000 trained military personnel infiltrated from the North into the South between 1959 and 1964, as every precaution was taken to conceal North Vietnam's support of southern Communist groups.

The systematic process of Communist infiltration into South Vietnam was accomplished by two major strategies. In 1959, the Hanoi government decided to help the V.C. in South Vietnam by opening a supply line to them. Agents departed from ports just north of the 17th parallel in boats disguised as innocent looking fishing vessels.

When the enemy quickly responded, the emphasis shifted to a 1,000-mile network of jungle and mountain trails—known collectively as the Ho Chi Minh Trail—

which wound through eastern Laos and into Cambodia, crossing the border into South Vietnam.

"Beginning in the North around the Mu Gia and Ban Karai passses, the trail zigzagged its way south inside a corridor up to 30 miles wide, within which parallel trails, connected by cross-tracks, granted a degree of immunity to aerial attacks. In the early years, the journey from the North took about six months; as the war escalated improvements were made. Permanent way stations were set up as supply dumps and rest centers, and anti-aircraft batteries were deployed. In the early 1960's, only about 400 tons of supplies a week could be moved into the South, mainly on porter's backs; ten years later, the trail had become a highway, capable of carrying over 10,000 trucks at any one time."

(Decisive Battles, p. 159)

When an infiltrator arrived at the Laotian border, his North Vietnamese was exchanged for a Lao "neutralist" uniform. Upon giving up all personal effects of an incriminating nature, a local guide directed him halfway to a series of way stations along the infamous Ho Chi Minh Trail. There, the next guide met him. Eventually the process would take him to a determined location in the South. In South Vietnam, he received two unmarked uniforms, a pajama-like uniform, rubber sandals, a sweater, a hammock, mosquito netting and waterproof sheeting.

The Enemy We Faced
The 199th Light Infantry Brigade's military publication, offers insight into the back-ground of Communist infiltration troops from the North.

"They came to my house and told my mother that I had been chosen to be one of them. They wanted me to become a chien si (soldier). My mother pleaded that I was too young. The North Vietnamese soldier said, 'He is old enough— the draft age is 15 to 40.'"

This is how 15-year-old Nguyen Van Qui became one of the enemy American soldiers faced. His story was typical. He was then taken to a training camp in the southern panhandle of North Vietnam. There, he and other recruits were given khaki uniforms and taught to aim and fire a weapon. The complete training cycle for duty as a regular chien si in the North Vietnamese Army (NVA) lasted six days.

After his training, Qui and 1,200 others were sent on a four-week journey down the Ho Chi Minh Trail. They moved about in small groups to escape B52 raids. About 700 of them were armed.

"Many died on the trail," Qui recalled. "Some died of malaria and others died from not enough food. It was very hard. Everybody was sick, but they kept pushing us."

(Tour 365, p.50)

By 1970, The NVA—uniformed North Vietnamese Army were armed with sophisticated weapons and backed up by tanks and artillery. Supplied by Russian and Chinese governments, they comprised over half of the total enemy forces faced by American soldiers. The remaining enemy was the pajama-clad Viet Cong guerillas from the hamlets (villages) of South Vietnam and infiltrators like Qui from the North.

The Geneva Accords called for a general election in 1955 to unite the two parts of Vietnam. The Diem government in the South rejected the possibility of a free election and the North protested loudly, but without sincerity. After the Geneva Accords, a high ranking communist official from the north was asked who he thought would win such an election. He replied, *"You know as well as I do that there won't be any elections."* *(Ibid. p. 15)*

Plans For Escalation

Hanoi planned to conquer the South with a three-phased warfare strategy outlined in the writings of Mao Tse-tung:

First: The enemy is harassed and weakened by guerilla terrorist attacks.
Second: Mobile warfare units of up to battalion size attack enemy positions.
Third: In all-out warfare by regular forces, an ultimate victory is won.
During phase one (1954 to 1960), the U.S. assisted the Vietnamese with economic aid and military advisors. Guerilla attacks intensified in 1960 and by 1961, phase two had escalated into open warfare. The 325th North Vietnamese, Regular Army Division, now reinforced the Viet Cong.

American presence in Vietnam had grown to approximately 700 men and it was apparent more help was needed to stop the expanding threat of Communism. In 1961 President Kennedy increased the U.S. commitment to South Vietnam, by adding pilots and support personnel to the growing number of military advisors. The decision had been made.

America would not allow a Communistic "Red Wave" to sweep over Southeast Asia.

Geology and Climate

When American soldiers first stepped foot upon Vietnamese ground in the early 1960's, they found a tropical land in an isolated corner of the world. Extending south from China in a long, narrow S-curve, Vietnam is about as large as California. The South China Sea lies to the east, with Laos and Cambodia forming the country's western border. Occupying the east coast of the Indochinese Peninsula, the people of Vietnam sometimes describe their country as "two rice baskets" hanging from opposite ends of a farmer's carrying pole. In the north, the Red River Delta forms one "basket" and the Mekong Delta in the south forms the other. A narrow stretch of land in central Vietnam forms the "carrying pole" that connects the deltas.

Vietnam extends about 1,000 miles from China south to the Gulf of Thailand. At its widest point—in the north—the distance between Laos and the Gulf of Tonkin is almost 400 miles. At its narrowest point—in central Vietnam—the country is only about 30 miles wide.

The country has a tropical climate and monsoons (seasonal winds) affect the weather throughout the year. The summer monsoon brings heavy rain from the southwest, whereas the winter monsoon brings lighter rainfall from the northeast. Most of the country experiences two seasons—a wet, hot summer and a drier, cooler winter. In the south the humidity remains high throughout the year. The average temperature in Saigon ranges from about 79 degrees Fahrenheit in December, to 85 degrees Fahrenheit in April. Most of central Vietnam is drier and cooler than the northern and southern regions, partly because of a much higher altitude.

MAP SECTION:

1.
Southeast Asia

THAILAND LAOS

DMZ
HIGHWAY 9
HIGHWAY 1
Khe Sanh
38
Hue
41
A Shau Valley
Da Nang
35
37
My Lai
Quang Ngo   I Corps
36
23
6
Pleiku
Qui Nhon
33
Ia Drang Valley   29
30   II Corps
13
22
Nha Trang
34   Ca Ranh
An Loc   42   27
31   Da Lat
8   24
40
Ben Suc   7   26   10   9
17   15
Long Xuyen   14   South China Sea
11   20   21   25   32   III Corps
1   39   16
44   Special
28   Capital Zone
18   12   3   43
4   IV Corps
2

Laos

Plain of Jars

North Vietnam

Dong Hoi
DMZ
Dong Ha
Thailand
Khe Sanh   Hue
Da Nang

South Vietnam

Cambodia
Pleiku
Qui Nhon
Mekong River   Ia Drang Valley   Tuy Hoa
Ban Me Thuot
Phnom Penh
An Loc

Saigon

Vung Tau

3.

The Ho Chi Minh Trail

IMPORTANT DATES IN VIETNAM HISTORY

111 [BC] The Chinese conquered what is now northern Vietnam.

939 [AD] China ended its rule over the Vietnamese, who then set up an Independent state. Nguyen Anh united the country and called it Vietnam.

1861 France captures Saigon and Da Nang

1900 Vietnam becomes part of French Indochina

1940 France falls to Germany in WW II. Japan controls Vietnam until its defeat at Hiroshima.

1946 Beginning of 8 year battle between Viet Minh and French.

1954 The Viet Minh defeat the French. The Geneva Conference divides Vietnam into two nations.

1957 Communist terrorists began to attack villages in South Vietnam. The fighting developed into the Vietnam War.

1973 U.S. ground troop participation ends in the Vietnam War.

1975 The Vietnam War ended on April 30, when South Vietnamese surrendered to the Communists. The Communists unified North and South Vietnam into the nation of Vietnam.

(World Book Encyclopedia)

Pieces of a Puzzle—The Complexity of War

In the Forword of "Portrait of a Tragedy", Retired Army Colonel, Harry G. Summers, Jr. analyzes the complexity of the Vietnam War:

"The Vietnam War is hard to understand fully, even for those who served there. One reason is that it went on so long. Compared to the less than four years the United States was involved in World War II, or the three years we were involved in the Korean War, America's involvement in Vietnam lasted almost twenty-five years.

Those twenty-five years became the longest and most controversial conflict in the history of America. Because the United States government never officially declared the conflict in Vietnam a war, it's hard to say just when it began. The first official American deaths in Vietnam occurred in 1959.

On a July evening in 1959, a Viet Cong raiding party killed two American military advisors and two South Vietnamese soldiers who were watching a movie in the mess hall of an army base outside Saigon. It was an unassuming start to a war, or more precisely to the American part in that war; but bigger things would soon follow.

For the more than two and one-half million American men and women who served within the borders of South Vietnam during those twenty-five years, the war was very much time and space dependent. The soldier who served as an advisor to South Vietnamese military forces in the southern tip of South Vietnam in the Mekong Delta in 1959, fought an entirely different war than the soldier or marine who served in the mountainous northern region along the Demilitarized Zone in 1969.

One fought a war against black pajama-clad Viet Cong guerrillas armed with primitive weapons. The other fought a war against uniformed North Vietnamese Army regulars armed with sophisticated weapons, backed up by tanks and artillery. The war in the Delta was a counterinsurgency war; the war along the DMZ (demilitarized zone) was virtually a reenactment of the trench warfare of the First World War. Yet both represented the "truth" about Vietnam."

U.S. Involvement

The history of the U.S. involvement in Vietnam began long before the first U.S casualty in 1959 and spanned the administrations of four Presidents:

Dwight D. Eisenhower, 1959 ...The loss of South Vietnam would set in motion a crumbling process that could, as it progressed, have consequences for us and for freedom.

John F. Kennedy, 1961 ...The United States is determined to help Vietnam preserve its independence, protect its people against communist assassins, and build a better life through economic growth.

Lyndon B. Johnson, 1965... The central issue of the conflict...is the aggression by North Vietnam... If that aggression is stopped, the people and government of South Vietnam will be free to settle their own future and get on with the great task of national development.

Richard M. Nixon, 1969... It is beyond question that without the American commitment in Vietnam, Asia would be a far different place today...Asian leaders know why we are in Vietnam...and urge us to see it through to a satisfactory conclusion.

(Quotes from 1970 Tour 365)

Political analyst, Fox Butterfield, discusses the United States involvement in the war in the Introduction to "The Vietnam War —Day by Day."

"Although most Americans were unaware of it at the time, U.S. involvement really began in 1945 at the end of World War II with President Truman's decision to back France's reconquest of its former colony, Vietnam. Each succeeding president made a further commitment, narrowing the choices for their successor.

Eisenhower helped empower Ngo Dinh Diem as South Vietnam's first leader after the 1954 Geneva agreement ended France's rule.

Kennedy stepped up the number of American advisors and, by sanctioning the coup which led to Diem's death in 1973, increased America's sense of involvement.

Johnson made the fateful decisions in 1965 to begin bombing North Vietnam and dispatch U.S. combat troops to the south.

Paradoxically, none of these presidents had a plan to win the war. They were trapped between their fear of being blamed for the fall of Vietnam and widening the war so much it might bring in China or the Soviet Union.

…The critical turning point in the war may have been the Communists' Tet Offensive in 1968. Hanoi expected it would cause the collapse of Saigon. In fact, the opposite happened. By finally exposing themselves in open battle, the Communists suffered over 50,000 killed… But the ferocity of the attack stunned Americans, who had been led to believe they were winning, and it greatly undermined remaining popular support for the war at home. In the aftermath of Tet, President Johnson announced he would not run for re-election and halted further escalation of the war.

Ironically, in the period after Tet the United States finally began to make progress in the war. Militarily the local Viet Cong were largely wiped out while the North Vietnamese who came south to replace them were battered. The regime of President Nguyen Van Thieu proved more stable than its predecessors and by 1970, 90 percent of the country had been officially 'pacified,' compared with only 33 percent in 1965.

But the American public had tired of war, liberals believing it was immoral, conservatives that it was unwinnable. With increasing domestic pressure to end the war, President Nixon agreed in 1973 to what turned out to be little more than a face-saving formula for withdrawal—The Paris Peace Accords. The POW's came back, but North Vietnam did not have to remove its troops from the south."

Statistics from John S. Bowman's "The Vietnam War—Day by Day" reveal The High Costs of War:

Personnel: "Some 8,744,000 Americans served in four branches of the US military—Army, Navy, Marines, Air Force—during the main period of hostilities (August 1964-January 1973), which makes the Vietnam War second only to World War II in numbers of personnel involved. Because of the constant rotation of US servicemen in Vietnam—primarily one-year terms—a greater percentage of personnel saw duty in Vietnam.

The average age of U.S. combat personnel in Vietnam was only 19—compared to 26 in World War II. Black Americans constituted about 13 percent of the total troop force in Vietnam, about the same as their proportion of the U.S. population, but 28 percent had combat assignments, and only 2 percent of the officers were black.

Meanwhile, about 15,000,000 eligible American youth avoided the draft by gaining student or occupational deferments; and estimated 250,000 simply didn't register for the draft; and estimated 1,000,000 committed draft offenses; some 25,000 were indicted for draft-related offenses; but only some 3250 spent any time in prison."

(p. 220)

Casualties: "The U.S. military lost 47,253 in combat casualties and another 10,449 died in Vietnam; there were 313,616 wounded, of whom 153,300 were classified as seriously wounded. Only a small percentage of the U.S. military personnel actually fought against large Vietcong or North Vietnamese units, although 76 percent were the targets of enemy mortars or rockets, and 56 percent witnessed their comrades being killed or wounded.

Due to the use of helicopters for evacuation, and the advanced medical facilities available, 82 percent of Americans seriously wounded were saved (compared to 71 percent in World War II and 74 percent in Korea)—the highest rate of any modern war. Only 2.6 percent of those who reached hospitals died. However, because of the enemy's use of booby traps, mines, ambushes, and other guerrilla tactics, some 10,000 US serviceman lost at least one limb (more than all those in World War II and Korea combined).

Another 81 U.S. servicemen were killed in Laos and Cambodia. Some 1340 Americans were listed as Missing In Action (MIA) when the war ended. Some of these would be identified and their bodies returned to the United States in the years that followed, but most would remain as MIAs.

South Vietnam reported 185,528 of its military personnel killed in the war, with 499,026 wounded. North Vietnam and the Vietcong reportedly lost 924,048 dead in combat. Vietnam is estimated to have lost 415,000 civilians in the war, with at least 935,000 wounded. South Korea lost 4407 troops fighting in Vietnam; Australia and New Zealand lost 475 and 2348 wounded; and 350 Thais were killed fighting in Vietnam."

(Ibid.)

Costs: "It is roughly, but reasonably estimated that the war cost the United States $150 billion in direct expenses. Indirect expenses would probably total at least that much, while still other costs—such as payments to veterans, interest on debts incurred, etc. are all but unending.

On an average day, US artillery expended 10,000 or so rounds; at about $100 per shell, this item alone cost $1 million per day. One sortie by a B-52 cost

$30,000 in bombs alone. Some 4865 U.S. helicopters were lost in the war, each costing about $250,000, and 3720 other aircraft were destroyed. The total tonnage of bombs dropped over North Vietnam, South Vietnam, Cambodia, and Laos came to about 8 million (about four times the tonnage used in all of World War II). Although the bombing inflicted an estimated $600 million worth of damage on North Vietnam, it is calculated that the United States spent about 10 times that much on these raids, in which thousands of U.S. fliers were killed, wounded, captured, or missing. The Soviet Union and China are estimated to have provided about $3 billion worth of aid to North Vietnam and the Vietcong."

(ibid.)

Personal issues of the Vietnam War's outcome effected thousands of military personnel. In "Vietnam The Decisive Battles", John Pimlott discusses the cause and effect of a unique Vietnam veteran issue.

Between August, 1964, and January 1973, some 2,594,000 U.S. servicemen were posted to South Vietnam, with the vast majority serving tours that lasted 365 days. Approximately 80 percent of the soldiers were exposed to enemy attack, and about 40 percent participated in ground skirmishes. The vast majority of those who survived returned to civilian life without recognition or ceremony. Unlike the veterans of earlier wars, they did not receive warm public welcomes; instead, many returned to ridicule and taunts of "baby killer." Soldiers from all branches of the service were advised to not wear their uniforms or medals in public.

The majority of veterans were able to reintegrate successfully into society, but for some the experience of Vietnam and their return home proved too much to absorb. Facing a country seemingly apathetic to their sacrifices, and feeling guilty at having survived where their friends had not; these men found it difficult to settle back into a normal pattern of living. A significant number suffered a disproportionate incidence of social and personal problems. Psychiatrists who dealt with them labeled their condition "Post Traumatic Stress Disorder" (PTSD). Plagued by characteristic insomnia, reenactment of disturbing experiences from Vietnam, and acute depression, most sufferers carried an inescapable feeling that the war had been a waste.

The dedication of the Vietnam Memorial in Washington D.C. in November 1982 and changing attitudes in the United States have done much to alleviate the situation. But for a significant number of veterans, the Vietnam experience remains a constant nightmare.

Society and The Vietnam War:

In 1990, historian and author, James A. Warren described in the Preface to "Portrait Of A Tragedy", the psychological and political effects the war had upon the identity and beliefs of society, as a whole.

"...The American experience in Vietnam provides us with a wealth of clues and insights about modern American history and American values. When President John F. Kennedy was laying the groundwork for direct American intervention in Vietnam in the early 1960's, the United States had reached the height of its power and self-confidence. We were the unchallenged leaders of the free world. There was a belief among the nation's leaders that the United States was invincible, that it had not only the political and military might to do what it wanted, but also the moral authority to do so.

In 1975, Americans watched on television the humiliating evacuation of Saigon, the capital city of South Vietnam. The surrender of the city to the communists ended a terrible era in our history—an era that had changed us. America was an entirely different nation than it had been back in the early 1960's. We were no longer so sure of our path, no longer confident that we had the answers to all the important questions.

The war had come close to tearing the nation apart. The American public no longer trusted its government. The armed forces of the nation had become demoralized and fragmented. The soul and conscience of the nation had been deeply wounded. And more than 57,000 men had sacrificed their lives..."

The Aftermath of War

The trauma of Vietnam remains, but its lessons remain unclear. Military experts, historians, and veterans yet debate the unanswered question of 'what should have been done.'

In a speech at the 1994 dedication of the Lyndon B. Johnson Presidential Library, the former President's daughter, Lucy revealed a private conversation with her father during the escalating war years.

The weary Commander and Chief confided, " It's not doing what's right that's hard for me... It's knowing what the hell is the right thing to do."

Perhaps one clear message of the Vietnam era is that the United States cannot go to war without popular support. Retired General Frederick C. Weyland, the last American commander in Vietnam, once wrote:

"War is death and destruction...

The Army must have the price of involvement clear before we get involved, so that America can weigh the probable cost in involvement against the dangers of non-involvement. *For there are worse things than war.*" (Italics added)

(The Vietnam War Day By Day, p.6)

ACKNOWLEDGEMENTS

As this memorial tribute reaches completion, words become inadequate in expressing my sincere appreciation for the many good people who helped make it a reality. First of all, I wish to express my gratitude to my husband and children for their love, support and patience as the months and years of research and writing unfolded. We gained much as a family and wish to extend our love and gratitude to countless other families, whose personal loss and sacrifice, have yet to be publicly acknowledged.

My thanks to former Idaho Attorney General, Jim Jones, who had the foresight to realize this important era of Idaho history must be preserved for generations to come.

Interviews with veterans, casualties' families, retired military commanders, and state department officials, offered insight and added understanding. Family members and friends who contributed photos, letters, tributes, poetry and " feelings of the heart", can never be adequately thanked.

The willingness of county clerks, school and public librarians, newspaper people, and historical society volunteers from across the state was greatly appreciated. Each helped in linking together pieces of a difficult and confusing time in our state and nation's history. High school yearbooks, obituaries, newspaper articles, cemetery, and funeral records all provided significant and priceless bits of information. My apologies are extended to the families of those fine Idaho servicemen whose records we could not locate. It is my hope that this memorial will open a conduit, through which respect, appreciation and remembrance will flow.

During the concluding and challenging weeks of the book's final edit process, the expert advice and input of my good friend, and former State Department Foreign Services Officer, Blaine Jensen, have been an invaluable and much appreciated asset. I'm also very appreciative to my trusted friend and veteran, Larry Petersen, for sharing personal photographs and rare military memorabilia. I'm grateful for the talented artwork and contribution of my daughter, Chrystine Whyte. Last but not least, this memorial tribute has finally become a reality because of the dedication and gifted skills of a true professional, Steve Hansen, who created the layout and text design.

In addition to these fine individuals, I wish to express my sincere thanks to the following contributors:

Jeff Lambson, Granite Publishing
Dave Otvos
Freedom Bird Members
Freedom Bird Historical Record
Retired Colonel Jack Layton, SR71 Pilot
Retired Lt. Colonel Darrel Savage

Senator and Mrs. J. Stanley Williams

Congressional Medal of Honor Recipient Bernard Fisher

The Department of Defense Military Records

Friends and family members of Idaho casualties

The Idaho Historical Society (Troy Reeves)

"Twin Falls Times News" and Twin Falls Public Library

Mountain Home Public Library

Gooding County Historical Society

Gooding County Public Library

Minidoka Historical Society

Kellogg High School Library

Orofino High School and Public Library

"The Clearwater Tribune"

"The Lewiston Tribune" and High School Library

Moscow High School Library

Bonners Ferry High School Library

Idaho Falls Public Library and Skyline High School Library

Madison High School Library

Gonzaga University Library

Emmett High School Library

"The Coeur d'Alene Press" and High School Library

"The Soda Springs Newspaper" and High School Library

"The Post Falls Tribune", High School Library, and American Legion Post

"The Wood River Journal" in Hailey, ID

"The Preston Citizen" and High School Library

'The Post Register"

"The Idaho Statesman"

"The Morning News"

"The Blackfoot News"

Potlatch High School Library

Blackfoot High School Library

"The Payette Newspaper"

"The News Examiner", Montpelier, ID

"The Jefferson Star" and West Jefferson High School Library

"The Power County News" and American Falls High School Library

Challis High School

St. Maries High School Library

"The Buhl Herald"

"The Idaho State Journal"

"Minidoka County News"

Snake River High School Library

Bonners Ferry High School Library

NOTES & SELECTED READINGS

The historic timeline and military strategies were formulated from the following combined works:

"Vietnam The Decisive Battles" by John Pimlott, Macmillan Publishing, NY.1990
"The Vietnam War Day By Day" by John S. Bowman, Magna Books, Hong Kong.1989
"Portrait Of A Tragedy" by James A. Warren, Lothrop, Lee & Shepard Books, NY. 1990
"Vietnam A History" by Stanley Karnow, The Viking Press, NY. 1983

Vietnam "In Country" Military Publications:
"Handbook for U.S. Forces in Vietnam" Dec. 1968
"The Hurricane" II Field Force Vietnam April 1970
"Tour 365" US Army Vietnam Summer 1970
"The Hurricane" II Field Force Vietnam Jan. 1970
"UP Tight" United States Army Vietnam Winter 1970
"Redcatcher!" Yearbook, 199th Light Infantry Brigade May 1969
"9th Infantry Division" Vietnam 1968

"The Washington Post Magazine" May 28, 1989, "VN Flashback" by George Wilson
"Life Magazine" November 1992 Volume 15, Number 12. p. 24
"Life Magazine" November 1987 Volume 10, Number 12, p. 110
"Parade Magazine" May 30, 1993 NY, NY. p. 5
"The Navy Times" Vol. 16, No. 17 Feb. 1967, Eastern Edition
"Popular Aviation" May/June 1967
"Air Force and Space Digest" March 1967
"Project Checo Report" 18 April 1966 Former classified report of "The Fall of Ashau"
Internet Site www.virtualwall.org
Video production ABC News "The Fall Of Saigon" 1989
Video production Lyndon B. Johnson Library "Faces of The Vietnam War", 1994

"History of The Idaho National Guard", Orlan J. Svingen Editor, 1995
"Seven Years In Hanoi" by Captain Larry Chesley, Bookcraft, SLC. UT 1973
"The Vietnam Reader" Edited by Walter Capps, Routledge, London, 1991
"Student Handbook" Vol. 2, R.R. Bowker Publishing, New Jersey, 1993
"Don't Know Much About History", Kenneth C. Davis, Avon Books, NY, NY 1990
"Academic American Encyclopedia" 1992, Grolier Electronic Publishing, Inc.
"Shrapnel In The Heart" by Laura Palmer, Vintage Books, NY, NY 1988
"Writings On The Wall" by Jan Scruggs, 1994 Vietnam Veterans Memorial Fund

"A Time To Kill", Edited by Denny Roy , Signature Books, SLC, UT 1992

"We Were Soldiers Once…And Young" by Lt.Gen. Harold G. Moore (Ret.) and Joseph. L. Galloway, Random House, NY, NY. 1992

"The Pentagon Papers", Copyright 1971, The New York Times Company

"The Tunnels Of Cu Chi", Tom Mangold and John Penycate, Random House, NY 1985

"In Retrospect", by Robert S. McNamara, Random House , NY 1995

IDAHO VIETNAM CASUALTY INDEX

Major Lawrence Acre   B. 2-2-35   Died 10-9-69   Enlisted from Coeur D'Alene, ID Army - 94, 95, 160

Cpl. Leo Joe Adakai   B. 5-3-44   Died 8-7-69   Enlisted from Blackfoot, ID Army

Sgt. Thomas Oliver Ahlberg   B. 2-3-51   Died 5-4-70   Enlisted from Idaho Falls, ID Army - 101, 103, 125, 126

Pfc. Duane Charles Akkerman   B. 4-17-46   Died 10-27-67   Enlisted from Lewiston, ID Army - 158

Col. Gerald William Alley   B. 7-28-34   MIA POW   (declared KIA 8-16-78) remains returned to U.S. in the 1990's Airforce. Enlisted from Pocatello, ID

Major James Herbert Allred   B. 9-26-25   Died 12-14-63   Enlisted from Twin Falls, ID Army - 8

Major Harry Arlo Amesbury, Jr.   B. 22-13-32   Died 4-26-72   Enlisted from Caldwell, ID

2nd Lt. Reese Mark Andersen   B. 7-31-43   Died 4-19-69   Marines Enlisted from Arbon Valley, ID - 51, 53, 160

Staff Sgt. James Barton Anderson   B. 9-25-47   Died 1-25-68   Army Enlisted from American Falls, ID - 84

Sgt. Victor Edward Anderson   B. 4-11-43   Died 1-31-66   Army Enlisted from Stone, ID

Sgt. William Edward Anderson   B. 7-22-31   Died 8-1-66   Army Enlisted from St. Maries, ID - 123

Pfc. Allan Theo Aslett   B. 7-25-50   Died 9-27-69   Marines Enlisted from Twin Falls, ID - 86

Sp.4 Glen Lawrence Atkinson   B. 10-24-46   Died 2-3-69   Army Enlisted from Caldwell, ID - 49

Cpl. Gerald Lee Baldwin   B. 3-18-49   Died 12-12-69   Army Enlisted from Nampa, ID - 93, 94

LCPL/E 3 Michael P. Bartelme   B. 8-4-46   Died 5-2-67   Marines Enlisted from Buhl, ID

Sgt. Brent John Baumert   B. 1-1-40   Died 4-22-66   Army (Born in SLC) Enlisted from Twin Falls, ID - 82

HN Phillip Arthur Beasley   B. 2-2-46   Died 9-30-68   Navy Enlisted from Boise, ID - 111, 112

1st Lt. William Ronald Beasley   B. 1-16-42   Died 9-25-66   Army Enlisted from Boise, ID - 112

Sp. 5 Ross Michael Bee   B. 6-24-46   Died 1-19-67   Army Enlisted from Georgetown, ID - 80

Major Anthony Rodney Bellamy   B. 1-30-40   Died 5-5-68   Army Enlisted form Boise, ID - 85

Pfc. Bruce Rolland Bennett   B. 1-29-47   Died 9-5-66   Marines Enlisted from Boise, ID - 152, 153

1st Lt. Johnny William Benton   B. 5-14-47   Died 11-25-68   Army Enlisted from Jerome, ID - 147, 160

Capt. Gary W. Bitton   B. 6-28-36   Died 12-6-63   Air Force Enlisted from Blackfoot, ID - 7

Cpl. William Darwin Blenkinsop B. 6-26-51   Died 8-29-70   Army Enlisted from Couer D'Alene, ID

Major Jon Keith Bodahl   B. 12-18-37   MIA/POW 9-12-69   (listed as Killed in Action 5-30-74) Air Force
                                                                    Enlisted from Boise, ID - 141, 143

Sgt. Edward James Boggess   B. 6-29-46   Died 12-29-68   Army Enlisted from Lewiston, ID

Capt. Curtis Richard Bohlscheid B. 12-9-36   MIA/POW 6-11-67   Marines Enlisted from Pocatello, ID - 137

Cpl. Jess Burton Boicourt, Jr. B. 10-23-45   Died 3-11-68   Marines Enlisted from Nampa, ID - 123

Sp 4 Gary Ray Boushele   B. 9-16-47   Died 10-27-69   Army Enlisted from Hailey, ID - 160

Capt. Bruce Gregory Bowles   B. 7-2-41   Died 1-15-69   Army Enlisted from Boise, ID

Cpl. John Alex Boyle   B. 2-15-50   Died 1-26-69   Army Enlisted from Idaho Falls, ID - 85

W.O. Ray Eugene Bradley   B. 9-12-36   Died 2-16-67   Army Enlisted from Boise, ID

Cpl. Everett W. Brauburger   B. 1-22-49   Died 7-24-69   Army Enlisted from Soda Springs, ID - 132

Major Harry Milton Brenn   B. 4-28-33   Died 4-13-67   Air Force Enlisted from Moscow, ID

Sgt. Leonard Lee Broenneke   B. 6-21-50   Died 6-14-71   Army Enlisted from Moscow, ID - 80

Sp 4 Randy K. Bronson   B. 1-6-49   Died 5-13-69   Army Enlisted from Meridian, ID - 150, 151

Sp 4 Arlo Frank Brown   B. 5-13-44   Died 1-14-67   Army Enlisted form Idaho Falls, ID

2nd Lt. Michael Brown   B. 8-25-43   Died 3-7-69   Army 116th National Guard Unit Enlisted from
                                                                    Fremont County (St. Anthony, ID) - 47

Sgt. Ivan J. Broyles   B. 11-22-38   Died 4-21-66   Army Enlisted from Blackfoot, ID

Capt. Robert Newton Brumet   B. 10-22-27   Died 4-9-64   Air Force Enlisted from New Plymouth, ID (Payette County)

Sgt. William Bunch   B. 10-13-46   Died 12-28-69   Marines Enlisted from Ahsahka, ID (Clearwater Co.)

Sp 5 William R. Burt, Jr.   B. 9-21-44   Died 7-11-69   Army Enlisted from Hailey, ID (Born in Bronxville, NY - 113

Sgt. Richard Buck Carlson   B. 2-22-44   Died 11-4-66   Army Enlisted from Twin Falls, ID

Sgt. Clyde Robert Carrico   B. 8-15-48   Died 12-19-60   Army Enlisted from Orofino, ID

Sgt. Chad Leonard Carson   B. 12-14-49   Died 12-10-69   Army Enlisted from Boise, ID - 128

Pfc. Robert Stanley Chambers   B. 3-24-48   Died 11-24-67   Army Enlisted from Potlatch, ID

Cpl. Johnny Howard Chapman   B. 2-15-52   Died 8-20-71   Army Enlisted from Boise, ID - 99

AX2 David Roger Chatteron   B. 3-29-38   Died 7-18-67   Navy Enlisted from Twin Falls, ID - 26

Capt. David Edward Cinkosky   B. 9-9-45   Died 8-5-71   Army Enlisted from Post Falls, ID - 90

Sgt. Conn Kay Clark   B. 12-18-46   Died 7-31-69   Army 116th National Guard Unit Enlisted from Rigby, ID - 47

Cpl. Grant LeRoy Clark   B. 9-21-45   Died 10-30-65   Marines Enlisted from Pocatello, ID - 13

1st Lt. James Bradley Claybaugh   B. 11-20-43   Died 3-29-69   Army   Enlisted from Caldwell, ID - 96

Lance Cpl. Larry Dale Coats   B. 8-1-48   Died 9-3-68   Marines Enlisted from Twin Falls, ID

Cpl. Clyde Ralph Coburn   B. 7-10-47   Died 12-9-67   Army Enlisted from Preston, ID - 112, 113

Capt. Ralph Brent Cordon   B. 9-27-42   Died 5-2-71   Army Enlisted from Idaho Falls, ID - 47

Sp 4 Jess William Creason , Jr.   B. 7-23-47   Died 4-26-68   Army Enlisted from Cascade, ID - 147, 161

Pfc. Michael Lee Crouson   B. 12-6-44   Died 12-10-66   Marines Enlisted from Pocatello, ID - 79

S. Sgt. Clyde Arthur Crow   B. 6-23-40   Died 5-19-66   Air Force Enlisted from Boise, ID

Sp. 4 David L. Curtis   B. 6-15-51   Died 6-17-71   Army Enlisted from Weippe, ID (Clearwater Co.)

BM 1 E6 James Marvin Curtis   B. 3-21-35   Died 11-15-68   Navy Enlisted from Hagerman, ID

Sp 4 LeRoy Damiano   B. 9-30-47   Died 2-12-68   Army Enlisted from Harrison, ID (Kootenai Co.) - 33, 162

Pfc. Elmo Lee DeFord   B. 6-1-47   Died 5-2-66   Army Enlisted from Hansen, ID (Born in Montpelier, ID) - 122

Lance Cpl. Larry D. Defilippis   B. 8-3-46   Died 11-12-66   Marines Enlisted from Idaho Falls, ID - 122

SFC Richard Lester Dennis   B. 4-3-29   Died 12-8-67   Army Enlisted from Smelterville, ID (Shoshone Co.)

Warrant Officer
Thomas LaMonte Dives   B. 3-7-48   Died 8-2-69   Army Enlisted from Malad, ID

1st Lt. Jack LeRoy Dodson   B. 2-14-38   Died 5-26-67   Army Enlisted from Kimberly, ID - 83

Sp5 Lyle Eugene Drown   B. 10-21-47   Died 4-15-69   Army Enlisted from Kimberly, ID - 113

Sp4 Michael Lee Earp   B. 1-22-48   Died 6-18-69   Army 116th National Guard Unit Co. D Enlisted from Grangeville, ID - 47

Pfc. Donald Lee Eldridge   B. 8-20-47   Died 9-27-68   Army Enlisted from Emmett, ID (Valley Co.)

Sgt. Louis Craig Emery   B. 9-27-50   Died 3-16-70   Army Enlisted from Parma, ID - 89

Pfc. Franklin David Endicott   B. 11-28-46   Died 9-4-67   Marine Enlisted from Boise, ID

Sgt. Steven Glenn England   B. 7-5-51   Died 2-15-71   Army Enlisted from Pocatello, ID - 60-61

Lance Cpl. Jerry Duane Estes   B. 1-18-45   Died 2-6-66   Marine Enlisted from Boise, ID

Sp4 Gary Gene Evans   B. 12-22-46   Died 6-13-68   Army Enlisted from Heyburn, ID

Pfc. David Acel Fairchild   B. 5-24-45   Died 2-2-66   Army Enlisted from Buhl, ID - 126, 127

Pfc. Raymond Patrick Finley   B. 9-15-47   Died 10-1-67   Marine Enlisted from St. Maries, ID - 161

Lance Cpl. Winfield Scott Flint   B. 4-18-48   Died 5-14-67   Marine Enlisted from Payette, ID

Cpl. Fancisco John Flores   B. 9-12-45   Died 5-21-67   Marine Enlisted from Parma, ID - 90, 160

Cpl. Thomas Allen Foreman   B. 3-25-48   Died 1-20-69   Army Enlisted from Caldwell, ID - 114

Cpl. Gary Jack Foster   B. 4-14-45   Died 6-4-66   Marine Enlisted from Boise, ID - 83, 84

Pfc. Gary Virgil Frazier   B. 11-10-47   Died 3-2-68   Army Enlisted from Pocatello, ID - 121

ETN2 Thomas George Funke   B. 3-29-43   Died 1-1-68   Navy Enlisted from Coeur D'Alene, ID

Pfc. Garry Lee Gabriel   B. 3-3-49   Died 12-27-67   Marine Enlisted from Boise, ID

Sp 4 Albaro Quezada Garcia   B. 2-19-49   Died 6-24-70   Army Enlisted from Nampa, ID - 59

S. Sgt. Mervin (Dennis) Golden   B. 9-12-44   Died 6-9-68   Army Enlisted McCall, ID - 34

S. Sgt. Bruce Lynn Goodsell   B. 5-15-45   Died 1-6-71   Army Enlisted from Thatcher, ID (Franklin Co.)

Pfc. Robert Jerry Gordon   B. 7-25-49   Died 4-15-69   Marine Enlisted from Hayden Lake, ID - 145, 146, 160

2nd Lt. Ralph Shoup Gorton III   B. 11-26-42   Died 5-27-68   Marine Enlisted from Boise, ID - 42, 43, 108, 160

Sp4 Michael Frank Green   B. 1-23-47   Died 3-10-68   Army Enlisted from Pocatello, ID - 121

Capt. Robert Carrell Green   B. 10-10-43   Died 3-17-71   Army Enlisted from Donnelly, ID (Valley Co.)

Pfc. Larry Dee Greenhalgh   B. 9-13-44   Died 3-17-69   Army Enlisted from St. Anthony, ID - 134, 135

ATR 3 Charles Clark Gregory   B. 8-20-47   Died 7-29-67   Navy Enlisted from Montpelier, ID - 29

Major William James Griffin   B. 12-18-34   Died 3-14-69   Air Force Enlisted from Homedale, ID - 157, 158

S. Sgt. Donald Jack Haile   B. 10-12-38   Died 2-9-68   Army Enlisted from Caldwell, ID - 104, 105

Pfc. Craig Hayes Hansen   B. 8-8-44   Died 6-20-69   Army Enlisted from Soda Springs, ID - 149, 150

Lance Cpl. Robert Warren Hansen   B. 1-15-47   Died 5-10-69   Marine Enlisted from Naples, ID

Sp.4 Eric Thomas Harshbarger   B. 11-13-49   Died 11-1-69   Army Enlisted from Filer, ID - 100, 101

Sp. 4 Lonnie Hilton Hendrickson B. 4-16-48 Died 4-3-69 Army 116th National Guard Unit Enlisted from Orofino, ID - 47

Lance Cpl.
William Barton Hepburn B. 12-17-47 Died 8-23-66 Marine Enlisted from Lewiston, ID (Born in Omaha Wa)

Cpl. David Edwin Herbert B. 5-16-40 Died 7-2-66 Army From Rupert, ID - 120, 121

Pfc. Craig W. Hirschi B. 7-29-49 Died 9-15-70 Marine Enlisted from Rexburg, ID

Pfc. Teddy Merlin Hodges, Jr. B. 3-19-45 Died 6-6-69 Enlisted from Malta, ID

Capt. Gregg Neyman Hollinger B. 5-9-42 MIA/POW 12-14-71 Army Enlisted from Paul, ID - 63, 138

Ensign Hall T. Hollingsworth B. 6-29-42 MIA/POW 1-16-66 Navy Enlisted from Grace, ID - 138

Cpl. Sheldon Dale Hoskins B. 5-12-48 Died 10-7-68 Marine Enlisted from Blackfoot, ID - 92

Cpl. Douglas G. Howes B. 8-24-49 Died 3-16-70 Army (Family in Parma, ID) Records show he last lived in Roy, Utah - 79

M. Sgt. William Balt Hunt Born 7-31-35 MIA/POW 11-4-66 Army Enlisted from Sandpoint, ID - 23

Pfc. Jerry Antone Hurianek B. 6-24-47 Died 6-27-69 Marine Enlisted from Middleton, ID

Sp 4 John Allen Hurst B. 10-31-49 Died 1-7-70 Army Born in Idaho Falls, Enlisted from Dubois, ID - 111

Pfc. Terry Floyd Huston B. 1-2-47 Died 6-7-66 Army Enlisted from Caldwell Born in Nampa, ID - 91

Pfc. Elmer Glenn Ireland B. 6-29-48 Died 7-1-69 Army Enlisted from Star, ID - 96

Sp4 Lloyd Bruce Jensen B. 3-14-43 Died 12-12-66 Army Enlisted from Boise, ID

A3C/E2 Bob Jewett B. 10-5-47 Died 4-28-67 Air Force Born in Pocatello, ID (Enlisted from Challis)

Pfc. Henry David Johnson B. 12-8-48 Died 5-23-69 Marine Enlisted from Nez Pierce, ID

Cpl Brent R. Jones B. 6-25-47 Died 5-21-68 Army Enlisted from Firth, ID - 135, 136

Lance Cpl. David Samuel Jones B. 8-29-49 Died 1-4-70 Marine Enlisted from Fernwood, ID (Benewah Co.) - 84

Lance Cpl.
Howard Lemuel Jones, Jr.   B. 3-4-48   Died 2-24-68   Marine Enlisted from Post Falls, ID

CWO Tommy L. Kearsely   B. 7-1-47   Died 5-4-70   Army Enlisted from Buhl, ID - 57, 58, 78

1st Lt. Kay Kazu Kimura   B. 11-1-43   Died 3-7-70   Marine Enlisted from Nampa, ID (Born in Poston AZ) - 105

Cpl. Rodger Magnus Koefod   B. 7-7-48   Died 4-27-69   Army Enlisted from Moscow, ID - 151, 152

1st Lt. Colin Ed Lamb   B. 2-11-42   Died 7-3-68   Army Enlisted from Caldwell, ID - 107, 108, 161

Cpl. Robert Wilbur Larison   B. 12-17-48   Died 11-1-67   Army Enlisted from Pocatello, ID

Sgt. Dale K. Larson   B. 10-24-47   Died 11-12-68   Army Enlisted from Burley, ID - 48

Pfc. John Gilbert Larson   B. 9-12-47   Died 12-30-66   Army Enlisted from Blackfoot, ID - 23

AX3-E4 Delmar Leon Lawrence   B. 1-6-46   Died 4-1-68   Navy Enlisted from Riggins, ID - 111

Major William E. Lemmons   B. 1-12-42   POW/MIA   Declared Killed In Action 6-12-78 Army Born in Burley, ID Enlisted from Pocatello, ID - 27, 164

Pfc. Robert R. Lewis   B. 10-14-47   Died 5-31-69   Army Enlisted from Boise, ID (Record shows he was from Modesto, CAL)

Sp 4 Gilbert Ray Lish   B. 11-30-47   Died 1-2-68   Army Enlisted from Boise, ID

Sp 4 James John Lister   B. 5-13-47   Died 3-21-69   Army Enlisted from Burley, ID

Sp 4 James Alton Lockwood   B. 5-25-46   Died 9-17-66   Army Enlisted from Sandpoint, ID

Cpl. Herman Augusta Lohman, Jr. B. 1-24-48   Died 4-6-68   Marine Enlisted from Twin Falls, ID - 38

Col. Herlihy Townsend Long   B. 3-15-24   Died 1-27-68   Army Enlisted from Mt. Home, ID (Records indicates he was from Macon, GA)

John E. Lumbry   Army Enlisted from Caldwell, ID (No other additional information)

Cpl. Neile Cooper MacKay   B. 4-17-45   Died 1-10-70   Army Enlisted from Weiser, ID

Lance Cpl. Danny Joe Maggard   B. 12-14-49   Died 3-18-69   Marine Enlisted from Parma, ID

Sp 4 Eddie D. Mapes   B. 1-18-51   Died 7-12-70   Army Enlisted from Kootenai, ID

Sp 4 Clayton Arthur Martin   B. 1-12-44   Died 10-16-67   Army Enlisted from Idaho Falls, ID - 29

Pfc. Richard Peter Massine   B. 11-21-45   Died 11-20-66   Army Enlisted from Kellogg, ID

L.Cdr. Roderick L. Mayer   B. 3-2-39   MIA/POW 10-17-65   Declared Killed in Action 10-31-77 Air Force Enlisted from Lewiston, ID - 12, 69

Sp 4 Steven Michael McArthur   B. 2-8-49   Died 4-28-68   Army Enlisted from Coeur D' Alene, ID - 42

S. Sgt. Raymond Louis McCaslin   B. 4-8-37   Died 12-26-69   Marine Enlisted from Boise, ID

Pfc. Steven James McDonald   B. 6-20-51   Died 11-28-71   Army Enlisted from Ketchum, ID

Cpl. Donald Smith McGinley   B. 3-31-28   Died 7-29-68   Army Enlisted from Rupert, ID (Born in Albany, MO) - 161

Capt. Donald Vernon McGregor   B. 12-22-33   Died 8-13-63   Army Enlisted from Paul, ID (Born in Heyburn) - 6, 95, 96, 160

Lance Cpl. Jay Darwin McLain   B. 2-7-42   Died 5-28-67   Marine Enlisted from Bancroft, ID - 81, 82

Cpl. Michael Lee McMasters   B. 2-24-47   Died 6-27-69   Marine Enlisted from Mt. Home, ID (Born in Plainsville, Ohio) - 120

HN Jim Carl McNamar   B. 9-16-45   Died 4-17-68   Navy Enlisted from Mt. Home, ID - 114

ATCS Franklin DeLano McNary   B. 2-24-34   Died 6-13-67   Navy Enlisted from Coeur D' Alene, ID

Col. Richard Joseph Meechan   B. 1-6-28   Died 6-15- 72   Air Force   Enlisted from Payette, ID

Cpl. Steven Dee Merrell   B. 1-28-50   Died 5-15-70   Marine Enlisted from Pocatello, ID - 160

Lester G. Michels   B. 4-18-29   Died 3-21-66   Marine Enlisted from Blackfoot, ID (Born in Hackensack, NJ) - 120

Sp 4 Cecil Ray Millspaugh   B. 10-4-44   Died 3-26-68   Army Enlisted from Declo, ID - 89

Sp 4 John E.S. Mitchell, Jr.	B. 2-12-51	Died 7-1-70	Army Enlisted from American Falls, ID - 93
Pfc. Lonnie Ray Mitchell	B. 10-5-47	Died 12-6-68	Marine Enlisted from King Hill, ID
Sp 4 Gary O Mooer	B. 3-15-45	Died 7-23-67	Army (Originally from Rosebud Montana)
Sp 4 Dean L. Moon	B. 7-12-47	Died 3-19-69	Army Enlisted from Sterling, ID (Bingham Co.) - 50
Michael James Mooney	B. 2-9-51	Died 8-10-69	Marine Enlisted from Eagle, ID - 55
Lance Cpl. Dan Ross Moore	B. 8-31-48	Died 10-17-68	Marine Enlisted from Idaho Falls, ID - 119
Pfc. William Ralph Morledge	B. 2-24-48	Died 9-20-68	Army Enlisted from Emmett, ID
Sgt. Ronald Grant Mottishaw	B. 10-5-45	Died 2-16-67	Army Enlisted from Pocatello, ID - 26, 130, 131
1st. Lt. Lester Neal Moulton	B. 5-13-42	Died 5-25-70	Army Enlisted from Victor, ID
Pfc. Danny L. Naillon	B. 10-1-46	Died 9-12-66	Army Enlisted from Payette, ID
Pfc. Jimmy D. Nakayama	B. 11-19-43	Died 11-17-65	Army Enlisted from Rigby, ID - 14
Sp4 Robert William Nelson	B. 2-15-51	Died 9-29-70	Army Enlisted from Rigby, ID (Born in Montpelier)-133, 134
Cpl. Steven Harold Nipp	B. 8-6-48	Died 2-8-69	Marine Enlisted from Post Falls, ID (Born in Coeur D'Alene)
Pfc. Mark James O'Brien	B. 9-27-47	Died 12-14-68	Marine Enlisted from Tetonia, ID (Born in Driggs, ID) - 87
Capt. Troy R. Oliver, Jr.	B. 10-10-36	Died 5-19-68	Marine Enlisted from Boise, ID (Born in Twin Falls, ID) - 119
Sgt. William Whitby Olsen	B. 8-26-47	Died 5-23-69	Army Enlisted from Pocatello, ID
S. Sgt. Bennett Walfred Olsen	B. 10-3-37	Died 1-8-68	Marine Enlisted from Caldwell, ID
1st Lt. David King Omstead	B. 5-4-47	Died 6-16-68	Enlisted from Harrison, ID (Record indicates he was from Costa Mesa, CAL)
EN 1 Michael Harris Painter	B. 2-28-43	Died 8-8-69	Coast Guard Enlisted from Moscow, ID

Sp 4 Steven J. Perry	B. 7-23-50	Died 12-28-68	Army Enlisted from Boise, ID (Record indicates he was from SLC,UT)
S. Sgt. William Don Petersen	B. 3-6-36	Died 11-15-67	Army Enlisted from Boise, ID (Born in Phoenix, AZ) - 30, 31, 32
Sp 4 Bobby Gene Peterson	B. 7-23-47	Died 7-27-67	Army Enlisted from Idaho Falls, ID - 28
Sgt. Jon Dale Peterson	B. 8-10-47	Died 4-1-69	Army Enlisted from Shelley, ID - 51, 97, 98
CWO Jesse Don Phelps	B. 10-1-37	MIA/POW 12-19-66	Army Enlisted from Boise, ID (Born in Ogden, UT) - 109
Sgt. Samuel C. Phillips III	B. 7-7-43	Died 10-2-67	Army Enlisted from Homedale, ID
Louis Alphonse Pichon, Jr.	B. 1-7-28	Died 3-26-69	Marine Enlisted from Ketchum, ID (From Slidell, LA)
Cpl. James Edward Piva	B. 3-20-48	Died 2-27-70	Army Enlisted from Challis, ID - 106
L.Cpl. Michael Lee Poletti	B. 2-12-50	Died 9-10-68	Marine Enlisted from Pocatello, ID
Pfc. Robert Allan Powell	B. 6-3-48	Died 9-19-66	Marine Enlisted from Boise, ID (Born in Weiser, ID)
Sp4 John Lynn Powers	B. 10-13-49	MIA/POW 2-15-71	Army Enlisted from Mackay, ID - 98, 99, 106, 161
Pfc. Michael Lloyd Priest	B. 3-31-47	Died 4-8-67	Army Enlisted from Idaho Falls, ID
Capt. Lewis DeVern Probart	B. 3-27-43	Died 7-17-69	Army Enlisted from Pocatello, ID - 77, 78, 87, 88, 153-156, 161
Sp 4 Max Welker Pugmire	B. 4-10-49	Died 10-24-69	Army Enlisted from Montpelier, ID - 144, 145
1st Lt. Frank Reasoner	B. 9-16-37	Died 7-12-65	Marine Enlisted from Kellogg, ID (Born in Spokane, Wa) - 11, 161
Cpl. Christopher Ray Reed	B. 12-21-46	Died 6-9-69	Marine Enlisted from Boise, ID
E4 Keith H. Reitz	B. 10-25-48	Died 3-9-70	Army Enlisted from Payette, ID (Born in Ontario, Oregon) - 160
Sp 4 Michael Hugh Richards	B. 5-10-50	Died 3-15-71	Army Enlisted from Bonners Ferry, ID

Sp 4 Arturo Recio Rios	B. 2-19-47	Died 4-19-68	Army Enlisted from Idaho Falls, ID (Born in Alamo, TX)
HN Samuel Henri Rodriquez	B. 2-21-46	Died 5-19-68	Navy Enlisted from Wendell, ID
Pfc. Ralph Lee Rotter	B. 4-14-44	Died 1-2-68	Army Enlisted from Lewiston, ID
Cpl. Douglas Noel Rowe	B. 11-13-46	Died 3-9-69	Army Enlisted from Pocatello, ID (Born in Rupert, ID) - 50
1st Lt. Ronald Benton Rueppel	B. 3-30-48	Died 9-27-71	Army Enlisted from Moscow, ID (Graduated from Dreary High School) - 62, 160
GSGT-E7 Lynne Harlan Rutter	B. 9-5-31	Died 11-5-70	Marine Enlisted from Jerome, ID (Record indicates he was from Rahway, NJ)
Sgt. Vicente Diaz Sandoval	B. 4-10-45	Died 4-8-67	Army Enlisted from American Falls, ID
Sp4 Floyd Gwen Savell	B. 6-4-46	Died 2-14-67	Army Enlisted from Boise, ID
Pfc Maeshall Gust Schaffner	B. 2-2-47	Died 3-18-68	Marines Enlisted from Cataldo, ID - 41
Pfc Ronald Dean Shaff	B. 1-28-49	Died 2-19-69	Marines Enlisted from Filer, ID - 49
1st Lt. John Frederick Shiefer	B. 10-14-39	Died 8-29-70	Army Enlisted from Boise, ID - 127
WO Glen Emery Shropshire	B. 12-27-46	Died 7-31-67	Army Enlisted from Sandpoint, ID
Lance Cpl. Verle Jennings Skidmore	B. 6-4-47	Died 5-10-68	Marine Enlisted from Terreton, ID - 42, 113, 160
Pfc. Kenneth Lloyd Small	B. 2-24-50	Died 6-7-69	Marine Enlisted from Salmon (Born in Idaho Falls, ID)
Pfc. Fred Steven Smart	B. 4-27-50	Died 6-19-70	Marine Enlisted from Meridian, ID (Graduated from Twin Falls High School) - 117
Sp 4 Ariel James Smith	B. 12-19-43	Died 11-8-69	Army Enlisted from Shelley, ID
Sp 4 Billy Gene Smith	B. 5-9-46	Died 11-12-67	Army Enlisted from Gooding, ID (Attended schools in Filer, ID) - 110

Sp 4 Gary Clarence Smith   B. 11-5-43   Died 10-10-68   Army 116th National Guard Unit Enlisted from Pingree, ID - 48

1st Lt. James Anderson Smith   B. 5-1-46   Died 9-12-68   Army Enlisted from Blackfoot, ID - 114, 115

Pfc. Michael Allan Snyder   B. 10-17-42   Died 4-6-68   Army Enlisted from Lewiston, ID (Born in Tillamook, Oregon)

CWO Jon Michael Sparks   B. 2-24-50   MIA/POW 1971   Declared KIA 3-11-76 Army Enlisted from Carey, ID

Sp 4 Ronald Lee Stapleman   B. 3-16-45   Died 6-10-67   Army Enlisted from Paul, ID (Graduated from Minico High School- Burley)

Capt. Gary Lyn Steele   B. 9-15-38   Died 4-19-65   Army Enlisted from Bliss, ID - 130

Col. Mark Stephensen   B. 5-1-30 MIA/POW 4-29-67   Remains returned to US April 1988 Air Force (Born in Riverton, UT) - 68

Cdr. Clarence W. Stoddard, Jr.   B. 1-30-27   MIA/POW 9-14-66   Navy Enlisted from Atlanta in Elmore County, ID

Major Raymond LeRoy Tacke   B. 9-22-28   Died 3-8-69   Air Force Enlisted from Cottonwood, ID - 124, 125

Sgt. David Arlington Tanner   B. 4-1-48   Died 12-8-67   Army Enlisted from Boise, ID

Lt. Robert L. Taylor   B. 12-15-37   Died 4-4-68   Army Enlisted from Fruitland, ID - 129

Cpl. Daniel Cline Tedrow   B. 2-3-48   Died 11-27-68   Marine Enlisted from Mullan, ID (Born in Wallace, ID) - 106, 107

CWO Henry William Tews   B. 4-11-46   Died 12-29-68   Army Enlisted from Shoshone, ID (Born in Hailey, ID) - 95

Pfc. Terence Pierce Thomas   B. 6-20-46   Died 3-11-68   Army Enlisted from Hammett, ID - 40

CMS Larry C. Thornton   B. 3-3-32   MIA/POW 12-24-65   Declared KIA 1-27-74 Air Force   Enlisted from Idaho Falls, ID - 139, 140, 141, 161

Sp 4 James Edward Tooley   B. 9-15-46   Died 12-19-66   Army Enlisted from Parma, ID - 85

Major Edwin Newton Troxel   B. 12-29-29   Died 8-2-71   Air Force Enlisted from Boise, ID - 115, 117

1st Lt. Kenneth Eugene Turner   B. 5-9-41   Died 4-24-66   Army Enlisted from Bruneau, ID

Sp. 4 Rodney Carl Turner	B. 7-2-48	Died 11-8-69	Army Enlisted from Boise, ID (Born in Nampa, ID) - 104
Pfc. Wesley William Vermeesch	B. 6-4-47	Died 10-30-69	Army Enlisted from Pierce, ID
Capt. George Francis Volk	B. 12-29-40	Died 4-21-67	Army Enlisted from Boise, ID
Pfc. Douglas John Wade	B. 4-9-47	Died 2-19-66	Army Enlisted from Idaho Falls, ID - 131, 132
M. Sgt. Howard Bert Waldron	B. 5-18-26	Died 3-6-68	Marine Enlisted from Coeur D'Alene, ID (Born in Declo, ID) - 37
Pfc. James Lloyd Walker	B. 11-18-46	Died 10-30-66	Army Enlisted from Blackfoot, ID - 83
Pfc. Jimmy Lee Ward	B. 5-1-47	Died 11-30-67	Marine Enlisted from Nampa, ID - 32, 33
Sgt. Johnny Lee Ward	B. 11-28-47	Died 9-11-69	Army Enlisted from Cambridge, ID (Born in Weiser, ID) - 87
Sgt. Dennis Wartchow	B. 7-6-50	Died 9-4-69	Army Enlisted from Idaho Falls, ID
Pfc. Michael Leon Wasserman	B. 7-16-48	Died 10-12-68	Marine Enlisted from Boise, ID - 148, 149
S. Sgt. Russel Lee Watson	B. 2-28-42	Died 2-6-67	Army Enlisted from Post Falls, ID
CWO Edward Joseph Weidenbach	B. 9-30-24	Died 5-5-67	Army Enlisted from Nampa, ID
Noel Thomas West	B. 12-6-40	Died 6-19-67	Army Enlisted from Wendell, ID (Record indicates he was from Tacoma, WA)
Cpl. Michel T. Wheeler	B. 1-18-49	Died 3-16-68	Army Enlisted from Emmett, ID
Sgt. William Whitney	B. 8-28-47	Died 11-8-67	Army Enlisted from Pocatello, ID
Sp 5 Robert Leon Willey	B. 7-19-47	Died 5-10-69	Army Enlisted from Grangeville, ID - 118
Sgt. Bill Gene Williams	B. 3-14-44	Died 6-3-70	Army Enlisted from Hailey, ID (Born in Gooding, ID)
Sp 4 Daniel Eugene Williams	B. 3-15-48	Died 4-11-69	Army Enlisted from Hamer, ID
Sp 4 Morris Edward Williams	B. 10-9-51	Died 2-6-70	Army Enlisted from Boise, ID (Born in Emmett, ID) - 81

Airman 2nd Class
Thomas Murten Willis   B. 10-3-46   Died 6-5-67   Air Force Enlisted from McCall, ID   (Born in Council, ID) - 86

Sgt. Jerry Barber Wilson   B. 6-1-45   Died 12-14-66   Army Enlisted from Mackay, ID (Born in Caliente, Nevada) - 82, 106

1st Lt. Robert Evans Wise   B. 11-26 41   Died 3-5-67   Army Enlisted from Coeur D'Alene, ID

L. Cpl. Eugene Eben Wolters   B. 1-30-51   Died 8-30-70   Marine Enlisted from Coeur D' Alene, ID

1st Lt. Strather Franklin Wood   B. 4-26-44   Died 2-18-71   Marine Enlisted from Boise, ID (Originally from Eugene, Oregon)

Pfc. Robert Gene Yagues   B. 5-19-48   Died 5-3-67   Marine Enlisted from Mt. Home, ID (Born in Rupert, ID) - 104

Sp. 4 Kenneth Wilson Young   B. 8-23-45   Died 5-24-69   Army Enlisted from St. Anthony, ID - 47, 78